The 3D Manager: Dangerous, Derailed and Deranged

A Dictionary of Organizational Dilemmas

The 3D Manager: Dangerous, Derailed and Deranged

A Dictionary of Organizational Dilemmas

Adrian Furnham
Professor of Psychology, University College London

W

WHURR PUBLISHERS
LONDON AND PHILADELPHIA

© 2001 Whurr Publishers
First published 2001 by
Whurr Publishers Ltd
19B Compton Terrace, London N1 2UN, England and
325 Chestnut Street, Philadelphia PA 19106, USA

British Library Cataloguing in Publication Data
A catalogue record for this book is available from the British
Library.

ISBN: 1 86156 251 9

Contents

Preface

This is the third book in a trilogy. The first was called *The Psychology of Managerial Incompetence: A Sceptic's Dictionary of Modern Organizational Issues* and the second *The Hopeless, Hapless and Helpless Manager: Further explorations in the Psychology of Managerial Incompetence*. All three follow essentially the same format of short essays on modern managerial dilemmas. They are intended to be manageable bites about management in non-technical jargon – an easy, but challenging, read for the busy manager.

The feedback on the first two has been good. Of course, in following the formula one could be accused of being *change averse* and echoing that oft-heard and deeply annoying refrain, 'If it ain't broke, don't fix it'. On the other hand, it is true that this book does not have a single message. It does not belong to the silver-bullet, magic-formula school of business books. Rather it follows the wry outsider's vision of the anthropologists. It is a collection of observations about business and business people by a psychologist settled nicely in his ivory tower. It is about the odd ideas that managers have and the consequences of poor management.

What happens at work is often truly outstanding. Why more psychological thrillers do not take place exclusively in the work environment remains to me a mystery. As does the fact that we have not yet seen the *Oxford Book of Business Poetry*. Surely business engenders enough passion and can sponsor enough poets to do justice to the vicissitudes of organizational life?

As an academic and a consultant I am asked (and choose) to review certain ideas written in books and proposals; to comment on current debates; to lecture to students and business people; and to offer my opinions on certain organizational problems. I sit on final selection boards as an external, hopefully disinterested, observer. I am on the advisory council of a successful think tank. And I have friends who are well-known business people.

These experiences plus a reading of business magazines and pages of quality newspapers provide me with the material for my observations on business and organizational life. And the experiences often can leave one amazed and aghast in equal measure. It is no wonder that 'Dilbert' is as famous as he is – the humour, you see, reflects many people's actual experience of office madness.

These essays are meant to be opinionated in the best sense of the word. Hopefully they are strident, funny and, at least in part, valid. But there will be those who violently disagree. I have received hate e-mail for my views on topics as varied as absenteeism, graphology and surveys. Academics like debate and the adversarial method at arriving at the truth, even consensus. These essays then may present only one side of the argument.

It is not easy being a manager – nor probably was it ever the case. Some aspire to management; others have it thrust upon them: sometimes as a reward, sometimes as a punishment. Some are trained and some are well selected: many receive little of the former and not much of the latter. It is therefore not uncommon to come across managers who can't manage and who are a liability to themselves, their staff and their company as a whole. This book is for those who deal with them.

Adrian Furnham
London, May 2001

Introduction

This book is about the literally mad things that many modern managers do and believe about how to best manage the workforce and a company. Occasionally, one reads reports of the percentage of the general population who experience some sort of severe mental disorder at one point in their lives. It is often shockingly high – as much as 25–33% may be expected to have a 'nervous breakdown' requiring professional treatment, even hospitalization, at some stage in their working lives.

It is equally shocking to read the way families put up with, and adapt to, significant madness in one of their number. The paranoid uncle, the hysterical sister, the manic teenager are 'put up with' often at considerable cost to the family. The same happens in businesses, particularly if the illness grows slowly. It is often best seen in cases of addiction to such things as drink, drugs and gambling.

It is quite common when investigating the case of a chronic alcoholic in the workplace that many, many people knew about the manager's drinking over many, many years. The alcoholic's absenteeism, mood-swings, secrecy and drunken incompetence may be noted by dozens of people who are directly affected but do nothing. This may be due to various factors: some are simply embarrassed and do not know what to do; others fear reprisal; and still others may have something of a drink problem themselves and simply feel guilty.

In this sense, organizations may house, adapt to, and ignore mental illness in their midst. Whilst this may seem a sign of tolerance, it may equally be seen as a sign of either or both ignorance and apathy. These people need help not tolerance.

How does managerial derailment, incompetence and madness occur?

There are various reasons for this sad but common state of affairs: *selection* – the way the selection process occurs or the reasons why certain people are selected; *socialization* – the way the organization inducts and 'trains' them; *modelling* – the way the organization chooses role models and encourages or discourages particular beliefs and behaviours; *stress* – the way pressures inside and outside lead to managers buckling under the stress; *gurus and consultants* – who knowingly or unknowingly give bad, mad or sad advice and are listened to and obeyed. And all of these are done by managers themselves who select staff, model ideal behaviour, induct new employees and lure consultants.

Of course, it is possible that certain organizations attract the unstable. It is said that psychology and psychiatry attract those who are themselves prone to breakdown, but that may be something of an oversimplification.

On the other hand, organizations can easily provoke mental illness. There are many ways in which organizations can cause breakdowns that are much the same as in families. These may be a function of a manager's individual pathology, the corporate culture or structure, or even because the company is a changing, reducing or failing business.

Psychologists have always stressed the role of parents in childhood development. For many of us our boss is *in loco parentis* and his/her boss may be accurately implicated in one's long-term mental health. And so it is up to the organization that at each level one's mental health, as well as wealth and welfare, are dependent on the sanity of the people above one.

Consider the consequences of the boss who is:

- laissez-faire, who essentially avoids involvement and responsibility and seems unconcerned about the quality and quantity of output, morale or customer satisfaction
- warm and fuzzy, who avoids conflict, attempting to gain acceptance rather than results. It may be all very well concentrating on good, if superficial, relationships, but that can be at the expense or viability of the organization as a whole.
- an arrogant autocrat, demanding obedience and who relishes being feared and disliked. These hypocritical types tend to get short-term results by being critical and threatening but often have

little long-term goals and destroy morale leading to staff turnover, absenteeism, etc.

• a bumbling compromiser, who is an ambiguous idealist, overusing participation and produces grey, mediocre but acceptable decisions

• a constipated, introverted bureaucrat, whose role and procedure-following appears more important than understanding the business changes and satisfying customers

• an amateur psychologist and developer, more interested in training courses and personal development workshops than playing attention to the 'bottom line'

• a benevolent autocrat, who pretends to be caring and people orientated but won't really brook opposition.

This typological approach may be easy to use and understand, even if it is not good science. Typologies don't explain the relationship between types, and they tend not to explore the origin of the problems. For that, we must look elsewhere.

The Dangerous Manager

Doctors talk about checking whether colleagues are '*safe*'. By this they mean the doctor is competent enough to be 'let at' patients. It means that he/she is able to make accurate and sensitive diagnoses and apply to appropriate treatment. The latter expertise clearly depends on the specialties. Surgeons need fine perceptual-motor skills; radiologists a keen eye; public health doctors a good head for statistics. But doctors, like other people, work in teams – and they have to manage others. Indeed, medical care depends on teamwork from highly educated specialists, through well-trained nursing staff to a range of other support staff.

Few talk of a safe manager; though we still talk of a 'safe pair of hands'. Sometimes we think of a safe manager as one who will cope with stress well. The safe manager can endure, even thrive, in a Third World country and not be broken by culture shock. The safe manager can withstand the stress of organizational restructuring. The safe manager can be trusted with secrets. The safe manager supports his or her staff.

'Safe' may also mean honest and reliable. The safe manager can be trusted with money, with plans. The safe manager is reliable. The safe manager is good at negotiation. The safe manager will carry out company policy. The safe manager indeed has access to the safe.

But what of the dangerous manager? Dangerously unpredictable. Dangerously reckless. Dangerously unstable. Dangerous with safety procedure and equipment. Prone to mechanical and people accidents. Danger is ever present at work. We live in a changing world with many organizational competitors. We need be ever vigilant for danger – from the outside, but also from within. And we need to understand when and why the otherwise safe manager becomes unsafe for him/herself, the team, the section and the company as a whole.

Some organizations 'train' people how to advance. The young manager soon learns the rules that are mainly *maladaptive*. Below are the rules to become dangerously incompetent, *not* its opposite. These include the following:

1. Never let anyone know precisely what you do, how you do it, or why. It is particularly important to keep both HR and your boss/boss's boss in the dark. This will ensure that they will hesitate before 'letting you go' in case they don't understand how crucial you are.
2. Brook little disagreements and 'throw your toys out of the pram'. Be unpredictable, demanding, rude – you are unlikely to be challenged as everyone will be too concerned with saving their own position.
3. Ingratiate the top bosses – learn their values, preferred style and ape it/them. Flattery and faking are the oldest tricks in the book, but they work well.
4. Call meetings: they are only called by important people and offer a wonderful way to condition the masses and come to be seen as both important and productive in their own right.
5. Be the in-house guru: read the business magazines so that you have all the latest buzz-words on the tip of your tongue. Say ' Tom' rather than 'Tom Peters' as if you know him personally, or 'Charles' meaning 'Charles Handy'.
6. Be 'creative'; up to date; modern. Wear a bow tie occasionally; be snazzy during dress-down days. Create the impression that, whilst being technically superb, you understand the importance of art, design, *blah, blah*…

7. Control the office politics. Never underestimate the power of rumours. Divide and conquer by changing your affections periodically. Discreetly stab various people in the back at random. The office, remember, is a place of danger, excitement, humour, revenge, scandal.

8. Be analytically ponderous and hence indecisive: if you never make a decision you can't be wrong. To be a good executive you need to be right only slightly in excess of 50 per cent of the time.

9. Cultivate the press. Make sure you make use of the photo opportunity. Don't ignore the in-house magazines that can be very influential. Keep your name and face in the press always associated with good causes, having fun, making profane remarks.

10. Be known as litigious and even a whistle-blower in the right cause. This will deter adversaries from going too far and may even lead them to see you as particularly moral.

This may serve as a simple checklist if you have a manager who scores six or more of these: they may be well on the road to real danger.

The Derailed Manager

Why do we work? Freud argued that work gave one the best sense of reality. It is critical to our well-being because it helps give us a sense of a secure self-concept. We learn at work to master tasks, create symbols of ourselves in our work products and achievements. That is why midlife crises and retirement strike at the heart of the issue of self-definition through work.

For people whose achievements are symbolized in advancement titles, the mid-life crisis represents the falling off of achievement. When incomes and titles hit a plateau, the sense of self is threatened without reinforcement from external symbols. The need to achieve and have symbols of achievement does not stop, and many people need signs of accomplishment if early career success slows down. We all hope that the products of self remain after the time of their creation is gone. So 'flattening' an organization, like retirement, can signal a major crisis. There are, in the jargon of psychobabble, a cessation of concrete signs of self-definition. A destructive external work-world can cause an internally confused and disoriented world.

The derailed manager is nearly always the *sidelined, ceiling-reached manager*. Possibly a risen star, even once labelled a 'wunderkind' and *potential high flyer*, the manager has to cope with, adjust to, a new label, a new life, a new self-definition. And that is hard. You are what you do: if what you do changes, so have you to change; and change is hard . . . . harder as you get older. A very common cause of derailment.

Work also functions as a disguised source of love and affection, and hence security. Work can easily be a refuge. It can provide caring, considerate, attentive staff who are respectful and even adoring. Affirmation can easily come more from work than from home. The demanding spouse, the unruly children, the need to do domestic duties, can often seem a poor second substitute for the 'love and affection' found in the workplace. Work can feed a person's most basic needs. Managers say, ' I have to do this or that' when they could or should say either 'I want to' or 'I choose to', because they have to get the psychological benefits from work. One can be thus soothed in the work environment.

Equally, work can make one feel indispensable, irreplaceable. The power of the affection shown by colleagues, customers, clients, etc. satisfies many a manager's deep-seated need for security and love. But it can easily be taken away. Through restructuring, mergers and acquisitions, transfers and the like, it is less than likely that one is able to form close bonds with people at work. The environment that once gave security can very soon give the precise opposite. The derailed manager is very much an insecure manager.

Work at its best gives one the sense of competence, power and self-respect. Competence implies confidence, which implies power. Powerlessness is synonymous with low self-respect, with low self-esteem and with growing alienation.

Autonomy, responsibility and control at work are associated with happiness. Being over-monitored or supervised, no matter one's status and power can easily lead to demoralization. Self-worth, self-confidence and self-respect can be gained and lost at work surprisingly quickly. And it is very easy to get into one of those viscious cycles. The derailed manager may cover up his/her low self-worth by preposterous aggrandizing, but it is not difficult to see through this most of the time.

Work helps one conquer time. Time is a finite product. It is perhaps the first issue discussed in meetings. People do not have the time to do things. The experience of time is bound up with the idea of change, the perspectives of disappearance and loss. People want to master time – to 'make time' not 'do time'. Time represents the inexorable passage of experience. Getting older and the feeling of 'late in life', and with it the profound sense of loss, is an inevitable but horrid experience. Time is spent; it is lost; it can't be regained. Time is continuous, relentless and disappearing. If we can create an organization, a product, or a process that endures the passage of time, we are (we often hope) defying, defeating and controlling time. Thus obtaining time-defying tangible achievements is a powerful motivator at work.

Those who at work monitor time most closely are often driven, with greater pressure to work – to produce things that 'beat' time, cheat death and endure. Many organizations are monuments to the CEO's battle with loss and change, and attempt to achieve immortality.

Imagine, then, the manager whose mastery and control over time is lost; whose job and skills are made redundant; whose life's work is discarded, rendered worthless. The feeling of having wasted one's working time can lead easily to depression – to feeling that one leaves nothing behind, that nothing is remembered. The derailed manager is frequently a time victim – a person who has experienced a profound sense of change at work.

Finally, work offers one a way to 'amount to something'. Of course, the value of what we achieve is subjective and this can lead to preposterous over- or under-valuing of particular accomplishments. There may be a prerequisite for the feeling that one amounts to something – it is self-acceptance.

The derailed manager's pathology may take many forms. He or she may be educated to work: they cannot stop working. Addiction of all sorts is not defined or measured by what people do but rather what they cannot do. Workaholics seek skill-development, goal-oriented situations and are very uncomfortable when issues like emotions, fantasy and spontaneity are called for. Their EQ is often low. They are often super-analytical, categorizing and aggressive as they 'attack problems'. They live for the future, not in the present, and are dictated to the e-goals: efficiency and effectiveness.

Variously, these addicts have been delineated in such ways as:

- the aggressive, angry, hostile addict using work to discharge aggressive energy

- the ashamed, low self-esteem addict, who gets the recognition he/she craves only at work
- he competitive addict, who finds work the easiest place to score points and win the game to gain respect
- the defensive addict, who works to depress and avoid feelings, desires and wishes they cannot deal with by 'burying' themselves in their work
- the inadequate lonely addict, whose lack of social skills means they have few friends outside the office but a given set of friends in it. The office is where their family, team, gang belong
- the guilty addict, for whom work is self-punishment and a way to expiate guilt which may have arisen for various reasons
- the obsessive addict, whose drive for orderliness and perfectionism will be tolerated only in the workplace, as their compulsive and controlling need to categorize, define and organize simply won't be tolerated outside the workplace
- the passive, dependent addict, who enjoys being told what to do, eschews initiative and prefers to follow the rules and procedures set out by legitimate authority
- the psycho-addict, whose sense of reality and personhood comes exclusively from the world of work
- the sexually frustrated addict, who enjoys the flirtations in the workplace but they know they cannot be rejected because the flirtatiousness is tightly controlled, between roles not people and only symbolic.

Two other very common, seemingly opposite, factors need to be discussed with respect to the derailed manager. The first is narcissism that thrives on the appreciation and verification of self-worth by others. The narcissistic manager is frequently personally very insecure and depends on work to compensate for their unremitting and remorseless sense of inadequacy. The narcissistic manager rarely complains of being unhappy: it is others that do so because they are seen to be there to gratify needs; otherwise they are frustrating, pointless, and should be avoided. There is only 'take' with these characters, no 'give and take'.

Any feedback from boss, co-workers and subordinates must be positive. The slightest and most justifiable criticism is likely to lead to vindictiveness or depression. The narcissist's façade is a front to camouflage a deep-seated fear of rejection. And the narcissist is concerned with control, such that they may superficially seem to be caring about their staff but this, like the other mask, is just a façade.

It's tiring being a narcissist: they can't let their guard down for an instant and therefore can't relax and enjoy the present. Vigilance keeps a sense of self intact.

Along with the narcissistically derailed manager is the self-destructive manager. Again, the idea comes from psychoanalysis with its love of paradox. The idea that the self-destructive manager is success-phobic. They are actually dependent people who, paradoxically, require to be taken care of by others.

As success at work occurs so does approval, promotion and the growth of reputation as someone who is dependable. But this manager wants to depend on others: not the other way around. So they have to find out the message that they are deeply flawed or that their success is fleeting. Curiously, then, they never achieve anything much of significance in indolence, procrastination and incompetence.

The 'fear of success' manager has the desire and often the ability to win but dare not do so least their achievement is appropriately recognized and rewarded with responsibility. Chronic lateness, carelessness and forgetfulness and inattention to detail are all excellent self-handicapping strategies used by the derailed and derailing manager.

The derailed manager is not uncommon in current business. The workaholic, the narcissist, the menopausal and the self-handicapping manager are all these suffering from derailment.

The Deranged Manager

Are some managers simply mad? Derange means to disturb functions so as to lead to insanity. Some managers are definitely deranged.

Accurate statistics on madness in the population at large are difficult to come by. In lay language, 'the nervous breakdown' is not uncommon and it is hardly surprising that mangers are as susceptible to madness as the next person. Many assume that stress leads to madness or is at least a major provoking agent. Thus managerial stress at work may be seen to be a powerful factor which may lead managers to be over-represented in the population of the mentally ill.

Cynics have argued that you would have to be mentally ill to want to work for certain individuals in particular corporations. Or some have suggested job selectors actually look for certain personality disorders to recruit into the organizations. Thus, the extremely aggressive may make good security guards or soldiers; the obsessional perfectionist may be excellent health inspectors; the manically optimistic may be sought for sales.

But what is mental illness or abnormality? There are three kinds of practical criteria often used to define abnormality:

- Discomfort: This can be physical or psychological but usually involves physical illness (colds, headaches, back pain, stomach and skin complaints) worry and depression, but always subjective unhappiness. The mad manager is not a happy person.
- Bizarreness: For psychiatrists, this can range from the serious (delusions, hallucinations and memory loss) to the less severe (like phobias and compulsive rituals). These behaviours are culturally and socio-economically defined but some are clearly very bad for business. These include :
  ➤ misperceptions of reality (seeing/hearing what is not there)
  ➤ misinterpretations of events and others' behaviours
  ➤ disorientation not knowing the date, the place, etc.
  There is a difference between bizarre and illegal. The desire to harm others is seen as illegal, the desire to harm oneself is considered bizarre.
- Inefficiency: Abnormal individuals underperform against both their potential and their previous performance. Being disorganized and unable to manage personal affairs.

Unhappy, odd and inefficient managers abound. Whether they are technically mad is a matter of dispute. The above definitions emphasize maladaptive behaviour and emotional distress but the legal definition considers impaired judgement and lack of self-control. These too are readily seen in the manager.

Certainly, managers are prone to depression and breakdown. In the jargon of psychiatry, many managers have a personality disorder (see box opposite). Each may be manifest in the deranged manager.

Over 25 years ago, a psychiatrist wrote a very persuasive paper published with the title '*On being sane in insane places*'. His interest was in distinguishing the sane from the insane and his experiment was a fascinating one. Eight sane people gained secret admission to twelve different American mental hospitals. They included a psychiatrist, three psychologists, a pediatrician, a painter and a housewife. By claiming they were 'hearing voices' they all easily gained admission to the hospitals, somewhat to their surprise.

Personality Disorder	Description
Antisocial	Engages in behaviours destructive to self and others, often impulsively, without remorse or shame. Is unable to sustain consistent work behaviour. Is irritable or aggressive, often getting into fights or assaulting others. Steals, destroys property, engages in an illegal occupation.
Borderline	Has difficulty in interpersonal relationships, exhibits wildly flexible moods, shifting from normal to depressed or irritable. Demonstrates unpredictable and impulsive behaviour; inappropriate, intense anger, and recurrent suicidal threats or self-mutilating behaviour. Reports feelings of emptiness or boredom.
Compulsive	Strives for perfection, is preoccupied with trivial details, rules, schedules and lists. Often has poor interpersonal relations because of demands that everything be done in one particular way.
Dependent	Exhibits lack of self-confidence and a helpless or stupid self-image, depending on others to make decisions. Often defers to others and puts up with abusive relationships. Has difficulty initiating projects or doing things alone; volunteers to do unpleasant tasks to win other people's favour.
Histrionic	Is overly dramatic and emotional, always trying to draw attention to self. May be inappropriately seductive in appearance or behaviour. Is self-centered and has no tolerance for the frustration of delayed gratification. Is uncomfortable if not the centre of attention.
Narcissistic	Has a grandiose view of own importance and abilities. Demands others' attention but reacts strongly to criticism; takes advantage of others. Believes own problems to be unique; is preoccupied with fantasies of unlimited success, power, brilliance, or beauty.
Obsessive-compulsive	Is overly perfectionist, so fails to complete tasks. Is preoccupied with details, rules, lists, or schedules. Is excessively devoted to work, to the exclusion of leisure activities and friendships. Is indecisive and exhibits restricted expression of affection.
Paranoid	Expects, without sufficient basis, to be exploited or harmed by others. Questions, without justification, the loyalty or trustworthiness of friends and the fidelity of spouse or sexual partner. Bears grudges or is unforgiving of insults or slights.

In the hospitals, they behaved normally, indicated that they were fine and no longer experienced the symptoms. They did not take the prescribed medication but they then had the task of being discharged essentially by convincing the staff that they were sane. They were thus highly motivated to be friendly, co-operative, helpful and normal.

The experience, especially the strict segregation of staff from patients, left a powerful impression on the psychiatrist and the other pseudo-patients. This segregation resulted in very limited extended contact between the two groups. Those with the greatest control and power over patients – the medical staff – were the least available. More staff contact with patients might have led to greater awareness of the degrees of normality and abnormality present.

Segregation and isolation also promoted feelings of powerlessness and depersonalization. Perfunctory interactions, absence of privacy, deprivation of personal possessions, and reliance on drugs as principal therapeutic agents contributed to such feelings.

The psychiatrist concluded that the fault did not lie with hospital staff, most of whom he was convinced were basically sensitive and caring people. Rather, he attributed many of the problems to unenlightened attitudes toward the mentally ill. These attitudes promote ambivalence and avoidance, even among staff to whose care they are entrusted. The numerous manifestations of this attitude in psychiatric hospitals include custodial care, heavy reliance on psychotropic (i.e. generates psychological changes) medications as primary therapeutic agents, and rigid segregation of patients and staff. He concluded that the detection of sanity in such places is unlikely. Given this probability, it is also likely that perceptions of persons who are truly psychologically troubled can be markedly distorted under the same circumstances. Moreover, the consequences of such hospitalization appear to be ideally counter-therapeutic. Less reliance on psychiatric labelling, a more pragmatic focus on solving personal problems, and creation of environments that promote health and well-being can do much to promote a realistic assessment of what is normal and what is not.

For every safe, sane manager there may well be a dangerous, derailed and deranged manager. Some start off safe and sane but events conspire to change that. Others are a bad choice right from the start. And, if you go through the files you may be able to find the clues to their incompetence early on. It is easier to keep a job than it is to get one. Once accepted, the dangerous, derailed and deranged manager may have 20 years to create havoc in any organization. Worth thinking about.

This book contains over 60 essays, each typically between 900 and 2200 words. They consider, in part, mad managers, and mad management ideas and techniques. They are meant to be provocative, possibly funny – even on occasion practically useful. They are particularly concerned with the bizarre ideas and advice given by business gurus, 'snake-oil salesmen' and other 'silver-bullet-merchants' in the management consultant business. A basic tenet of this book is that some of the recommended practices in management actually lead to derailment.

Ageism in business

To many middle-aged (40–55) middle managers, the future looks bleaker than ever. Policemen and prime ministers seem to be getting younger. And the sight of e-commerce multi-millionaires at the age of 25 (or less!) is the final straw.

Those who have been out-placed and eagerly seek work are sometimes told that they are finished at forty, fetched up at fifty and certainly shagged out at sixty. It was only a generation ago when age meant experience, experience meant seniority and seniority meant security, money, power and influence. When service-based industries were replaced with performance-management systems, the role of loyalty seemed to go out the window. Long service was a badge of failure not success.

The career is dead, so the gurus say. We are all portfolio-knowledge workers now, irrespective of the 'time we have put in' (the loyalty, devotion and commitment we have shown); we are as dispensable as old technology – typewriters in a word-processor world, experts on LPs in a CD world, old money that has been withdrawn from circulation.

But is it true that age alone is a barrier to work in the new millennium? The answer is age is associated with three things that make one employable: skills, attitude and reputation. And it is for these three things we are hired and fired.

The issue of skills is essential to keeping a job. Skills are not the same as abilities but related to them. And, of course, skills are related to age as some skills become redundant. We grow up with the technology of our age but have to learn new skills as it changes. The question is whether people do continually pick up and fine-tune new skills. Acquiring new skills does take ability, effort and practice. You can teach an old dog new tricks but you have to teach it differently.

Older people may find previous skills have to be unlearnt before new ones are learnt as the latter can interfere with the former. Further, and most importantly, there is an issue about self-confidence, shame and 'face' that is more germane to the middle-aged worker. Older people are afraid of being exposed as ignorant and therefore resist training that shows them up. And this can lead to a vicious cycle. Fearing that they have insufficient skills and knowledge, older people shun opportunities that teach, refresh and hone those skills.

You are what you can do. All outplacement consultants do an initial skills diagnosis that attempts to ascertain the level of both hard and soft skills. Hard skills are often knowledge-based – and can range from fairly basic but useful skills like touch-typing and basic numeracy to higher-order skills like understanding advanced computer programs, speaking a foreign language as well as being able to write in different styles (technical or non-technical, tabloid or broadsheet).

Soft skills that are valued are typical managerial skills of planning, appraising, negotiating, etc. These are more difficult to measure accurately and therefore easier to fudge. Many come naturally with experience, because people are given the opportunity to practise them. The soft skills are not necessarily easier to acquire. In fact, they are rarely explicitly taught. You are supposed to acquire them osmotically. Some Darwinian process is supposed to happen such that those who acquire these skills get on and those that do not never really get promoted.

There are many reasons why the older employee has fewer hard but more soft skills than a young 'whipper-snapper'. Educational opportunities, both formal and company-sponsored, were fewer some years back. People left education earlier and hoped the university of life would support them. Second, the development of technology and globalization has resulted in the need for skills like computer literacy and speaking foreign languages that were unimportant 20 years ago. However, many older people have picked up delegation, negotiation, communication and other skills because they have been required to do it for many years and have watched others do it.

Psychologists have distinguished between fluid and crystallized intelligence. The former is the ability to solve problems, the latter the ability to answer *University Challenge*-type questions. The young have more of the former, the old more of the latter. Both are useful and necessary but in a fast-changing and complex world the former may be more and more important.

Core-skills portfolios are the first jump. The second is attitude – attitude to change, attitude to development, and attitude to the future. Attitudes to change are often related to self-confidence and beliefs about ability and control. A cynical, negative, sour attitude towards the company, the young or the new, is a sure predictor of limited shelf life.

We hear a lot about life-long learning, about constant improvement (KAISEN) and about adaptation to new conditions. It's all true.

But what determines the acquisition of skill is often 'attitude'. That idea covers a multitude of sins. It is about self-confidence, about dispositional optimism, about being forward looking. Ambition is a powerful driver. The old joke about how many psychologists it takes to change a light bulb is totally relevant. The answer is one – but the light bulb needs to want to be changed.

We have all seen seriously old people pick up and enjoy practising new skills, because they enjoy learning, are future-oriented and want to keep up. Given the choice between a sour, backward looking but bright 60-year-old and an enthusiast forward looking but of only average ability, I would choose the latter.

It is indeed a paradox that whereas abilities cannot be changed attitudes can, but it is the latter that seem more immutable as we get older. Often, these attitudes can be predicted early in life. If you are optimistic, 'can do', ambitious and sociable at 15, you are equally likely to be at 50, even with the vicissitudes of life and the slings and arrows of outrageous fortune. Elite survivors – those octogenarians who keep their marbles and lead active happy lives – remain young at heart because of their attitude. They are curious, participative, willing to have a go. They know their limitations but are not weighed down by them.

You are not necessarily finished at 40 but, if you want to believe it, you will be. The power of self-fulfilling prophecies is immense. Rather, you may be flourishing at fifty, sailing a sixty, successful at seventy and an eager beaver at eighty.

Assessment centres

Some business people are quite simply more important than others. The decision to promote someone to the board, send them overseas or invest in major retraining cannot be taken lightly. The question is how best to make that decision. Or at least to begin with: what data to collect to inform one's decision?

If an employee has been working for the organization for some time, there is inevitably some sort of data of their service record. At worst, there is little more than gossip and a few inconsistent and superficial appraisal reports. At best, it is a frequently collected, behavioural report by supervisors, colleagues and reports matched with actual output data. Alas, most companies are amnesic with regard to human resources issues, logging very little data upon which to make serious people decisions. Bureaucratic organizations manifest their constipation by extensive file keeping but also make sure the records carry very little worth to the decision maker.

Inevitably, the longer a person has worked for the organization, the more is known about him or her but most often this is reputational, as opposed to hard, data. Most promotional decisions are no longer based on time served, but on ability shown or potential to be realized. It is therefore important that anybody considered for serious promotion, or investment, or whose job could have real consequences for the company, is seriously evaluated.

Often, these sorts of decisions will be made on the basis of hearsay, rather than on what the senior people actually know about the candidate's suitability for the job in question. At worst, the decision is seen in the light of 'turn-taking', reward for long service or the best of the bunch available.

One option is to get a second opinion by sending the person to an assessment centre. Just as one may have to go through a 'medical' (checkup) before moving job, there may be every reason they also undergo a 'psychological' checkup at an assessment centre. But why an assessment centre? They are, after all, very expensive: they may last from two to three days and the final report, which is all the customer gets, may cost then anything from £1,500 to £5,000. Is it worth it? Can it really make a difference to the quality of decision making?

There are many types of, and ways of getting, information about individuals. Psychologists usually differentiate between three types of data: self-report, observational and test data.

Self-report data are obtained primarily from interview or question-naire. Most senior people are skilled interviewees, as are politicians. They know how to answer even pretty astute questions to show them-selves in the best light. Personality tests, learning-style inventories, atti-tude forms and value questionnaires are also forms of self-report. The person answers a set of specific questions carefully designed to measure a particular phenomenon. There are various problems asso-ciated with questionnaires, including the problem of lying, distorting the truth or not being able, rather than willing, to report accurately. Most people, for instance, believe they have a sense of humour, which is patently not the case. They also believe they are brighter, better drivers, more intuitive, etc. – all of which is frequently wrong. Although psychologists have developed rather good ways of catching what they politely call 'dissimulators' such as by lie tests or demanding forced-choice answers, still they can be got round.

The fact that interviewees like interviews is testament enough to the fact that they may not yield very accurate data about such things as a person's ability, teamwork or how they cope under stress. The limitations of self-report are pretty self-evident; the question, however, is what is the best alternative?

The second source of data is *observational data* – that is, based on the observations of another. Indeed, 360-degree feedback data are based on observations by boss, peers, subordinates, clients, etc. And a great impact it often has. Nearly always, it is the feedback from the subordinates that shocks managers most. There are many reasons for this but the predominant one is that it is the direct reports of managers who best know their particular management style.

Psychologists have distinguished between things that people do and do not know about themselves, and things that others do and do not know about them. Thus, we all have things we know about ourselves that we are happy to share with others and those that we prefer to keep hidden. But there are often things about ourselves that we do not know that others do. This may refer to ability or lack thereof, morality, mental health, etc. You do not have to be deluded to not be able to give a fully factual account of your temperament.

Indeed, the things that people seem least able to report on accur-ately are their motives. Some are easier than others. We all know about the pathologically ambitious, the obsessional control freak and the domineering bully. But people know much less about the deep-seated needs of people for autonomy, diffidence, exhibitionism or understanding.

After all, why do people apply for promotion – power, money, status, to please their spouse (or long-dead parents) or simply to bump up their salary prior to retirement? Often, they cannot tell you, but observers at work can and, when asked, will do so. You don't have to be a psychotherapist to see patterns of behaviour that tell of the motives of people.

Spouses, long-time colleagues, teachers and past employers make reasonable observers. Hence the use of references. But sometimes they become spiteful or more often disingenuously nice because they fear litigation from written documents.

So a better alternative is to get trained observers to write about someone's behaviour while doing a range of tasks over a period. If the tasks are salient to the job, the observers trained, and there is more than one of them, there is a pretty good chance they can come up with some pretty interesting and important observations, which will certainly help make better decisions.

The third sort of data are called *test data*. Psychologists often make the distinction between tests of power and tests of preference. The former are like IQ tests, the latter like personality tests. The former do, but the latter don't, have right or wrong answers.

Research teaches us very clearly that the best predictors of work performance are, not surprisingly, work-sample tests. General IQ is a better predictor, but best of all are specific abilities. In other words, it is ability more than personality, experience or reputation that is the best predictor of work success. And it is ability data that selectors have least real information about. There is reputational evidence about ability, but little real data.

IQ tests can measure special ability – mathematical or verbal – and they can measure problem-solving ability. They can warn about an ability level that may be rather too low to find learning and adaptation easily. Equally, they can indicate very high levels of intelligence, which may indicate a person would become seriously bored if not sufficiently stimulated.

Assessment centres often require that participants do real, valid, up-to-date tests of ability: numeracy, reasoning, vocabulary, problem-solving.

Business-babble and political correctness

Business-babble is a growth industry. To be fluent in corporate-speak may be a requirement for advancement. Being an inventor of business jargon terms, and having them exclusively identified as one's own, is practically a necessity of being called a 'business guru'. No wonder then that journalists supposedly favoured the word 'guru' because they could not spell 'charlatan'.

Most people know about the systematized buzz-word generator. This was actually no more than a list of three columns of words with a dozen or so in each column. The joke was that you could combine the three into an utterly meaningless, but serious sounding, buzz-word. For instance, a 'responsive transitional contingency', 'synchronized third-generation capability' or a 'systematized incremental programme'. This gives one impressive obscurantist semantic possibilities, whose terminological inexact options can seriously inhibit documentary clarity! In short, one could easily invent meaningless buzz-words.

Reports and presentations are littered with this nonsense. Indeed, some companies appropriate, even rejoice in, this in-house, semi-secret language precisely because it is a marker of being 'one of us'. Knowing, or at least thinking that one knows, the meaning of this gobbledegook, and using it frequently, shows loyalty, corporateness and the ability to speak more than one language. Because there are few English-Business-Babble dictionaries, the tongue remains obscure except to anthropologists and missionaries who stumble on these tribes and have the time, patience, and motive to try to understand them.

7

The rise of corporate-speak and guru-speak is attributable to many factors. Being fluent in business-babble can help distinguish them from us, insiders from outsiders, top management from junior management and those with and those without an MBA. It can similarly give the impression of sophistication while obfuscating. Speaking an obscure tongue means one can have a secret language or at least a marker of education and group allegiance. Some gurus strive to invent, change or colonize words to make them their own so that, whenever used, they themselves are thought of. They are the catchwords of comics, the sound of big success. The writing of mission statements added to business-babble in a big way.

But perhaps the major reason for the increase in imaginative business-babble is an attempt to present the unpalatable in an acceptable way. Corporate language is used as a balm, a bandage or, at worst, a blanket not to solve problems but hide them.

A second sort of corporate-speak is the precise opposite of the above. The buzz-word generator makes up obscure concepts that sometimes have a simple meaning – that is if they have one at all. The opposite is to use simple, everyday phrases that have a special meaning within the organization. Thus to 'adopt an attitude of watchful waiting' means, of course, to do nothing. 'Taking a long hard look at', 'under active consideration', 'in a holding position' and 'evaluating the possible prematureness of this idea' are other synonyms for the same thing. 'Channels of communication' are trails of interoffice memos or interpersonal e-mails.

Then there are new management techniques, all of which are a form of impression, as opposed to real, management. Managing by Post-its: use these little pads to shower offices. Then there is management by reorganization. BUA management is popular: management *by using a*bbreviations.

Jargon can also be found in job titles. In the old days, you were 'clerk of works' or 'technical supervisor'. Now the latter are 'laboratory stewards' and the former 'managers of infrastructural support'. The idea of a job title is to inflate the ego of the holder – often in exchange for a reasonable income – while baffling, but possibly impressing, a client. As the title 'manager' becomes overused so everyone is then a director. Soon we shall reach the American standard where the first job in the company, like the last (bar one), is executive vice-president.

In the old days, one had 'strengths and weaknesses'. Now we still all have strengths but we have 'developmental opportunities'. Those who can't calculate are 'mathematically challenged'. You don't sack people any more but offer 'outplacement counselling'.

Business-babble now surpasses psychobabble in its imaginativeness and impenetrability. This is based on all sorts of things. The airline industry gave us phrases like 'I am in a holding position', 'Can I be upgraded?' and 'Old Curruthers is in the departure lounge of life'. Computers have helped or hindered the business-babble industry, depending on your view. To 'download a preformed intuition' is to have an idea.

Companies develop and enjoy their own in-house terms and jargon, particularly for grades and customers. Sensitivity to being a 'level-4 manager' or 'grade-5 supervisor' means little to the outsider but everything to those in the organization. And some customer-facing groups develop a funny, telling but deeply derogatory set of epithets to describe customers. Some are unprintable, most unattributable.

Those who support political correctness, though ironically it is not PC to describe it as such, proffer a simple explanation for its support. They argue that PC places emphasis on protecting the rights of minorities, 'respect for diversity' or accepting (even celebrating) differences. The philosophy is clear in the point that the right to free speech or airing unpopular opinions must be subordinated to the right of guaranteeing equal protection under the law where comments may be seen as degrading, disrespectful or hostile.

PC philosophy argues that linguistic titles and labels used to describe others, usually minorities, convey a substantive political message. It is philosophy about the power of language. Hence the fascination with Eurocentrism and male bias – hence all the changes in words like 'manpower', 'chairman', etc. Words don't involve just meaning: they carry, enshrine, and enforce attitudes both positive and negative. The 'gender' of words thus implies the gender of the occupant of the title. Even the etymology is suspect. Hence, an academic wanted 'seminars' changed to 'ovulars' because of etymology. But that is feminism, not neutral PC-ness, where one de-genders (as opposed to emasculates) words.

Is there proof for the PC position? Does changing words change attitudes? Does pro- and prescribing acceptable and unacceptable words have a long- or short-term beneficial effect? Or is it nothing but time-wasting flimflam – a pleasant alternative to dealing with business problems? Alas, the jury is out; the evidence is missing.

Critics of PC see it as a repressive orthodoxy that, paradoxically, attempts to achieve tolerance and harmony by tyrannical censorship and ideological coercion. They contend that by ensuring the veneer of polite language the underlying problems, if there are any, are ignored. The anti-PC lobby see PC as empty rhetoric and a hollow attempt to quiet the discontent and appease the complaints of certain bodies.

Whatever the motives or the theories of the pro- or anti-PC camps, the business world is alive with people constructing buzz-word generators or subtly censoring the language. Some terms have passed into history: 'The captain in the cockpit could not take tea from the stewardess as he had both hands on the joystick' is something you would not hear any longer.

Business consultants as psychotherapists

Most people in business have probably been surprised by the extent to which a clever, clear-headed colleague has come under the seductive power of management consultants. Some become dependent, seemingly unable to make even banal decisions without checking with their favourite guru. Others appear to turn their back on received wisdom and MBA training to pursue wacky, modern, airhead ideas favoured by the more 'alternative' consultants.

Even when the consultancy is over, some business people clearly carry a light for those consultants. Cynics suggest two causes of this, sometimes bizarre, behaviour. First is that old favourite 'cognitive dissonance' or 'buyer's nostalgia'. It is about reconciling two contradictory facts. At great expense, you hired consultants to do a job who did not produce the results you wanted. One solution is to redefine the result and point out how good the consultants were at diagnosing the 'real problem' and helping a 'long-term' solution. The more they cost, the greater the disappointment, the stronger the need to rationalize the mistake – and, paradoxically, the better the consultancy is considered to be, the more strongly it is defended.

Others point out that stressed, bewildered-by-change, work-aholic managers need the use of a confidant outside the business, to whom they can talk about a range of issues. The consultant becomes part confidant, part confessor, a friend, a sounding board, a second opinion – in short, a psychotherapist.

Studies on the effectiveness of psychotherapy give the best insight into what clients get from business consultants. For years and years, therapists from different theoretical traditions fought it out, trying to demonstrate how only their therapy worked. The Freudians lambasted the behaviourists; the cognitive therapists ridiculed both, while the existentialists astutely implied that the efficacy of other therapies was simply impossible. Eclectics tried a reasonable compromise, suggesting that maybe it depended on the problem: behavioural therapy was best for phobia, cognitive therapy for depression, psychoanalysts for narcissistic tendencies, drugs for schizophrenia, and a long hike in the country for adolescent ennui.

But the real shock came with the publication of meta-analysis, which vigorously examined the outcome of many hundreds of studies. They found that all therapies – except the very outlandish – appeared to work *equally* well. The benefits were modest but measurable. Despite remarkably different therapies based on strikingly different theories, the outcome was the same. It was the explanations preferred for this observation that may explain the warm and positive response to many business consultants.

- *Expectations of improvement.* These may be self-fulfilling expectations or old-fashioned placebo. The idea is simple – leading a client to believe their problem is solvable increases their morale and optimism, which in turn helps to solve the problem. The clever consultant knows the importance of fully pointing out the complexities of the problem, the difficulties that lie ahead (blah, blah = big invoice) but also assuring, and constantly reassuring, the client they can make things better. The client's morale improves. They feel they will cope, overcome their problems and triumph in the end – and they (sort of) do. The sugar pill will work – and it does. Consultants that don't accentuate the positive make problems for themselves and fail to explain the greatest medical breakthrough of the twentieth century – the placebo.
- *The therapeutic alliance.* In therapy, the relationship between therapist and client is usually characterized by acceptance, attention, caring and respect. This is a formidable cocktail to the rejected,

ignored and despised business manager. And it gets better and stronger over time. A good business consultant knows that he/she is in the relationship business and that it is the social support provided that often gives the courage for business people to act decisively. There are problems in the alliance, of course, as so many struck-off psychiatrists and psychologists note. But the Freudians knew the power of transference and counter-transference where feelings towards people and issues are transferred on to the consultant. Beware the manager who wants the consultant to attend meetings, or keeps quoting them. One has to walk a very delicate line in the relationship, but its power is unquestionable.

- *Diagnosis and self-understanding.* Therapists attempt to help people to introspect, to examine themselves, and to record their behaviour. They encourage the monitoring of everyday events and processes and so encourage self-understanding about motives, responses and habits. Some try to help clients to understand fully their conflicting motives for actions, while others insist on the rigorous diarization of everyday behaviour (e.g. smoking). Often, the insight is the cure. The consultant does likewise – all are hot on measurement and monitoring, often of features of the business activities forgotten, ignored or neglected by the business person. And, in that sense, the consultant helps the client (cures the patient) because they become much more self-aware.

- *Commitment to change.* Patients simply coming to the therapy session reaffirms their commitment to attempt to overcome the problem. Moreover, they are obliged to work on that change between sessions so that they come to each session with reports of progress. Often, they have to show commitment because of the cost of the consultancy. Clients have to make and sell the idea of bringing in consultants; then they have to support and pay them. This commitment is often done publicly and therefore risks ridicule and humiliation if it goes wrong.

The implication of this is that it may not matter too much what type of consultant you bring in because they all have exactly the same effect. The IT techie, the west-coast weirdo, the smart-arse strategist or the manic marketer may all bring about the same benefits – small, but noticeable benefits, and probably at great cost.

But there is one other finding from the psychotherapy world that does cause a little concern. Its called 'spontaneous remission' and it means that, over time, people seem to get better without any professional help at all.

Career counselling

It used to be called 'vocational guidance'. Then it became 'career advice and counselling'. Now the closest any adult gets to this topic is in outplacement counselling, which often involves trying to get a burnt-out, middle-aged, executive a new job. Or more likely persuading them that downshifting, or some other euphemism for stopping real work, is a good thing.

Since the late 1920s there have been various tests of vocational preference used to help guide bewildered and guileless school-leavers into job categories suited to their interests and abilities. The trouble is that many are attracted to glamorous jobs for which they have little or no talent. Occasionally, they may have great talent – to be, say, a concert pianist – but the jobs are too few and the competition too great.

The concept behind career counselling is pretty simple. It is the old 'round pegs in round holes' idea of fitting the person to the job. Fitting the job to the person is really more about ergonomics than about guidance. The 'fit' idea is simply that a person's productivity and satisfaction will be greater in jobs that they are temperamentally better suited to. Hence extroverts are advised, wisely, to go into sales and marketing where they thrive on the variability, people contact and air of optimism. Introverts, on the other hand, find the quiet work of accounts, stores and engineering more to their taste, where they can work alone in a less people-oriented and frenetic atmosphere.

We know extroverts trade off accuracy for speed, and introverts speed for accuracy. We know extroverts respond better to promises of reward than to threats of punishment. We know that extroverts work better than introverts in the presence of distraction (open-plan offices). We know extroverts are more likely to have accidents (of a particular kind) and we know their boredom threshold is easily reached.

But good vocational guidance people need to look at various other personality traits like conscientiousness, creativity and neuroticism, but also ability. Having the right personality profile without the specific abilities won't do. And we understand what abilities are required from a job analysis.

One starts then with the job, rather than the person. The theory says one does a careful, thorough and multifaceted job analysis to determine what skills, abilities and temperaments the ideal job holder should have. It is now popular to judge ability, motivation and personality under the term 'competency', which is an unhelpful term. Thus, one needs to know requisite levels of numeracy, literacy, as well as speed and ability to learn. Data on all this can be acquired from assessment centres, biodata, psychometric testing, references and even (least reliably) the interview.

Traditionally, however, selectors seem to spend more effort on analysing the person rather than the job, while for vocational guidance experts it was the other way round. But some notions of career counselling are deeply flawed for various reasons. First, they are far too static: they fail to take into consideration the fact that people adapt to, and change, their jobs.

People *adapt* to the job they are in. They can show fairly striking changes in attitudes, beliefs and work-related behaviour because of the incentives and requirements of the job. Most organizations attempt, through various explicit (induction, mentoring, training, appraisal) and implicit (reliance on observation) techniques, to shape and mould behaviour into a currently acceptable pattern. This means, inevitably, that attitudes, leader- and followership-styles and even aptitudes of employees may change over the first year(s) of employment; sometimes, but not always, in the direction desired by the organization. Thus, a fit may easily and quickly develop into a misfit *and* vice versa.

But individuals also *change* their jobs (without leaving them). They rearrange furniture, use space and technology differently and 'personalize' different aspects of the job. They can negotiate with others, earn special privileges or simply ignore various constraints and precedents. In this sense, very soon they are doing the job rather differently from their predecessors, and possibly from the way recommended by the company. Thus, the job for which they may or may not have been carefully selected becomes changed. Again, fit may become misfit (or vice versa); further, the change may have a significant effect on individual and group productivity.

However, both adaptation of personal work style, and attempts to change the way of doing the job, are more likely to lead to a higher rather than a lower level of fit because the changes made are all attempts to increase fit. It may also be the case that a person does change the way a job is done (to fit their own preferences) so that it turns out to be less efficient. In this sense, it is possible to increase satisfaction and reduce productivity at the same time.

Jobs themselves *evolve* and change. Organizational restructuring, the development of new technology, changes in the market, etc. all means that jobs evolve fairly fast. Thus, it is possible that a well-planned fit can quickly change as the job evolves with technology, market forces or customer demand. Indeed, over time it may be that people find the degree of fit varying substantially as a function of job evolution. It is no doubt the case that changes in the way jobs are performed will be greater than changes in one individual's preference or skill over time. Thus, it may be predicted that, in those areas or sectors that show the greatest job evolution (e.g. computing), patterns of individual fit may be most volatile. Conversely, where jobs remain fairly constant (e.g. agriculture), patterns of fit are likely to be much more longitudinally stable.

The whole concept of career counselling seems outdated precisely because we are constantly, and probably correctly, being told there is no longer such a thing as a career. A career is defined as 'a field or type of employment that offers a long-term series of opportunities for advancement'. We shall all have, if lucky, multiple careers – we shall be personal-portfolio managers. And therefore what advice we need will be quite different.

Because of the speed of change in technology, all jobs were and are in a state of flux. Job analysis will therefore be less relevant. And person analysis will have to focus on potential rather than current knowledge and skill. So the key features will be the speed and thoroughness in the acquisition of *new* knowledge and skills, as well as motivation.

Perhaps the three factors that are most predictive of these abilities are intelligence, personality and biography. Intelligence is probably the best predictor of speed of learning. Often, intelligent people are curious and self-confident and hence happy to tackle new tasks. Intelligent people are better and quicker at analysing problems, be they logical-deductive problems or more creative problems. It has been argued that there are distinct, but related, types of intelligence which relate to ability in particular issues. Thus, Gardner distinguishes between seven types of intelligence:

1. *verbal* or linguistic intelligence (the ability to use words)
2. *logical* or mathematical intelligence (the ability to reason logically and solve number problems)
3. *spatial* intelligence (the ability to find your way around the environment and form mental images
4. *musical* intelligence (the ability to find, perceive and create pitch and rhythm patterns)
5. *body-kinetic* intelligence (the ability to carry out motor movement, e.g. being a surgeon or dancer)
6. *interpersonal* intelligence (the ability to understand other people)
7. *intrapersonal* intelligence (the ability to understand yourself and develop a sense of your own identity.

The single, best predictor of multiple-career success is multiple intelligence. But it is not the only one.

Probably the personality dimensions of greatest importance are conscientiousness and neuroticism. The latter predicts absenteeism, low morale and stress-proneness. So one wants a high score on the first dimension and a low score on the others. Conscientious people are prudent, hard-working and therefore reliable. They soon get a good reputation, which serves them in good stead. Coupled with ability, this trait is a sure-fire career winner. On the other hand, neuroticism is a deep and abiding handicap. It is not easy to 'cure' and can have a long-lasting effect on a career. The neurotic is unhappy and tends to be dissatisfied, stressed and complaining in all jobs they have. Again, the consistency of their behaviour leads them to develop a poor reputation, which, of course, can be self-fulfilling.

Biography may be a good indicator of the deep and often-murky springs of motivation, which helps one understand what drives a

particular individual to achieve. Precisely what keeps people going
and ever striving while others are happy to relax on their laurels is
unclear. Motivation is the engine, ability the chassis, and personality
the design. The longevity, adaptability and popularity of the car are
dependent on all three.

Success in the job in 2020 can be assessed now. We have little
idea what the world of work will be like but we can do a reasonable
job in assessing the potential of the individual to carry it out in over
20 years, because we know the predictors of success.

Just as we need pet passports and car-history documents, so all of
us are going to need our career-portfolio papers. It is to these that
selectors and counsellors need to attend, if they are to give the best
advice and employ the best people.

Competencies in the new millennium

It is over 25 years since McClelland (1973) began to popularize the
concept of competence and nearly two decades since Boyatzis's book
The Competent Manager was published. Since then, the concept has
spread like wildfire in HR circles, and companies have felt the need to
have a personal framework.

Competency frameworks are seen to have quite specific benefits.

1. *Language:* At best, a common, shared, rich, descriptive language to
   describe people and performance. At worst, it introduced jargon,
   psychobabble and imposed particularly specific meanings on
   everyday words, which were not properly understood.
2. *Measurement:* The idea that performance needs to be measured to
   be managed and that measurement could improve feedback. This
   leads to the recognition of the importance of good HR databases
   to improve decision-making. It also made people aware of the
   problems of measurement and attitudes like: 'What is important
   isn't measurable and what is measurable isn't important', which
   can be replaced by 'What is important must be measured'.
3. *Consistency:* Nearly always the idea was the competency approach
   led to better consistency across the whole organization in the way
   people managed (selection, development, appraisal). HR was
   consistent, up to date, sophisticated, but with consistency often
   came bureaucracy and rigidity.

4. *Development:* Competencies certainly helped organizations focus on the need for development, but also how to go about it. It also often helped trainers develop courses and measures like the 360-degree feedback forms.

Over the years, various issues have occurred again and again for researchers, which need to be addressed.

1. *Should we use the term 'competency'?*

Whilst this may be a relatively minor point, it remains for some non-HR people an important and contentious issue. Because the whole competency movement is past its fashion-peak in the 1990s, the term is now not as widely accepted as it was. To a large extent, the earlier organizations introduced their framework the more likely they stuck with 'competency' language and concepts. Some are quite happy with this situation; others have sought to change it.

Those who have chosen not to use the term have done so for various reasons. To many, competency sounds mediocre. Further, not *having* a competency or *being* competent implies incompetence, which is a serious issue in business.

Others have preferred to use their own terms, like *high performance behaviours, management practices* and *standards*, that they can identify with. They argue that they are better understood by line managers and have the individual stamp of their company. They're genuinely unique to them.

2. *How many competencies do we need?*

Most organizations end up with a list of competencies through their particular chosen research method. This list is typically between eight and 15, though some organizations may have as many as 30 general competencies (each with a number of behavioural indices).

One lesson that many companies report is that a list of 10 or 15 competencies is probably too long. It becomes unwieldy for the managers and adds much to the bureaucratic burden. However, others, who are tied into industry standards, find that they can cope quite adequately with as many as 20 supposedly unique competencies.

There is always a trade-off between comprehensiveness and bureaucracy and the best, most parsimonious, level of description.

The systems that work best are short, simple and comprehensible rather than comprehensive. This is, and has been, an important issue in explaining why frameworks have failed: even those in HR complain about the time taken to complete documentation and the perceived overall benefit of the exercise.

3. How is the competency list/framework derived?

There are a number of issues here: should one do the research in-house or use consultants? Is the initial research essential to the buy-in process? How important is it to do research across all sections/departments of the organization? How long should this phase last? Is any one methodology more useful than another to generate a useful, and unique, framework?

Where the team responsible for introducing competence has done extensive pilot work across the organization, the introduction has tended to be more successful. Line managers like to be consulted – often individually rather than in focus groups and meetings – and taken seriously. Failure to listen to specialist groups, particularly in engineering/finance, has often led to later problems.

Many, many organizations attribute problems of the competency approach to the time taken to generate the framework from deciding to go down that route to producing agreed and finalized documentation. It seems not unusual for it taking 2-3 years between announcing the initiative and the documentation appearing. Expectations have been badly managed and this often leads to cynicism and scepticism.

The critical issue lies in timing and managing expectations about when the framework will be finished and how it will help line managers in particular and the organization in general. Communicating clearly about purpose and progress right from the beginning can solve many of the problems.

4. When and how best to use consultants in the process?

To a large extent, this depends on the consultants used, the relationship between HR and the particular consultants, and the general use of consultants in the organization.

Consultants can be used at various stages, typically:

A. early research in designing the framework
B. launching the project
C. specific training associated with the framework
D. auditing the process
E. redesigning and updating the project.

Some line managers resent consultants and it can become an issue in the initial stages of the project. Without doubt, the stamp on the final competency framework and process is more a function of the consultants used (if so) than the uniqueness of the organization itself.

5. *Should the consultancy framework be applied across the whole organization?*

Most organizations start with the explicit aim of trying to devise a framework useful for all people in the organization above a certain level. Thus, it is hoped that it is generally applicable across all departments, sections and regions for those at a specific level of seniority. Thus, for instance, part-time or support staff are not initially included and may never be so.

Once again, this is an issue of balance: allowing specialists to have a small number, 3–4 competencies, to add to a short but manageable list of 6–8 general competencies, works well. This is the 'compromise position' that many organizations find themselves in. Those that resist introducing specific competencies often have the use of the whole framework threatened.

6. *Who needs to champion the project?*

The issue of an organizational champion or organizational support is not unique to the problems of introducing competency frameworks. However, the issue seems more crucial when considering the design, introduction and maintenance of HR projects.

Where competency frameworks have failed, research has frequently noted two related things: the loss of the champion and/or the withering of board-level support.

Just as importantly, if the board does not endorse the introduction of the framework, it seems doomed to failure. This includes going on training courses, attending early research meetings and being seen to use the system. This support is needed not only at the initial phase but also right through the process.

7. How often and why do competency frameworks need updating and revising?

There are three phases to the successful implementation of all frameworks: planning/creating, implementing/launching and maintaining. Typically, the money and energy are exhausted in the first phase, which takes longer and proves more difficult than expected. Whilst there is, of necessity, money and energy left for the launch and the training support of the competency framework, this can easily evaporate in the really important phase: maintaining the system and ensuring that it is used in the organization.

Typically, there is a call for changing and revising the system a few years after launch. This is a normal and healthy reaction. However, it is not easy to reproduce or adapt the manual. There is also the natural resistance of those who have spent considerable time on the manual. Hence, it is rare to see frameworks thoroughly revised and updated as much as they should be. Indeed, there appears to be a negative relationship between the amount of work done in the initial 'manualization' and the desire to change the system.

It seems to be the case that, like all systems, there needs to be a balance between continuity and change. Competency frameworks clearly need re-visiting every 2–3 years to ensure they are still relevant. Resistance to updating is a common source of failure. Many report that, when frameworks were introduced, they were all concerned with the *current*, rather than the *future*, needs of the organization.

8. For what function should the competency framework/architecture be used?

One of the initial attractions of the competency framework idea was that it would help integrate a variety of people management functions, specifically: recruitment and selection, development and training, and performance appraisal. The idea was that the system would generate both the concepts and the data bank for each of those systems.

Different companies began at different points: some started investigating the idea of introducing competencies because they had problems with retention, others with development and still others with appraisal. The research seems to suggest that implementation through personal development programmes (either 360° feedback at senior level or certificates at the junior level) works best.

Most companies use frameworks for training, some for selection and fewer for appraisal. The last nearly always has serious problems associated with it. Most line managers need to be introduced to the language of competency by first applying it to themselves and understanding their own behaviour. The language of general management competence helps managers focus on what they should be doing and also provides company-wide consistency around these issues.

9. *What training is required around competency frameworks?*

There are three types of training that need to be done to support all and any competency frameworks:

- *Individualization of work-plan*: Many frameworks find they need to have two parts to them, i.e. those that apply to everyone, at their level, and those that apply to them only (generic vs. personal). These may be called 'key objectives', 'key result areas', 'key practices', etc. but require personal specifications. Individuals need training in writing their own work-plan, particularly specifying success criteria. Whilst it is not difficult listing competencies and behaviours, they frequently find it problematic coming up with measurable criteria to evaluate each competency. There needs to be training and facilitation around this issue.
- *Progress/interim reviewing*: Most managers are poor at, and fundamentally neglect, giving staff feedback on their performance. This is not in the context of a final, end-of-year appraisal but an interim discussion about progress on specific competencies. They need to be taught how to structure and conduct these sessions so that they feel confident in giving both positive and negative feedback to their staff.
- *Rater Training*: Where competencies are rated by line managers for selection appraisal, it is most important that they know the pitfalls of rating and do not fall into one of the many traps, which seriously undervalues the numeric (or even verbal) feedback generated. Rater training courses are about the measurement and

assessment of competencies to ensure that measurement is accurate and reliable.

10. *What are the problems of linking competencies to pay?*

This is an enormously complex and sensitive issue and explains why so few competence frameworks drive performance-related pay systems. The issue revolves predominantly around the reliability of the ratings of competence, who rates (boss, peer, subordinate), comparability of ratings across raters (soft, tough boss), the size of the pay reward relative to base rate of pay, etc. Certainly, the evidence suggests that the introduction of competency frameworks other than through developmental issues raises the expectations that performance/competence will be rewarded (possibly by pay). Whilst competency frameworks in appraisal are sold on their ability to improve consistency and equality, the opposite is often the case. Both managers and staff are deeply sceptical, even cynical, about all appraisal systems. By introducing a competency framework in the hope that it cures all the problems of appraisal and performance-related pay is to expect too much.

So what are the characteristics of a good, competent framework? In essence, the need to be:

1. *Simple*: Parsimonious, not overcomplex, more understandable than fully comprehensive competency frameworks.
2. *Salient*: They must be relevant to line managers, staff, senior managers, and the business objectives and plan.
3. *Supported*: They have to be fully supported in terms of staff, money, and, most importantly, morally championed consistently from the top.
4. *Flexible*: It must be recognized that all systems are temporary and in need of updating regularly, based on changing circumstances.
5. *Rewarding*: The application of the system must be rewarded, particularly for line managers and staff. The former need to see it helps the process of good management and the latter need feedback, qualifications, etc.
6. *Developmental*: The idea that the system needs to be initially linked into developmental opportunities for senior managers.
7. *Communicated*: The aims, deadlines and benefits of the project need to be spelt out clearly, regularly and simply – and best not oversold.

8. *Adaptable*: The system must allow for certain individual depart-
    ments to add specific or technical competencies. Having both
    unique and shared competencies.

Conferences

Bored with the same old faces at meetings? Want a day out of the office
with a good lunch? Have to use up your training budget? Want to
network, benchmark or do a bit of headhunting? Want a bit of a fling
in an anonymous smart hotel? Yes? Then go to a conference.

It has been said that business conferences have the same reputation that Open University residential courses once had: alcohol,
adultery and aspirations. They implicitly offer many temptations for
the stressed, but mildly bored, executive.

Training and HR managers will tell you that they get inundated
with flyers and junk mail advertising conferences. They certainly
vary more in topics than in cost, which is typically £200 to £400 per
day. They are often held in upmarket hotels offering a good lunch. A
day conference is often surprisingly short – registration 9.30-10.00
supposedly to allow one to get there, and final discussions end at
4.30. So, what with lunch, tea and coffee breaks, total time listening
may be as little as four hours.

What makes a conference popular and successful – or not?
There are at least four aspects of the conference that are important
and certainly affect the 'happy-sheet' evaluations at the end. And
only *one* refers to the programme or the speakers.

The first factor is the *venue*. Conference-goers, like theatre critics,
are a fairly jaded lot and difficult to please. They have been to the
best hotels (in this country and abroad) and even attended conferences on ocean-going liners, barges and boardrooms. They become
picky and concentrate heavily on peripheral factors like the biscuits
with coffee, the choice of desserts at luncheon, the state of the loos
and whether their peculiar gastronomic requirements are met. It is,
after all, easier to judge and rate food and amenities than conference
content. And, if it is a very desirable 'overnighter', there are the
shower caps, the soap and the silence of the bed springs that can be
rated.

As a consequence, there is a small army of amateur Egon
Ronays happily judging conference hotel facilities and food. And just

as the theatre critic perks up when Macbeth is set in punk outfits or Salome is sung in the nude, so the conference addict is ever on the lookout for new, different, unusual conference settings. Castles have become more interesting than hotels, but there is a limit to innovation, mainly based on cost.

The second factor is give-aways or *conference trophies*. Again, inflation has meant conference organizers moved on from a giveaway folder to a file, to a briefcase (bag), to a full party bag containing a few books written by speakers, pens and other stationery adverts, as well as other discreet little presents. Like in-flight wash bags their total value is often minimal. But, once again, the folder and the briefcase are tangible and easily comparable. Note also the way in which some conference attendees place files ostentatiously in their relatively book-free offices as signs of training and education. Never underestimate the value of the adult party-bag.

A third factor is the *attendance list*. This partly confirms that the conference is worth attending. If person X from company Y attends, it probably means that it is worthwhile. Further, the more who attend the better. Popularity is a sign of success. Note the disappointment on conference faces when they pitch up to a meeting where there are only a dozen or so other attendees.

Another factor in the attendance list revolves around networking, benchmarking – and industrial espionage. Benchmarking is all about comparative processes. It is also about copying ideas, even, quite frankly, stealing ideas and practices from others. Within every business sector, there are companies with fine reputations for products, services, innovation, etc. And professionals are nosey. They want to meet the people in those organizations, hear what they have to say. And conferences are ideal places for this activity. They are also ideal for affairs – testimony to which may be found in many divorce court cases!

And fourth, there are the *conference speakers*. What appears to be the most successful mix is one or two famous names, the odd token academic and a few real-world, hard-bitten practitioners. Famous names are expensive and can be very prima donna-ish and they are a risk because, to pay their £3000 an hour (upwards), one needs many more 'bureaucrats'. It is quite simply a risk calculation. Some gurus – Handy, De Bono, Harvey-Jones – have been heard before so the good conference organizer is always on the lookout for new, different, speakers. Often sports stars or television newsreaders 'do the ticket' very nicely despite the fact that few know anything about the topic under discussion.

People like speakers who tend to the entertrainer model – a few ideas, a lot of funny stories, a memorable case history. They like some, but not a lot of, participation, and can feel cheated if they are forever in syndicate groups doing the work for the speakers.

So what are the criteria of a damn good conference? A new, posh, interesting venue a varied and full take-away package; the opportunity to meet and 'get to know rather well' others doing the same job as you – oh yes, and a few speakers who provide a few ideas in an entertaining way.

Creating the right impression

We all make disastrous people-selection decisions, even when we collect lots of data over long periods of time. The divorce statistics are testament to that. We make errors whatever selection method we favour: the mysticism of graphology, the codes in references, the expense of assessment centres or the realism of actual work samples.

But whatever procedure HR professionals might favour, either for an initial sift or for a confirmation of their intuitions, most people expect, demand, and use interviews.

And the interview is literally that: an inter-view where both parties, selector and selected (appraiser/appraised), view each other face to face.

Both the problems and the joy of the interview are that, being adults, we are all skilled at impression management: putting your best foot forward, showing your best side. The snappy suit, the firm handshake and the confident smile have been known to sway the decision. This renders the interview more like a hall of mirrors or a charade of bluff and pretence rather than a 'clinical surgery' for the collection of vitally important information.

Just as interviewers become more experienced, so do many job seekers. Like the development of assault and defensive weapons, so selectors and selected become ever more sophisticated in 'sussing each other out'. These days, the advent of video-conferencing means that we can interview, negotiate with or just chat to people face to face from all over the world. Thus, both verbal and, particularly, non-verbal presentational skills, observation skills and questioning skills are becoming ever more important for all managers, particularly those in HR.

We communicate by e-mail, by phone and by face to face albeit over a video link for speed. In letters and e-mail, all we have to go on is the meaning of the words. People can hide behind the documentation, not disclosing possibly crucial things about them – their sex, age, ethnicity or disabilities.

At least on the telephone one has vocal cues – the tone of the voice, the accent, articulateness. And these vocal cues can be important in detecting anxiety, uncertainty, even telling downright lies. Vocal cues and clues of interest include response latency (how long they take to reply), slow and uneven speech (as if they are thinking about something else), eagerness to fill silences (feeling guilty that they are not believed) and 'pitch raises', which means the voice goes up at the end (with the implied question: 'Do you believe me now?').

Accent, speed of talking and pitch, as well as 'firmness' of the voice, all have an effect on the attractiveness of the voice, as actors know well. They can convey class and education, confidence and sex appeal.

But the face-to-face meeting or the video conference allows us to see and hear the person. Still, most business is done face-to-face. But what is it we want to see? What are the non-verbal cues that supposedly can tell us so much?

Most researchers in the area tend to break up the topic into discrete areas, showing how such apparently trivial or fleeting phenomena like a firm handshake or a habit of looking at the ceiling when one speaks carry considerable communicative content. These differ enormously from culture to culture, making communication all the more difficult. The nine sorts of areas that are researched are:

1. **Eye gaze**: When, where and why we look at, signals dominance, liking or shame, interest or communicative intent. Gaze is determined partly by distance (which is why we tend not to look at each other when standing too close), topic of conversation (which is why Catholic confessionals and psychiatrists' couches are arranged to exclude eye contact and encourage introspection). Extroverts do more looking than introverts. People wear dark glasses to prevent people knowing where they are really

looking. Just a fleeting glance, say, between bridge partners or lovers can have extraordinarily powerful communicative content, if one understands the context and their relationship. Pupil dilation can tell us about a person's emotional state, specifically if they are angry – or randy!

2. **Facial expressions**. These are innate and universal, unlike most other non-verbal behaviours. Facial movements – raised eyebrows, blushing skin, down-turned mouth – all create a particular impression. The smile is relatively easy to fake, and it is known that ventriloquists, sales people and sophisticated liars tend to smile more than other people. Women understand the power of make-up to hide, change and enhance features. Some facial features like a nervous tick or a false eye can be very memorable. And we have a great deal of control over these expressions, which we can use to our benefit.

3. **Gestures**. There are polite and rude gestures, gestures that beat time or try to change the pace of proceedings and gestures particular to accompanying and amplifying speech. The clenched fist and the V-sign have a powerful symbolic quality. Self-touching, particularly if it is excessive, may be a good indicator of anxiety, especially during tense negotiation moments. People fiddle with the hair, their jewellery and their pens. Some are very characteristic of individuals and easily mimicked. We come from a gesturally poor country, having only half a dozen well-known gestures, while the Italians have over 30. People use gestures when they don't have words: they gesture directions, they gesture size and shape, and they gesture pain to doctors.

4. **Orientation**. The angle we choose to stand or sit in relation to another person is important. The shape of tables and where one chooses to sit, or is appointed to sit, is frequently deeply symbolic. One can include, exclude, marginalize and integrate others by simply orientating the body appropriately, while standing or sitting. All skilled negotiators know that being able to 'shape' the room by an astute movement of the furniture can ensure a small but significant advantage. A combination of the angle and distance one sits from another, as well as relative height, can signal a great deal about the rank and status of parties. Think of how a law court is arranged. Consider how the layout of the House of Commons affects what goes on there! One can signal that one

wants an intimate, an adversarial, or a co-operative meeting by room layout and the sensitive use of chairs and tables.

5. **Posture**. The tense, upright posture of the interviewee clearly signals anxiety, while the laid-back posture of the film director on the chat-show couch can be a show-off's sign of super confidence. Posture is most interesting when it changes: it could be nothing but an attempt to get more comfortable, but it could equally reveal an inner discomfort. They say that posture is more sincere than gesture because people are less conscious of it. Posture, like deportment, can signal breeding or height differentials or depression. Note the posture of two people who are introduced: their relative rank is easy to see.

6. **Body contact**. Because we live in a non-contact culture, we are very sensitive to touch. Most of us can readily distinguish between the professional touch of doctors and the social touch of the handshake, and between the friendly touch on the sports field and the sexual touch of a lover. Waiters know that touching a customer may increase the likelihood of a tip. When, where and why we touch is strictly regulated by our culture. And there remain very strong taboos in the area, as most of us have learnt. Hence the discomfiture of going to a society where the rules are different. One reason we British are thought of as cold is because we so rarely touch one another, though this may be changing.

7. **Dress**. Signals about our wealth, taste, values and social differences are sent by the way we dress. Hence the number of consultants eager to help business people to create a better impression. Badges and cuff links, designer labels and even the material (like fur) do make conscious statements about who we are or (but rather) who we want to be. One can try to intimidate others by dress and signal membership of groups. National dress and formal dress are easy because there are strict rules. But dressing down or going casual is more difficult because there are fewer guidelines. Being over- or underdressed at a party is a great embarrassment and a testament to the importance of clothing as a signal.

8. **Odour**. People douse themselves in scents to disguise their natural smell, which can give important cues about diet, health and anxiety. Businesses know certain smells – baking bread, freshly ground coffee, cigarette smoke, disinfectant and boiled cabbage can evoke powerful memories, change moods and alter

behaviour. The discriminating can literally smell fear in their negotiating. Recent research on smell-recognition has pointed out the power of smells. In one study, men were shown to over- or underrate the specific skills of a potential PA based exclusively on her perfume.

9. **Territory**. Appraising someone in your own office, instead of theirs, feels different. We have both public and private territories both at home and in the office. Our behaviour is affected by how conscious of surveillance – or free from it – we feel. Hence the importance of where negotiating meetings take place. The concept of neutral territory is important.

Not all of these nine non-verbal behaviours are relevant to video-conferencing. Orientation may be a function of studio requirements, and odour is not detectable. Further, the territory may be neutral for both parties. But still the video link can provide some excellent cues to understanding how comfortable the other is.

There is a lot of nonsense said about body language: that every action is symbolic, that Prince Charles fiddling with his cuff links means he feels handcuffed to the monarchy. Others give a spurious percentage saying that body communication is x% more 'powerful' than verbal communication. If that is true, why are charades so difficult?

Many consultants on the issue also say that a knowledge of body language means that you can 'read people like a book'. That is simply not true, but it is a fact that being observant as to both *what* is being said and *how* it is said does help one understand others.

There are two aspects to communication competence: sensitivity and flexibility. The first is being sensitive to the cues – both verbal and non-verbal – that one is receiving. The second is responding to those cues. Being sensitive but not flexible means you are observant about what is going on but unable to do much about it. Being flexible, but not sensitive, means you know what to do but not when to do it. Being neither means you really have low EQ. And having both means you are a really skilful manager.

Many training courses – whether they are selection, appraisal or negotiation skills – teach flexibility. They teach tactics and strategies: how to ask questions, how to give bad news. But few teach sensitivity, though a lot of social and interpersonal skills courses say they do. The good news is that both can, and must, be learnt. The hallmark of any manager, and particularly HR managers, is that they are good (flexible and sensitive) communicators.

Creative workers

It seems to be an unstated, but widely held, assumption that all businesses need creative people. Some assume that creativity is both necessary and sufficient for business success. Creativity, whatever it may be, is clearly a very desirable characteristic and worth developing a reputation about.

The way people most often use the phrase 'to be creative' is both different from, and certainly more desirable then, being innovative. Innovation is about doing things radically differently. It seems to be implicitly assumed that creativity is special, innovativeness ordinary, and that creativity is a rare gift, while innovativeness can be learnt.

It is certainly true that one of the pathways to success in organizations is indeed through innovation. Some have rejoiced in the innovative product route. Disney, Polaroid, Sony and Windows typify this route to success. Others have developed innovative technology like Benetton, Honda and Evergreen. Some have tried to be innovative in the way in which they have a 'relationship' with their customers. Some of the airlines (Virgin) and credit-card companies have been successful doing this.

But other organizations have been extremely successful without any particular innovation. Some have simply exploited the rigidity of their competitors, like Federal Express or Easyjet. Others have turned around a slowly declining business, like the Hilton Hotels. Saatchi and Saatchi arguably were successful not because of amazing creativity but rather by capitalizing, mobilizing and manipulating market forces. Some airlines have found success through the exceptional-service route.

But still the received wisdom is that we all need highly creative people. And the search is on to find, recruit, manage and retain them. But is the gain worth the pain? If you can find them, can you manage them effectively?

Curiously, empirical research into creativity remains something of a backwater. Essentially, there have been four rather different approaches: those who study the creative *process*, those who are fascinated by the creative *person*, still others who are interested in the creative *product*, and more recently those interested in the creative *situation*. The problem for the social scientist is finding agreed real-world criteria for creativity so that the issue can be properly investigated.

It may be based on product criteria (patents awarded, number and type of publications), professional-recognition criteria or on social recognition, all of which are open to fashion, political correctness and the like.

There is both good and bad news when looking at the scattered scientific literature on creativity. The first is that it is true that both 'creatives' and psychotic mental patients share the ability to produce more unusual associations between words and ideas compared to that large but undistinguished group called 'normals'. In the jargon, this means creatives and certain mad people have common information processing patterns, which could be seen as deficits.

They seem unable to inhibit irrelevant information from entering consciousness. They find, whether they like it or not, unrelated ideas become interconnected – and this is often bizarrely a very creative process. They also both have high resting levels of activation and tend to be oversensitive to stimuli. Hence, they may demand a special environment in which they can feel comfortable.

The extant research on creativity and madness suggests persons genetically related to psychotics are often unusually and statistically improbably creative. Creative persons often suffer bouts of serious breakdown and psychopathology. And psychotics and creative achievers have strikingly similar ways of thinking.

But, of course, madness is neither necessary nor sufficient for creativity. Most mad people (psychotics) are far from creative. And many highly creative people are more prone to neurosis rather than psychosis. Certainly, many creative writers have been prone to depression but few (with some notable exceptions) have ever been hospitalized.

A recent study comparing equivalent groups of creative and non-creative 'normal' people brought to light the problems with managing creatives. The creatives were marginally more extroverted but much less conscientious. They were all less efficient, less dependable, less organized, less responsible and less thorough. In short, they were lazy and self-indulgent – but they were creative, by all accounts.

However, the creatives certainly were artistic, curious and imaginative. They were marked for unconventional, introspective and unusual thought processes. But they were also distinctly neurotic. They tended to be self-pitying with brittle ego defences; they tended to be tense and prone to depression. People noted they were anxious and touchy. They are certainly impulsive and moody. Many seem overly concerned with their levels of adequacy. It may be that neurosis is associated with creativity in 'normal' populations and psychosis in 'abnormal' populations. Certainly, if one has been around talented 'arty-farties' for any time, it is not difficult to notice rather high levels of neurosis. But once again it must be emphasized that not all neurotics are creative – one does need raw talent.

Now you know why advertising agencies have account managers. These are relatively normal people who intercede between the client and the creative. Put the latter two together and you may expect sparks and a quick end to the business.

Don't be fooled at the interview. The creative person is not the marginally flamboyant figure in coloured bow tie dressed a little like George Melly. The charming person with a steady history, both personal and professional, is unlikely to be the real creative. Real creatives are likely to be pierced and have tattoos in places you never thought possible. Further, their daily intake of legal and illegal substances would also probably make you shiver.

By definition, the real creative is difficult to manage. They are cold, manipulative and uncaring and they do not easily work in teams. Frequently absent, they often let you down. But some are clearly worth the investment and pain – but which? All, however, are difficult. After all, they score on both neuroticism and psychosis. How do you manage the anti-social, egocentric and unreliable? The answer is: with difficulty. But, if you really care about creativity, you may have to.

Detecting liars

Can you detect people telling lies? If so, what do you look for? Is the mismatch between verbal behaviour (*what* they are saying) and non-verbal behaviour (*how* they are saying it) sufficient to detect lying? Are some people simply better liars and, if so, why? Extensive and very careful research by experts in the area has revealed that betrayal of concealed information is organized by the type of information. Indirect speech, pauses, speech errors and decreased illustrators indicate that the verbal lie is not prepared. Slips of the tongue, tirades, micro-expression or squelched expression often indicate powerful emotion. Blushing, gazing down or away means embarrassment, while decreased illustrators, and slower and softer speech can mean boredom.

Social psychologists with an interest in non-verbal behaviour have been particularly interested in the non-verbal behaviour associated with lying. I have summarized this literature elsewhere. I state that it can be noted first that you can observe stress signals produced by that autonomic nervous system: dry mouth, sweaty palms, shallow and uneven breathing, 'tickly' nose and throat, blushing or blanching. These are noticeable when someone is under stress, whether he or she is lying or not. It is very easy to confuse the two. People can be anxious for many reasons, only one of which is that they are caught lying.

People are less conscious of their feet or legs: the further you are from the face, the nearer you get to the truth. Sudden changes in foot-tapping, pointing feet to the exit ('I want to get out of here'), simultaneous tight-arm and foot-crossing have all been taken to indicate lying. Active extroverts fidget more, as do young children. Foot movements may be as reliable an index of boredom as they are of lying. The frequent crossing of legs may simply indicate an uncomfortable chair.

Posture is more sincere than gesture: it can be seen as more unnatural and forced when people lie. Because people seem less aware of their total posture, they may secretly signal various desires (to leave) or that they are holding back the truth.

Giveaway, expansive gestures decline during lying; because they feel they may be caught, liars tend to sit on their hands, fold their arms or clasp their hands together. The lack of spontaneity may be an index of lying or fear: the fear of being caught. But some people are simply not as generally expressive as others: they are still not frozen. Liars have shifty gazes: when children are lying, they look down or away. They look guilty but do not look you in the eye. Many an innocent person has been accused of lying because they avoid eye contact. But people avoid eye contact for many different reasons – they feel uncertain about their opinions, they are tying to remember facts or they feel social embarrassment. Indeed, it is impolite in some cultures to look someone in the eye.

There are both verbal and non-verbal cues for lying. Indeed, some argue that it is easier to spot lying on the telephone than actually seeing people face to face. There are five clear *verbal* cues to lying:

1. Response latency: the time elapsing between the end of a question and the beginning of the response. Liars take longer. They hesitate more than they do when not lying. But beware the thoughtful introvert: they take longer to respond than extroverts.
2. Linguistic distancing: not saying 'I', 'he', or 'she' but talking in the abstract, even when recalling incidents in which he or she was involved. Thus, they talk in legalese: e.g. 'It could be said', etc.
3. Slow but uneven speech: the individual tries to think while speaking but gets caught out. He or she might suddenly speak fast, implying something is less significant. It is the change in pace in response to a particular question that gives a clue that something is not right. Changes in behaviour are always interesting to the lie detector.

4. Overeagerness to fill silences: to keep talking when it is unneces-sary. Liars overcompensate and seem uncomfortable with what are often quite short pauses. Hence interrogators tend to remain silent after a person has given an answer. Liars worry that they are not believed and hence continue to answer.
5. Too many 'pitch rises': that is, instead of the pitch dropping at the end of a reply, it rises like a question. It may sound like, 'Do you believe me now?' Curiously, the resulting accent is not unlike that of Australians.

There are also various non-verbal behaviours that are linked to lying. They include:

1. Squirming/shifting around too much in the chair. They seem to be saying: 'I do not want to be here.'
2. Having too much – rather than too little – eye contact, as liars tend to overcompensate. They know that liars avoid mutual gaze so they 'prove they are not lying' by a lot of looking – but a 'tad too much'.
3. Micro-expression or flickers of expressions – of surprise, hurt, anger. These are difficult to see unless frames of the video are frozen. The eyebrows are often an interesting place to look for flashing micro-expressions.
4. An increase in comfort gestures – touching his or her own face and upper body. Some people even hug themselves or caress their own bodies.
5. An increase in stuttering, slurring and, of course, 'Freudian slips'. These are mistakes where what one really believes 'comes out' and one says really what one means rather than what one intended to say.
6. A loss of resonance in the voice – it becomes flatter, less deep, more monotonous. Often, the pitch goes up. This is a direct result of physical arousal, almost a constriction of the throat.

Why do liars get caught? It has been suggested that there are five reasons why liars get caught.

First, lack of preparation: not ensuring that their story line is developed, consistent or verifiable; not checking certain facts. The more complex the lie, the more preparation is required so that the story is consistent over time and between different parties telling it.

Second, lying about feelings (emotional escapes): it is easier to lie about facts than feelings; sadness, anger and so on return in the re-telling, but, if they're not there, this may indicate lying. It is particu-larly difficult to sustain a lie about an event that really moved one.

Third, of course, there are feelings about lying: old-fashioned guilt, the more people realize or believe they are telling a serious lie, the more likely they are to show guilt. Such deception-guilt arises more from the action of lying than from the lie itself. It increases when the lie is selfish, when the deceit is unauthorized, when the liar is ill practised and when the liar and his or her target are similar in terms of personality and social values. Moral, religious people thus may be easier to detect because of their guilt; unless, of course, they genuinely believed they are lying in a good cause.

Next, there is the ever-present fear about being caught (detec-tion apprehension): the more serious the threatened consequences of the lie, the more nervous the liar. Detection apprehension occurs most strongly when the target has a reputation for being suspicious and difficult to fool, when the stakes are high in terms of rewards and punishment, when the liar is less practised or has been an unsuccess-ful liar in the past and when the target benefits little from the lie. Thus, letting a person know one is an expert lie detector (a psycholo-gist, a police officer) may beneficially induce detection apprehension.

Finally, one can get caught after the lie by duping delight (relief after the lie): the observable and puzzling relief shown after a lie has been told. A person is caught for duping delight most often when the target of the lie poses a challenge because he or she has a reputation for being difficult to fool. It also occurs when others are watching or can appreciate the skilful performance of the liar.

How ordinary people (in, say, a job interview) can try to detect liars:

First, establish base-rate behaviour. This means noting what they are like when they are normal, relaxed and telling the truth. Give people time to relax and see what they are like when it is unlikely they are lying. Some people fidget more than others. Neurotics are more anxious than the stable most of the time. They twitch and stutter more. There are numerous idiosyncratic but stable non-verbal behavioural differences between individuals. It is too easy to mistake particular signs such as sweating or avoiding eye contact as a betrayal of anxiety and a function of lying, when it is perfectly normal, everyday behaviour for that person. Talking in public, being cross-examined or even being interviewed by a stranger can make people very uncomfortable (some more than others, and, paradoxically, non-liars more than liars).

Next, look for sudden changes in verbal, vocal or visual behaviour such as movements. It is when behaviour alters noticeably that it is most meaningful. Note any mismatch between what is being said and how it is being said, as well as any differences in anxiety level as certain topics are raised. When the eyes, the voice and the words spoken are not in emotional synchrony, it may well be a very good sign of lying. A forced smile or laugh to accompany the carefully prepared verbal line can be a powerful indicator that 'something interesting is going on'.

Then formulate a hypothesis as to the cause: what are they lying about, what is the sensitive issue? Not everything is a lie. Why should they be lying about some issues and not others? What would cause them to lie?

Finally, test the theory by bringing up a particular topic (the area of the lies) and see if the non-verbal pattern re-occurs. If there are persistent indicators of discomfort when particular topics are reintroduced into the conversation, one may assume a stronger possibility of lying.

Of course, we all know the difference between white and black lies, between lies of omission and commission, between 'impression-management distortion' and real lies, and between the 'naughty porky' vs. the immoral, illegal and unjust lie.

But it is not only the job selector or negotiator who needs to know about lying. Colleagues, customers and subordinates may well have cause to lie and there are times we need to sniff them out. It is not easy or totally reliable, but a careful reading of the vocal and non-verbal signals will certainly help the process.

Dissent: using the power of the freedom to disagree

To dissent seems much more gentle than to disagree. It means to withhold assent, be of a different opinion, to hold an opinion different from the majority or the established orthodoxy. Dissenters both in the religious and the secular sense are non-conformists.

What sort of organizations encourage or suppress dissent? What sort of people for personal reasons or 'matters of principle' habitually choose to dissent? Some organizations fear dissent and disagreement, talking about positive thinking, believing in the cause, etc. For them, dissent is a dirty word: something to be avoided and discouraged at all costs. Some organizations, like people, are conflict averse. They fear and thus suppress argument and dissent. They see only its negative side and try to suppress it. Others relish it, almost flourish in it.

Taken to extremes, this can easily lead to 'groupthink'. When group members become tremendously loyal to each other, they may ignore information from other sources, if it challenges the group's decisions. The result of this process is that the group's decisions may be completely uninformed, irrational or even immoral.

Some of the potential consequences of groupthink include:

- Few alternatives are considered when solving problems; preferred accepted solutions are implemented.
- Outside experts are seldom used; indeed, outsiders are distrusted.
- Re-examination of a rejected alternative is unlikely.
- Facts that do not support the group are ignored, or their accuracy challenged.
- Risks are ignored or glossed over; indeed, risk is seldom assessed.

There are supposedly eight classic signs of groupthink (see the table on page 41).

But some people believe that dissent can be an organizational asset. They argue that ideas and practices from unchallenged organizations tend to be bland, uninspired, repetitive and second rate. Dissenting, it is argued, leads to innovation and better ideas. Tension can create involvement, interest and creativity.

The pro-dissenting school believes that in defending the views both the majority and the dissenters are forced to clarify their views. They thus have a chance to test their ideas and capabilities. Further, dissent allows long-standing, even festering, problems to surface and be dealt with.

Faced with dissent, organizations (and individual managers) tend to adopt a number of characteristic positions. These include:

Classic signs of groupthink

Symptom	Description
Illusion of invulnerability	Ignoring obvious danger signals, being overly optimistic and taking extreme risks
Collective rationalization	Discrediting or ignoring warning signals that run contrary to group-thinking
Unquestioned morality	Believing that the group's position is ethical and moral and that all the others are inherently evil.
Excessive negative stereotyping	Viewing the opposing side as being too negative to warrant serious consideration.
Strong conformity pressure	Discouraging the expression of dissenting opinions under the threat of expulsion for disloyalty.
Self-censorship of dissenting ideas	Withholding dissenting ideas and counterarguments, keeping them to oneself.
Illusion of unanimity	Sharing the false belief that everyone in the group agrees with its judgments.
Self-appointed mindguards	Protecting the group from negative, threatening information.

- Domination: This involves the authoritarian position of might is right. They assume – sometimes by a sort of divine-right principle – that they are right and (all) dissenters wrong. But how they deal with the dissenter may also reflect the corporate culture. Some tend to try to suppress, ban or exclude the dissenter; others try to humiliate or publicly punish them, while still more try to modify dissenters and let them down easily.
- Containment: This involves denying or rejecting dissent talking about 'sight differences in opinion', 'virtual agreement', 'time will sort this out'. The aim is to mitigate or temporize dissent by containing it. Often, the organization is prepared to charm or seduce dissenters and 'play the long game' to wear them down. But the bottom line is that dissenters are wrong and dissent is undesirable.
- Capitulation: Some organizations/majorities give in to dissenters if they believe they are right, that they will win in the end or are faced by litigation, strikes or worse. Few like to be seen to capitulate, and will strive hard to do a good PR job to present their capitulation as something very different.

- Compromise: This is the most British of approaches because it seeks to take the dissenter's views into consideration by modifying the policy, plan or decision. The organization likes to see itself as fair but responsible. The question, of course, is whether the result is a strengthened hybrid or essentially a fudged and weakened solution.
- Integrated solutions: This is supposed to be the best approach because this approach aims to satisfy fully the demands of both (or all parties) rather than a compromise, which attempts to lower demands. People and groups that favour this approach tend to follow rules like: forget domination, clarify real intentions, re-evaluate goals, analyse demands and be open.

Emotionality at work

Emotional intelligence is all the rage. Whilst it is self-evidently true that you need more than raw intellect to succeed in life, you can't do without it to succeed in business.

Whilst there remains no agreement as to the fundamental components of emotional intelligence, nearly everyone agrees that two aspects of it are pretty fundamental. The first is *self-awareness*, which involves understanding of one's moods, emotional states and drives and more particularly how these affect others. The self-aware manager, at least in our culture, tends to be marked by self-confidence, charm and self-deprecating humour.

The second fundamental component is *self-regulation*, which is more than self-control and impulse control but the capacity of thinking before acting and of coping under pressure. The well self-regulated manager tends to be a safe pair of hands, trustworthy, known for their integrity and open to new experiences and change.

The bell curve of all human characteristics: intelligence, height, personality, by definition, means that most of us are 'in the middle' – neither very bright nor very dim, not extreme introverts or extreme extroverts. And, presumably, emotional intelligence is also distributed normally.

But just as some managers are very tall and others conspicuously 'vertically challenged' so one does find managers with rather extreme emotionality scores. They are equally dangerous for the business and problematic for their colleagues, but for opposite reasons. The two extremes may be characterized as the manic marketing manager (though they do not have to be in marketing) and the introverted internal auditor (though they, too, can be anywhere in the organization).

The first is the *manic marketing manager*. They are certainly tiring to be around. Energy, enthusiasm and optimism they have in bucketloads. They seem supremely self-confident, courageous to the point of recklessness, and often creative. They can intoxicate all those that have contact with them. They embody charisma. They can, if clever and articulate as well, electrify an audience and give people a profound belief in themselves and their destiny. They seem to be on a double dose of Prozac. And they never seem to run out of steam. They are often attracted to marketing, sometimes PR. They talk a good deal, have unlimited ideas and possibilities and have grandiose visions of the future.

But these hypomanics have low EQ and can be disastrous for organizations. They have turbulent social relationships, and their financial extravagance can lead to serious problems. A tendency to break rules with regard to sex and drug taking also leads to problems.

Most of all, they react badly to setbacks. They can quickly and easily switch from sparkling enthusiast to irritable, impertinent, fault-finding viciousness. Trifles can lead to tears.

The manic manager needs help. They are not very self-aware, at least in terms of the consequences of their behaviour. And they are very poor self-regulators. Most people have heard of those with manic-depressive bipolar disorder who move from extreme highs to pitiful lows and need medication to maintain a more stable emotional state. But some manic managers are not prone to long bouts of depression yet they do need help of family, friends, colleagues and others.

The problem is that some organizations attract, even reward, manic behaviour. For the manic manager, the manic state is wonderful: it is characterized by a euphoria, rapture and a deep sense of strength, exaltation and omnipotence. They can inspire others with a real sense of mission. But they can easily become moody and destabilize well-formed groups. They can inspire distrust as quickly as they inspire trust. If you can stand the roller-coaster life and being with a manic marketing type, OK. And, if you are prepared to trade off the highs for the lows, they may be an asset.

The second type, the *introverted internal auditor*, is at the other end of the emotional expressive scale. They are the detached, detail-oriented drones of the organization, who are as emotionally flat and as unmovable as a polished granite courtyard. They have flattened emotions themselves and seem quite uninterested in the emotional lives of others. They are emotionally illiterate, reflecting neither on their own emotional state nor that of others. They have little realization of how they 'come across', or much ability to fake emotions.

They tend to be very literal with emotions and have a very small emotional dictionary. You need to weep in front of them before they realize you are upset, and have a serious temper tantrum before they can comprehend you are angry. They certainly are out of touch with their inner child – if indeed they have one!

Naturally, they turn away from people-oriented jobs to technicalities, machines and numbers. They can be found in finance and stores. And they can be very good because nothing seems to ruffle them. They are analytic, cold and restrained. To most people, they seem dull and uncommunicative. They can describe details, physical and technical aspects of human problems, but have no insight into how others react to them.

They have little imagination, no creativity, and rarely express enthusiasm. They may be excellent data processors but poor managers. Some organizations are scared of any emotional expressiveness and hence can cope with these dead fish. They certainly get poor 360-degree feedback, though it does not worry them unduly. They need emotional education – how first to recognize and then respond to emotional communication via verbal and non-verbal signals. It is not easy to educate an emotional illiterate, but it is possible with sustained effort.

The ability to understand and manage emotions at work is important. The bandwagon interest in emotional intelligence reflects many people's personal observation that social skills, empathy and assertiveness are crucial factors in the workplace. Some organizations, for historic reasons, have preferred the emotionally restrained, others the emotionally expressive. But most quite naturally prefer the middle of the road. Nothing succeeds with excess.

Employee theft: causes and cures

Some call it 'shrinkage' or 'fiddling' and accept it as inevitable. Others resort to psychobabble, describing it as 'a form of non-violent property deviance'. We all know about embezzlement and petty theft but there is also grand theft. But the simple fact is that employee theft is one of the most prevalent, costly and hidden problems confronting current businesses. It is a white-collar crime against the company – employee theft.

Repeated incidences of minor theft add up over time so that it has been estimated that employee theft is 10 times more costly than street crime and accounts for over one-third of all business failures.

Some companies lose about 10 times as much from employee theft than shoplifting, and the situation seems to be getting worse. One reason for this is that in a devious way there is a culture of acceptance with respect to employee theft. It seems that in Britain people are happy to victimize organizations (but not individuals) and feel and express little guilt over the issue. More importantly, perhaps, employee thieves are caught and prosecuted very infrequently.

Both the observers and enactors of theft see themselves as latter-day Robin Hoods stealing from rich, smug, disdainful organizations and giving it to the poor (themselves). Also, organizations seem loath to prosecute caught thieves, possibly because they do not really see it as criminal behaviour. They prefer internal sanctions like repaying the company for the loss, which signals that theft is a breaking of company rules, rather than a breakdown of basic social values. Prosecution also brings bad press, requires impressive evidence of theft, may involve expensive legal battles, and may simply be unwise if an employee is extremely efficient. This may account for the fact that employee theft is, for most people, stealing without guilt.

People steal cash, goods and time. And they are remarkably ingenious, rivalling the techniques of those great escape war heroes. But it is also an organized crime. Gangs, groups or rings of employees conspire together to make theft more efficient.

Various group norms have been shown to exist that condone, even promote, employee theft. Some theft is provoked by staff imitating their supervisors. If it is OK for the boss, it must be OK for me. Dishonesty starts at the top and works slowly, inevitably and corruptly downwards. Many employees see theft as informal perks to which supervisors feel entitled. Also, people steal because their supervisors allow, even encourage, them to do so. It is true that supervisors pre- and proscribe what may be stolen, by whom and to what degree. Some have called this a system of controlled larceny, while others see it as part of an invisible wage structure. Theft becomes a sort of managerial tool that is faster and more efficient than promotion or calculating performance-related pay.

When managers utilize hidden economic rewards to supplement their staff's overall rewards, they pay a great price. This supervisory collusion can be serious because theft-based rewards are often sizable. Some managers even see theft as a major source of satisfaction – a source of fun and excitement in an otherwise dreary job.

To a large extent, work group norms seem to regulate and support employee fiddling and pilfering. Some organizations are schools for dishonesty in the same way that prisons are universities of crime. Employees learn what, and what not, to steal, how to help others and how not to whistle-blow. In fact, it has been shown that people are more restrained and encouraged by their co-workers than by formal management threats. Employees share tips about stealing, share the loot appropriately and get praised by colleagues for their efficiency and knowledge. In fact, the group support helps thieves to continue to think of themselves as honest, upright, organizational citizens.

Many work groups, like individuals, collectively rationalize their deviant, illegal behaviour. Thieves develop characteristic techniques of neutralization, which help them psychologically distance themselves from their crime. They deny responsibility (the nature of the victim), condemn the condemner and appeal to higher authority.

Groups have stories they tell about fiddling, which function to communicate acceptable and unacceptable behaviour. For all sorts of reasons, some things are fair game, others completely off-limits. Thus, waiters can take some foods but not others and on some nights more than others.

Psychologists have attempted to understand employee theft in terms of distributive justice and equity theory. The idea is that people have a notion of fairness about how they are treated in the workplace. They give and they get. Stealing is a way of redressing grievances equitably, seeking revenge on a company when the equitable or fair situation has changed to become inequitable. When employees feel underbenefited, unbalanced, short-changed, in not receiving appropriate pay and recognition, they try to 're-establish distributive justice' in their exchange relationships with their employer by 'nicking wot's available'.

What evidence is there that there is a close association between employee satisfaction and theft? Not only do people believe this to be the case (the common-sense argument) but the data support them. However, it could be that theft causes dissatisfaction because people need to justify their reactions. Equally, it is possible that other factors (e.g. alcoholism, low work commitment) cause both stealing and dissatisfaction.

What the research shows is that theft can be both restitutional and retaliative. The former is about 'evening the score' for being treated unfairly, while the latter is about reciprocity. Employees seem enticed to steal because of the way they are treated but this link can be ameliorated by the way they are treated. Thus, in one study, researchers found that, when told their pay had to be cut, those who were given an inadequate explanation stole twice as much in 'restitution' as those who were given an adequate explanation. The extent to which the employees display social sensitivity is also important. The combined effects of treating people inequitably (pay below market rates) and without dignity lead them to retaliate with typical 'reciprocal deviance'. In other words, it is not only the magnitude of perceived injustice that makes a difference but also the way inequity is presented to the workforce.

So how can the manager reduce employee thefts? The first is to break the social norms that accept and rationalize theft. Some companies have had success with simply printing theft statistics on the intranet. It is essential to stop employees seeing their theft as appropriate and desirable. Business ethics talks can help this.

Profit-sharing also helps align the interests of employer and employees. Activities that lower profitability (pilfering in employee-owned companies) soon become taboo. Where this is not possible, having a clear social contract prohibiting theft may help.

If perceived (note, not actual) fairness is an issue, it is important to emphasize continually the fairness of the company's compensation system. Company hotlines for just whistle-blowing have been shown to have a significant effect. Some companies have suggested that the issue of theft should be brought into the open and employees should be encouraged to discuss how it is to be defined and treated. This helps to flag that the company is serious about theft and helps ensure employees' commitment.

Companies are now so worried about the issue they are attempting serious preventive, proactive, rather than reactive, methods. This involves integrity testing and background checks at selection. It also involves employer publications but, more ominously, a tightening up of internal controls and security. The following are guidelines for stopping theft:

1. Install security systems and implement internal controls for any process involving money or company assets.
2. Use valid *integrity* tests in the selection process.
3. Conduct background checks in selection appraisal as thoroughly as the law allows.
4. Review and revise, if necessary, any job or organizational information presented to prospective employees, stressing honesty, integrity and the costs of being caught.
5. Conduct orientation programmes that discuss the company's code of ethics and formal procedures to be followed in case of problems.
6. Initiate and model a culture of honesty in the organization, with clear reinforcement for honesty and punishment for dishonesty.
7. Provide support or encouragement for employees' personal and skill development.
8. Counsel 'troubled employees' out of the organization.
9. Review compensation and benefit packages for internal and external equity.
10. Get to know employees through effective communication and implement programmes that create bonds between employees and the company.

The equity contract

Worker anger is, it seems, all the rage. Many companies are finding their biggest enemies are not the management team, clients and customers, service providers or suppliers – or even competitors. It is their employees, particularly those unhappily on a short-term contract.

Forget the partnership, stakeholder, guru-babble of modern business. The adversarial relationship between employee and employer has never really gone away. Workers in many sectors are still seen as 'objects of production'. It almost seems as if a Marxist analysis of labour may regain fashionability because of the changing patterns of work.

If certain reports are to be believed, manifestations of workplace discontent are becoming endemic. Naturally, one has to question these statistics, particularly as consultancies that 'release research reports' on worker rage, or whatever, have a vested interest in taking up the problem. Companies, on the other hand, naturally want to downplay the problems they experience. So the truth is difficult to establish. But what is admitted by all parties is the increase in dishonesty, fraud, leaking secrets and theft/destruction of property.

The old rage rituals of strikes, or threatening strikes, has been replaced by white-collar individualistic crime. The demise of the unions and the reduction in manufacturing industries mean that organized, collective protest is a thing of the past. Occasionally, one still gets 'work-to-rule' protests, which is usually a euphemism for slothful, sour service.

In many ways, organized industrial protest was easier for all parties. It was easy to predict and control. There were even arbitration bodies set up to regulate negotiations. Now the isolated, angry, knowledge-worker can easily feel helpless and powerless. And all they need is the well-publicized example of others to have a bit of copycat fun at immense expense to the organization. Often feeling let down with broken promises, the new worker can and does exact a great price for their unhappiness. There is nothing so dangerous as a worker scorned.

Signs of rage and disaffection are well known. *Stealing* time is popular through absenteeism and poor, erratic punctuality. *Stealing goods* like stationery products, even furnishings, seems pretty rife. A philosophy of entitlement encourages not so much stealing but abuse of company facilities like use of fax, e-mail, transportation and other facilities for personal and non-authorized use.

There are other nastier signs, which are far less 'acceptable' to admit, even to a sympathetic ear. There are twentieth-century Luddites who spitefully damage and destroy company property. But there are also twenty-first century Luddites, usually computer hackers and their fellow travellers who can break into and, if they want to, destroy company records, processes and systems. Given the way things are automated these days, one clever, but malicious, employee can do more damage than a dozen of his/her father's generation and probably the whole workforce of his/her grandfather's.

Then there are the blackmailers and bombers. This group is, mercifully, probably the smallest but potentially the most destructive. Probably the most currently popular form of work-anger expression is whistle-blowing. There is an eager audience for the whistle-blower – the press in particular but also the competitors, sometimes the union, and in certain instances the police. The whistle-blower can act both courageously and pusillanimously. The latter used to be called 'squealers' and they can easily hide behind a cloak of anonymity, sending multiple letters to the press.

There is case after case in all sorts of sectors detailing the destructive power of the delusional employee. The secret and security services have had their fair share of problems. *The Higher Educational Supplement* published with *The Times* has a regular whistleblower column where the incompetent and nepotistic world of higher education is regularly put under scrutiny.

The central question is how to account for this growing trend. Why the increase in evidence of disloyalty and disaffection? And, perhaps more importantly, what can be done about it?

There is a global trend to what used to be called 'atypical employment'. Whether they are called 'interim managers' or 'fixedterm employees', they are often called 'contractual workers'. They are, in fact, short-term workers. Of course, all workers have contracts, be they formal, legal written contracts as well as personal understandings between employer-interviewer and employee-interviewee.

Those personal understandings have been called the 'psychological contract'. It is often implicit, never written down. It is about expectations on both parts – employer and employee – about work and conditions of employment. It is often really about nebulous, abstract concepts like loyalty, equity and fairness. Psychological contracts are open-ended, dynamic, implicit agreements specifying what the individual and organization expect to receive from one another over the full course of the working relationship. They are about diffuse responsibilities and rewards.

When a person starts a job, they have expectations and hopes about many issues like a career path, promotion, training, etc. Their legal contract, and possibly their discussions with an HR interviewer, have settled matters of pay, holidays, etc. called 'comps and bens' (compensation and benefits). These are usually non-negotiable and simply explained. Curiously, the things that often matter most to individuals – job security, career paths – are passed over. And for good reason. No employer should promise what they can't deliver. Further, most prefer the short-contract worker in the flat organization, which means for the worker no security, no future and no promotion.

Most of us know the lifetime career in one organization is dead. Consultants despise lifers for having no ambition, whereas in the past they were models of loyalty. But everyone, over 30 at least, wants some stability and predictability in their lives. It seems natural to be rewarded for service. But the current philosophy talks about performance management – not service management. Just as actors are only as good as their last play, so accountants are seen as only as good as their last audit, surgeons their last operation, lecturers their last course.

The word 'experience' used to cover a multitude of virtues. Middle-aged people justified all sorts of benefits – usually promotion and pay rises – on the basis of this nebulous term. But in the new world it counts for little. This is mainly because, with ever-newer technology, no one has relevant experience.

As a result, many middle-aged and older people feel letdown, even betrayed. Most just disengage - the 'quit but stay' brigade doing as little as possible. There may be a generational effect working here – where older people (over 50) disengage, those 30-50 become politically active, or fraudulent, 21-30 whistle-blowing, and those under 21 engage in good old-fashioned arson and destruction.

The answer is not a simple one but might be found during the interview process, when expectations may be clarified and the causes and consequences of change fully explained. Employers and employees need to clarify, discuss and where appropriate modify their expectations of the employee. Like sex and death, promotion in some organizations has become a taboo topic – as has job security.

Problems are exacerbated by a refusal to discuss issues or, worse, sending ambiguously coded messages which are easily misunderstood. At the selection interview, the probationary interview and at the annual appraisal, the psychological contract needs airing. Unless the employer has some idea of the expectations of his/her employees, he or she can do nothing about modifying them. And this means biting the bullet on promotion and pay policy – traditionally the hottest, and therefore most undiscussed, topics.

As long as policies are implemented equitably and communicated clearly, there is rarely too difficult a problem to deal with. Issues arise if there are exceptions to rules or there is a noticeable chasm between 'official' policy and what happens in reality.

Clarify the psychological contract about objective work issues but also about trust, responsibility and loyalty and you go along way to preventing the consequences of the spiteful, vengeful, angry worker.

The ethical business person

Business ethics is the application of general ethical ideas about right and wrong to the world of business. Despite the wry smile when the idea is mooted in some circles, nearly all business schools devote valuable curriculum space and teaching time to the area. Most middle managers and supervisors avoid ethics talk. Quite rightly, they see it as a threat to harmony: it's intrusive, confrontational and invites prejudice and recrimination.

Others believe it a threat to efficiency; ethical principles are simplistic, inflexible, inexact and definitely not adhered to by the opposition. And, of course, ethical debate can be a threat to the image of power and effectiveness. Moral talk and ethico-babble is esoteric and idealistic – fine for business-school types with nothing better to do but definitely not appropriate at work!

Having a really (as opposed to PR-governed) ethical business is supposed to bring various benefits: fulfilling public expectations, improving business relations, employee productivity, even profit, and protecting the business from unethical employees and competitors. The idea – without much evidence – is that all companies should have a clear, explicit and closely followed corporate ethical policy about numerous issues regarding employees, customers and suppliers. Thus, companywide policies about affirmative action, childcare, pollution and green issues and safety at work are all thought of as ethical issues. So are the old chestnuts of nepotism, discrimination and sexual harassment.

Each functional area is supposed to state and obey various rules. Thus, the accountants have to ensure their reports are characterized by accuracy, integrity and comprehensiveness. Marketing and sales have to be honest in their advertising: to price fairly and not to use or accept gifts/bribes to ensure sales. The IT people have to adhere to rules about privacy and security. The idea is that the firm, the bosses or selfish interest should not dominate. All very well – but is this driven by legal requirements, clever PR or a belief in a genuinely ethical system?

The problem with ethics is a bit like philosophy in general. It attracts ignorant busybodies, who believe that ethics is either a pretty common-sensical sort of topic or else an opportunity for them to ride a particular hobbyhorse and convert others to their ways of thinking. The worst solution to resolving ethical issues is the most common – appoint an ethics committee from all representative areas of the organization and let them either formulate a position or rule book and/or act as adjudicators when the need arises. There are many problems associated with this approach not least of which is the assumption that ethics is common sense, that all views are equally accurate, valuable and viable, and that no knowledge or expertise is required to solve ethical problems and issues.

A cursory glance at the library or the web will reveal many weighty, complex, philosophical tomes on ethics. Ethics is often a set paper in divinity schools and philosophy departments. Medical ethics now exercises some of the best minds in the area. Problems – like genetic engineering – are considered from various positions, (e.g. the famous utilitarianism) and their implications considered. Thus, consequentialists disagree with deontologists. Utilitarians are a specialist subgroup of the former, while those favouring egalitarian-ism are one type of deontologist.

Ideally, ethical systems are consistent and coherent. They are reliant and clear on principles, which are applied accurately and fairly on all occasions.

Everyone has experienced the dynamics of the meeting where the socially unskilled, the pedantic and the attention seeker disrupt the business. The less technical and the more 'moral' the issue under discussion, the more likely everybody is likely to put their oar in, and defend, often rather rudely, their positions. The result – long, catty, unhelpful meetings that leave few satisfied. Those meetings rarely result in a clear, consistently applied, internally coherent policy. Often, they are between individuals or groups who favour certain positions but cannot really articulate them clearly or coherently.

Consider moral judgments: First, individuals assume that good consequences can always be obtained, but people who are less idealistic admit that bad consequences are often mixed with good ones. Second, people who are highly relativistic in their moral outlook believe that universal moral principles are of little value when making moral judgments. Less relativistic individuals underscore the use and importance of fundamental principles.

People high on both idealism and relativism can be called 'situationists', those low on both 'exceptionists'. High on idealism and low on relativism make one an absolutist; whereas the reverse means one is essentially a subjectivist.

Situationists feel that people should strive to produce the best results possible but they are also relativistic for they believe that moral rules cannot be applied across situations. Adherents of this ethical ideology believe in a close analysis of each situation (i.e. looking at possible consequences of each action in terms of its context) before reaching a situationally appropriate moral decision. Situationists do a type of cost/benefit analysis before acting, in order to maximize good outcomes and minimize bad ones. Absolutists are also idealistic; they support actions that yield a greater number of positive consequences than negative ones. Absolutists differ from situationists in that they add to their cost/benefit analysis a condition that their actions should conform to some sort of overall moral code. Thus, whereas a situationist may justify lying (or even killing) under certain circumstances, an absolutist would insist that it was wrong to lie under any circumstances because doing so would violate the strict codes of justice and fair play.

Subjectivists are like situationists, because they are sceptical of moral principles, and much less idealistic than situationists, because they feel that in many cases it is impossible to avoid negative actions. This ideology is termed 'subjectivism' because its adherents describe their moral decisions as subjectively based, individualistic evaluations that cannot be made on the basis of more 'objective information like general moral absolutes' or 'the extent to which the action harms others'. Subjectivists essentially believe in the dictum that morals are a matter for the individual and his or her conscience and therefore it is pointless to try to extrapolate general rules because every moral action depends on the individual's perception in the immediacy of the moment in which the action is taking place.

Exceptionists support the existence of general moral codes or values but, as their name implies, in certain circumstances they do allow for exceptions to those general codes that they support. Exceptionists are described as being non-relativistic and pragmatic, and they will break their moral codes if, by doing so, they avoid the negative consequences that a moral action may incur if activated at that particular juncture. So, exceptionists can be termed as those people who have and uphold general moral rules but break them when these rules prove to be inadequate or unacceptable for a particular situation. Imagine sorting this out with a group of middle managers!

The solution – hire an ethicist and a lawyer. The Jesuits make fine ethicists with their understanding of casuistry and sophistry. Make it the job of those two, who need to meet only very occasionally (especially given the hourly costs of lawyers), to draft policy that follows an ethical system as stipulated by the business. The problem, of course, is giving them a clear enough brief in the first place.

Experience is a poor teacher

When asked to justify promotion on the basis of time-serving, few talk about loyalty or commitment to the organization. But they do frequently mention 'experience' – this semi-mystical term presumably means that having seen and solved problems in the past one can do so now with more speed, accuracy and precision.

That is, of course, if the present is like the past. But that was when change was gradual, orderly and predictable. Today it's non-linear, recursive and ad hoc. The procedure-driven have to learn to become issue-driven. One has to learn that every problem presents an opportunity. And many new problems are quite different: no one has experience of how to solve them.

The problem with experience as a teacher is that it is too slow. Experience in so many business-related fields may not only be irrelevant, it may well militate against you. Take the issue of learning a new computer package that may be radically different from the last. Old learning can impair new learning. *Tabula rasa* is beneficial.

During the Second World War young men learnt to fly before they could drive. And they did so more speedily and efficiently precisely because they did not have to unlearn some of the natural and spontaneous reactions they might have acquired while learning to drive a car.

Following medieval guilds some organisations still have an apprenticeship model of training. One works with the master for maybe as long as five to ten years, starting out doing very meagre and trivial tasks, ending up by taking his or her place. Training in the arts is still like that: hence the master class. But that is in part because music has not changed much. Playing a musical instrument may have changed little in a hundred years, hence one can pass on the skills through a succession of master teachers.

However, as technology and practice change, skills acquired through experience are worthless. You don't have to be very old to remember the old technology: how to use a slide rule, how to 'cut a wax stencil' on a Gestetner machine, how to feed a computer card into a mainframe – lost skills for a lost work. The experience is not at all useful.

But there is a far worse problem. And that is where the learning and experience handicaps or inhibits further learning. Here experience does not become redundant, it becomes divisive; and this is, or can be, a long process. It is a double process and often takes more than twice the effort and time. We all become wedded to familiar technology. The operating system becomes one's mother tongue, and to have to relinquish it is met with tremendous resistance.

Many times in the last century Asian dictators like Mao targeted middle-class professionals for re-education. Their experience, which shaped their view of the world and the way they did things, was deemed to be politically inappropriate. Pol Pot redrew up the calendar, calling the year: Year Zero. He wanted to start again: clean the slate, forget the past. So those with most memory of the past and fondness for the ways things were done – these must be dealt with.

The past, they say, is another country: they did things differently there. And that experience may be a poor teacher; indeed, a handicap.

That may be all very well with technology, but what about managing people? Surely people have not changed fundamentally over hundreds of years, so that managing people is a long lasting and transferable skill? Experience in people management must be a good thing – or is it?

Generational differences are mainly about values, not fundamental biological differences. The 'Baby Boomers' are different from 'Thatcher's Children', who are different again from 'Generation X'.

And the way they work reflects it. Job security, empowerment, training opportunities are valued quite differently by different generations. They have different carrots and sticks. Those who manage an international workforce soon discover this.

Twenty years managing garment workers in Bradford hardly provides one with much expertise for managing front-line staff at Heathrow. Again, then, experience may be a poor teacher.

The lesson of experience is that one really does need constant learning. Just as the actor and the cook are frankly only as good as their last production or meal, so the manager is likewise. One has to learn to discard and unlearn – to declutter one's management style and technique shelf and to embrace the new.

And so the best experience is learning to learn. Then it is a good teacher.

The ex-pat

One of the many consequences of the economic success of the Pacific Rim countries is that they now attract a fairly sizeable number of ex-pat managers, consultants and workers from North America, Europe and Australasia.

From Kota Kinabalu to Kyoto and from Taipei to Tokyo one can 'unearth' the ex-pat. Some may be in chameleon disguise of the native, while others are conspicuously and proudly chauvinist, going out in the midday sun. Others talk consistently of home and live according to seasonal patterns quite out of synchrony with the local time.

The ex-pats can be found at the club famous for its poor food, cheap gin and faithful retainers but also at the new, smart and expensive sports club. But they can also be found in the local church, the Rotarians and, more often, business associations. Others are not so obvious, preferring either to blend in with the locals or keep very much to themselves.

But how do the ex-pats adapt to living and working abroad? Are some with years of colonial experience better than others at finding a niche in Asia?

An ex-pat is usually definable as someone who makes the decision to live and work abroad. They should have some choice in the matter and be of an age when they can be self-sufficient. Many ex-pats start out as an adventurer, as someone who, at a relatively young age, with few responsibilities and a taste for sensation seeking, set out abroad 'for a while'. Many don't plan to be ex-pats but they find themselves in the role. But how do they change over time? What happens to these fleeing bounty seekers?

It seems that various ways of adapting are open to them. These different styles may change over time, and indeed they may be more common in some countries than others. But most are immediately recognizable.

Upwardly mobile. This ex-pat soon discovers that with some technical training, a Western education, English fluency and a white skin they are of the top pecking order. Demographically speaking a lower middle-class European is treated like an upper-class group member. Instead of being a servant, one has servants; instead of taking orders, one gives them. And it's a good feeling, so much so that return becomes unthinkable because it means downward mobility.

Sojourners. This group is more pragmatic, with a long-term plan. They are abroad for a specific goal and usually a set time period. It may be to accrue capital to pay off a mortgage or start a small business. Or it may be to do one's duties in the company and earn promotion on return. Strictly, they are not ex-pats but tempor-ary sojourners on a foreign posting, though they usually mix with ex-pats.

Nomads. These are sequential sojourners in the sense that they pitch their tent in one country after another, apparently aimlessly. A new pasture seems all they are after for they follow no long-term plan. The relatively buoyancy of national economies may be enough to spur a move as they trade a bear market for that of a bull. But the longer they spend abroad, the harder it is to go home. They are condemned to being the wandering albatross of the ex-pat world.

Financially trapped. This group is one of the saddest. They have stayed too long at a place in decline. They do not have the option to return 'home' because they are tied into a pension plan and, indeed, a weak economy. The financially trapped may be found in badly managed, newly independent countries where the currency has been chronically devalued. They cannot move or come home because they simply have no capital. Whilst they may be 'all right' if they stay put, their lack of foresight or simple bad luck has meant they are condemned to exile.

Gone Troppo. One of the most curious and maybe pathetic reactions of the long-term ex-pat is when he or she has gone native. This may be quaint or downright peculiar. It is, of course, much more than becoming thoroughly acquainted with the language, the dress codes and the norms of the natives, but a rejection of one's own values. This is not the stuff of the White Rajas but more that of Lawrence of Arabia. More often, however, it can look regularly pathetic and may be induced as much by a love of alcohol and adultery as the values and behavioural norms of the local culture.

The Never Lefts. The most odd reaction is that of the ex-pat who behaves as if they never left home. They may be marooned in a tropical paradise or isolated in the primitive bush, but they are slavishly faithful to their old ways of dress, food and social behaviour. Caught in time, they maintain the style and preferences of the country they left, which now no longer exists. The past is indeed another country.

Colonialism may have been replaced by 'cocacolonialism', but in some places the ex-pats exist as if nothing has changed since the great days of empire. The Dutch in Indonesia, Americans in the Philippines, the French in Vietnam and the British in Hong Kong, Singapore and Malaysia, still lead a colonial lifestyle. They are happy to be abroad so long as the natives are waiters and drivers. And they may have a deeply ambivalent attitude to the mother country and the thought of coming home. To re-pat the ex-pat is indeed a major challenge.

Fads and fashions in business

Management by technique is both a cause and a consequence of gurus' business books. To be a successful guru, you need to christen, personalize, and proselytize a magic-bullet technique. Without an eponymous technique, the guru is nothing. But, because they have a short shelf-life and almost predictable sell-by-date, one has to invent, re-invent, re-name or somehow come up with a new technique every couple of years to stay in the public view and make lots of money.

What matters is the name and the packaging hype. Whether it works or not is secondary. To do well, the idea must echo the Zeitgeist. There is a very long history of fads beginning just after the Second World War. Consider the following list of fads over a 40-year period:

Decade	Buzzword	Fad
1950s	Computerization	Installing corporate mainframe computers
	Theory X	Giving people more say in their work so they will produce more
	Quantitative management	Running an organization by the numbers
	Diversification	Countering ups and downs in the business cycle by buying other businesses
	Management by objectives	Setting managerial goals through negotiation
1960s	T-groups	Teaching managers interpersonal sensitivity by putting them in encounter seminars
	Centralization/ decentralization	Letting headquarters make the decisions/letting middle managers make the decisions
	Matrix management	Assigning managers to different groups according to the task

(contd)

(contd)

Decade	Buzzword	Fad
	Conglomeration	Putting various types of business under a single corporate umbrella
	Managerial grid	Determining whether a manager's chief concern is people or production
1970s	Zero-based budgeting	Budgeting without reference to the previous year's numbers
	Experience curve	Generating profits by cutting prices, gaining market share and boosting efficiency
	Portfolio management	Ranking businesses as 'cash cows', 'stars' or 'dogs'
1980	Theory Z	Adopting such techniques as quality circles and job enrichment
	Intrapreneuring	Encouraging managers to create and control entrepreneurial projects within the corporation
	Demassing	Trimming the workforce and demoting managers
	Restructuring	Getting rid of lines of business that aren't performing, often while taking on considerable debt
	Corporate culture	Defining an organization's style in terms of its values, goals, rituals and heroes
	One-minute management	Balancing praise and criticism of workers in 60-second conferences
	Management by walking around	Leaving the office to visit work stations instead of relying on written reports for information

So much for supply. There is also a voracious appetite on the part of confused, perplexed and desperate managers who want a quick, successful solution to their intractable problems. Most managers are desperate for the magic bullet. Hence demand.

The whole thing is a bit like the diet industry. Miracle diets come and go. They are invented by gurus of that world – doctors, dieters, second-rate actors and sports stars past their best. And they are consumed at great expense but little long-term effect by hopeful fatties who know this technique, like all the others, is probably an example of the triumph of desperate hope over experience.

Management techniques of all sorts fail for a variety of reasons:

- They are not relevant, appropriate or salient to the particular situation in which they are applied.
- They need to be customized to the particular situation but no one knows how to.
- The technique needs many years, not months, to have a measurable and meaningful effect.
- One may need different techniques used at the same time – not just the one to achieve the desired outcome.

There is nothing wrong with using these techniques per se. But they can be dangerous, if they limit thinking and flexibility. The techniques that have tended to be well known over the past couple of years include benchmarking, business process re-engineering, and total quality management. They are indeed a mysterious trinity.

Benchmarking (sometimes called 'best practice') is a very simple idea: find out what the world's best performers are doing and copy them. The problems for the managers are manifold. How do you define the best company? What if you are the leading company? But more importantly, how do you know there is not a better way to do the job?

To follow benchmarking is to be a follower, not a leader – to replicate not innovate. The real, and ignored, question is how the best practice affects outcome. This is a process question. Indeed, analysis may reveal that the most successful company's results occur *despite*, not *because* of, best practice.

Really successful companies innovate, not copy. They seek first to understand the problems and business process and overcome the former by changing the latter. Benchmarking can involve a massive but misguided research process, which always, perhaps rightly, leaves one feeling second best.

Re-engineering (also called 'core process redesign' or 'process innovation') took the world by storm over a decade ago. The idea, like all magic bullets, is deceptively simple. Most companies – manufacturing and service – are arranged around specialization not process. Thus, one follows how people or forms get processed by one department (accounts, stores, transport, HR, etc.) and then redesigns the process radically.

Perhaps the reason why this idea was so popular was that it justified laying off large numbers of people. Yet a decade or so after this enthusiastic slash-and-burn fervour of the gurus, they recanted, being very self-critical of the idea that re-engineering really was much help.

Why did it, like many other super-fix ideas, fail? First, it nearly always suggested massive reconstruction and radical restructuring. Hence this claim that there is massive incompetence and inefficiency everywhere. If it were true, surely the company would have gone under earlier? The more radical the re-engineering, the more the gurus got paid and the higher the expectations of success.

Re-engineering is another word for 'rationalization'. But it remains true since Adam Smith and Max Weber pointed it out that specialization is a major key to efficiency. The difference lies in specializing around a natural business process.

If re-engineering encouraged one to have a renewed and thoughtful reconsideration of the business structure and process, it did a good job. But it led too many to make radical changes that never bore fruit.

Total Quality Management sets out to acquire high quality products and services (defined by customers) by getting employees to do a systematic analysis and improvement of business processes. The idea came from a statistically minded engineer – an unlikely guru. Again, the magic bullet was forming TQM groups and employing their recommendations.

But are groups of employees able to understand the full aspects of technical efficiency? It helps to cut waste but rarely offers an overall company strategy for change. Real questions like how, when and where it should be applied remain unanswered.

Beware the snake-oil salesperson guru. Companies, like individuals, are both complex and unique. Many of the techniques advocated are good ideas. But, to be successful, they need to be applied carefully, continuously and in a customized way that suits the needs of that particular organization. Just as diets don't work unless the dieter changes their whole lifestyle, management techniques don't work unless the whole business process undergoes a serious shake-up.

Feedback, not feedbag

There is a splendid cartoon depicting a man talking to a horse. He says, 'You are a wonderful animal, canter well, have a beautiful mane...' and the somewhat disgruntled horse looks up and replies 'I said *feedbag*, not *feedback*!'

Most managers now have either experience or knowledge of 360-degree feedback. For the uninitiated, what this effectively means is that various people such as the *boss* from above, colleagues and *peers*, and *subordinates* from below fill out a fairly detailed question-naire on how they see your work-related behaviour. The employer also often rates himself or herself on the same questionnaire. The questionnaire addresses all sorts of things (initiative, leadership, team participation, customer service) but twice, and on two different scales: how well they did perform and how relevant the behaviour was (its importance). The questionnaires are statistically processed and typically lead to a report that describes managers through the eyes of others.

The feedback reports come in many forms. Often, the reports categorize behaviours – four boxes: *celebrate* (high performance, high importance), *fix* (low performance, high importance), *ignore* (low performance, low importance), and *investigate* (high performance, low importance). Some reports highlight those ratings where there is considerable difference between the two raters.

What the research teaches us is that the differences are greatest between self- and other ratings, no matter who is being rated or what is being rated. That is, it may be between self and boss, self and colleagues or self and subordinates. And this is not only for the deluded. One reason for this difference is called by psychologists the *fundamental attribution error*. What it means is that people explain their own behaviour in terms of situational and variable factors, while they explain the behaviour of others in terms of personality traits.

This is best illustrated by asking people if they are introverts or extroverts. Most people hesitate then explain they are both and it all depends. Ask them about their relations or work colleagues and the like and they are quite confident: he is a strong extrovert, she an introvert, and so on. We are aware of the variability in our behaviour but not so much that of others. We change according to the situation; they do not.

Another example of this is to ask a presenter (the actor) and the audience (the observers) about a business presentation that goes wrong. The presenter explains it in terms of the nature of the audience, and the latter in terms of the character or ability of the presenter.

This is not merely a manifestation of defensiveness. It is also about focus. The presenter focuses on the audience and they on him. And they explain things in terms of what they see.

Further, it is about knowledge. The presenter (the actor) knows about past performances: the audience does not. We know if we have a consistent history of good (or bad) presentations; they do not. They assume what they see is typical, which it may not be.

All this partly explains why different people have rather different perceptions of, and explanations for, the same behaviour. It also explains why feedback ratings are so different. More importantly, it explains why some feedback is so difficult to accept. Consider the case of the typical performance appraisal. The boss (the appraiser) knows that feedback is, or should be, good and bad, though he/she has learnt to call it strengths and *developmental opportunities*.

So how does one give feedback about poor performance? Most bosses dread this and avoid appraisals because of it!

The typical scenario goes like this: The manager (the appraiser) knows the appraisee will focus not on the good, but the bad, feedback. They know they will be asked to justify the three 30 per cent scores given to the candidate (even if 30-odd are rated 60 per cent and above). So they prepare their case with quasi-documentary evidence of typical incidences that illustrate the poorer behaviour.

During the appraisal feedback session, the appraisee typically challenges both the details (i.e. memory for) and the interpretation of the event. A heated discussion then occurs about an incident in the past. The appraiser is pressurized to change the rating; the appraisee is upset and demotivated. The 'problem' is solved by not giving the appraisee any low marks in the first place. This accounts for the fact that 5-point rating scales become 3-point scales (only 1, 3 and 5 are used); 7-point scales usually become 4-point scales, etc.

What this means, in effect, is that few people get honest feedback. The weakest get an average of 3.28 out of 5, the best 4.17. The difference in feedback is practically imperceptible; the difference in productivity glaringly obvious to any internal or external observer. And, if pay is linked to appraisal ratings, all get pretty much the same, and often very little. Hence, there is neither feedback nor feedbag.

A better approach is to be forward-looking. It is extremely important that appraisers give honest and differentiating feedback.

That means both the good and the bad. It is unlikely that people are good at everything. And they themselves know their strengths and weaknesses. In fact, all but the deluded often feel their appraiser does not know them well or has no insight, if they score them highly on certain things (for example, uptake of new technology, creativity).

The most important aspect of feedback is that you can do something with it. Hence the appraiser should prepare not a justification of low marks but a close and clear description of the different, ideal behaviours that merit a higher score. This focuses on the future not the past. It focuses on behaviour not personality. It focuses on improvement not failure. And it specifies to the appraisee what the appraiser wants.

In some jobs, feedback and feedbag are the same. For a salesperson working predominantly on commission, the salary cheque is a good index of how well they are doing. In call centres – the fastest-growing job sector in the country – people are given daily print-outs of their performance: calls answered, sales per call, total revenue generated, time spent on the phone, etc.

But for those in jobs where performance is more difficult to measure, feedback is less common. Hence the power of the 360-degree reports. It is not uncommon for middle-aged managers with 25 years' experience being stunned in every respect by the report. They are in fact receiving feedback (mainly from reporting staff) for the very first time. It can hurt. Hence the army of consultants who 'facilitate the feedback'. What that means is 'help the appraisee make sense of it and plan for behavioural change where appropriate'. Being surprised is not enough – being able to do something about it is more important.

But feedback should not be an end in itself. One can have 360-degree feedback fatigue if it is done too regularly without sufficient processing of the material. After all, feedback should help productivity, which relates to the feedback.

Fight the good fight

Most of marketing is about the acquisition of new customers. It has been said that the aim of marketing is to make advertising and selling superfluous. The aim is to understand customer needs so well the product or service sells itself. And most of us have heard about the five *p*'s or six *s*'s, or whatever, of marketing and selling. But how do marketees think? What metaphors do they use and what, if any, are the consequences of these metaphors?

Scientists have looked at how ordinary people think about their health. Some researchers have identified the various ways people conceptualize illness. Consider the following different metaphors for the cause of ill health:

- *Time running out* or degeneration, where illness is attributed to the wearing out of the body
- *Mechanical* faults or damage, where illness is attributed to broken or faulty body mechanisms
- *Imbalance* or lack of harmony, either between various parts of the body or between the individual and his or her environment
- *Invasion* or penetrations of the body by germs or other foreign bodies causing illness
- *Debilitation*: a weakness of the body that results from overworking, being 'run-down', a chronic disease or a weak spot in the body
- *Stress*: usually from work, relationships, environmental sources
- *Environmental irritants*: such as allergies, pollens, poisons, food additives, smoke, etc.
- *Hereditary proneness*: genetic transmission of a particular illness, quality or trait, which includes general weakness.

And these metaphors are important. After all, you starve a cold (because it has invaded the body) but feed a fever (it results from debilitation). Lay people think, speak and act in terms of metaphors that powerfully influence their behaviour.

Organizational gurus have also noted that people think and talk about their organization in terms of quite specific metaphors. These include the organization:

- *machine* – designed and operated as machinery and, indeed, making humans conform to its needs
- *organism* – a live, adaptable mechanism like our bodies
- *brain* – rational, problem-solving, self-critical and innovative
- *culture* – a set of shared values, principles, attitudes and beliefs about what is important and how the world works

- *political systems* – an institution with set power, authority, responsibility, order; about control and influence
- *psychic prison* – a collection of myths and fantasies that are confined by their own representation of themselves to the outside world
- *flux and transformation* – a generative system that develops, grows and regenerates
- *vehicle for domination* – a mechanism to impose its will on others by domination and control

Clearly, if you want change at work and think of your organization as a machine, you recommend re-engineering; if you believe it is a culture, you try mission statements; if you use political system metaphors, you might try empowerment and, if you think it's a psychic prison, you leave.

Curiously, the world of marketing, so full of hype and promise, is not rich in metaphor. Without doubt, the predominant metaphor for customer acquisition is that of *warfare and conflict*. One 'mounts an aggressive campaign', is clear about 'strategies, targets and tactics' and one makes sure of the prime state of one's marketing armoury, weapons and ammunition.

The macho image and language of the marketing world (where *Campaign* is the major journal) is further evidenced in recruitment advertisements for marketing experts. These also extol the virtues of aggression, referring to conquering new challenges, being a cut above the rest and contain all that 'no pain, no gain' language.

Salespeople are steeped in 'win-lose'-speak. The consumers, as much as competitors, are engaged as adversaries in a game of semi-lethal combat. The idea, of course, is that consumers subjected to skilful thrust and parry eventually succumb and 'sign up' and 'cough up', presumably feeling vanquished.

But there is a new alternative to the warfare metaphor – indeed, a very opposite alternative. It's called *relationship marketing*: the principles of personal selling as essentially transactional. However, those interested in those elusive concepts: *repeat sales* and *customer loyalty* now talk about relationship marketing.

Relationship marketing is about caring. It's win-win. And it can pay off handsomely with customers who have long time horizons and high switching costs. Thus, each seeks to develop a solid long-term working relationship with the other.

But this leads to 'in' and 'out'-suppliers: the former try to make switching difficult with incompatible systems, proprietary ordering systems – in short, indispensable. Out-suppliers do the opposite by trying to make the change easy. They make compatible, user-friendly, cheaper products – until, of course, they become the in-supplier.

The metaphor of a relationship is so much nicer. But it begs lots of questions. Is the relationship like a marriage or more cohabitation – is it binding, semi-binding or committed-ish? Is the marriage one of monogamy or polygamy? Are affairs allowed or severely punished?

Or is the relationship merely a friendship, or more an acquaint-anceship without the emotional charge of marriage? Of course, a one-night stand comes more from the conquest-metaphor school than from the relationship school.

And do you, the purchaser or the consumer, really want a relationship with a marketeer, a salesperson or a company? Most people want convenience not commitment! This is not California! We don't do retail therapy – we simply go shopping! And anyway, who sets the terms for the relationship?

It seems too much of a one-way traffic where companies want a relationship with customers, even if the attraction is not reciprocated. It can all too often end in tears with companies who have more the pathological profile of a stalker than a secret admirer. It smacks too much of dating agencies for insecure inadequates.

A major problem is that the two metaphors – warfare and relationships – are pretty incompatible. The aims, the concepts and the practices learnt in the one world do not easily translate to the other. Those schooled in customer acquisition by assertiveness, aimed totally at the process of 'closing the sale', may find it difficult to manage and understand the customer in terms of a steady ongoing relationship.

Relationship marketing has far-reaching implications for the overall customer proposition, for internal communication, for the corporate culture, for service provision and for all associated processes. But too many old hands cling on to the old metaphors. The warm and fuzzy talk of relationships is simply not as sexy as the phraseology of cut-and-thrust and conquest. It somehow seems unlikely that the magazine *Campaign* will change its name to *Relationship Building*.

But as with all good marketing, one should start from the viewpoint of an intimate understanding of what the customer needs, wants and expects and not what the company would like them to want.

Focus groups

It may come as a surprise to those who believed focus groups were an invention of third-way spin doctors of the late 1990s to find they were first used nearly 60 years ago. They were devised by American researchers during the Second World War to try to understand public reaction to radio programmes. While listening to radio programmes, people had been asked to indicate their reaction by pushing buttons (positive, negative) but the researchers (American sociologists) needed to know why they did so and when. Afterwards, they had a sort of wash-up discussion about the 'experiment'. Thus evolved the focus groups of today.

But this research method – if it is that – disappeared from the battery of techniques used by researchers until it was revived in the late 1980s. There was a sudden interest in the focus group from essentially two different quarters. Market researchers had always kept the methodology alive and used it to test the acceptability of products (cars, cereals), services (mental health services, hospital facilities) and people (political candidates).

The researchers had mixed motives in using these groups. Some wanted to hear 'the truth' in the language of the 'ordinary consumer'; others wanted 'secret insights' and counter-intuitive ideas when looking at issues. Others simply wanted to know if people would like a new untried product. However, many believe these groups present very spurious data concerning whether or not people will like or buy a product.

The output is a report that somehow summarizes what people said. They are peppered with 'sexy quotes': Sort of vox-pop sound bites that hopefully encapsulate an attitude. What those who commission the report want is understanding but, also, nearly always some direction for decision-making. Ideally what they like to hear are consensual views or at least easy and valid ways to predict the behaviours of a segmented market. This, they believe, might help them to price or market products better and, if necessary, make certain changes before they get too far in their development.

The other users of focus groups – the post-modernist social scientists – rejoice in the opposite of consensus. They celebrate argument, counter-argument, claims, rebuttals and disputations. Nearly all have rejected empiricism as a means to understand the world, and adore all forms of relativism. They argue that different data-collection methods in different contexts lead to data with different meanings. And, of course, they argue that all perceptions are equally valid. Indeed, they often love to see establishment positions challenged and eagerly record the often wacky, highly unrepresentative views of articulate minorities.

Sociologists often claim that focus groups are flexible and are the most efficient way to comprehensively elicit a person's view. Focus-group methodology is very simple, though it comes in rather different forms. It has been defined as: 'an informal discussion among selected individuals about specific topics'. Not much different from a dinner party, then! There are, as one may predict, no strict rules. But they all have a *moderator*, whose job it is to 'keep discussion focused on issues and ensure a wide range of opinions are solicited and debated'.

There are many variants on the theme that have, of course, important implications for how the groups are run and the resultant data. Some of these are:

1. Who is in the group: strangers vs. an established group; to maximise group homo- or heterogeneity.
2. Whether the group meets only once or many times.
3. Whether the data from the focus group 'stand alone' or are supplemented by other sorts of data from questionnaires or experiments.
4. Whether groups are audio- or video-recorded: both or neither.
5. How directive or controlling the moderator is and how much he/she encourages others to challenge speakers by asking for elaboration, demands examples, etc.

But, as researchers have found out, all these factors do make a difference to the overall outcome and report. One American study published in a marketing journal found outcome very dependent on moderator style. Thus, the level of sophistication with scientific theory and concepts in the moderator has a significant effect on both the focus-group dynamics and outcome reporting.

Another study by the same researcher in the area – Dr William McDonald from Hofstra University – found research objectives inevitably lead to very different outcomes. He isolated three different rationales: to understand the everyday experiences of consumers, to generate scientific constructs and to validate them against everyday experience, or, third, to provide a sort of clinical judgment defined as second-degree scientific constructs without numerical measurements. He found the reports of everyday-oriented moderators superficially appealing but lacking the depth provided by scientific moderators. In short, focus groups may be very unreliable, depending on the education and approach of the moderator.

Focus groups do show how people engage in the process of collective sense-making: of how views are constructed, expressed, defended and occasionally modified within the context of debate with others. But is this what spin doctors and marketing managers want to know? Their key features are of getting at ordinary people's language, concepts and concerns. In a sense, it is the opposite of the public understanding of science; it is the 'scientific' understanding of the public.

But focus groups also try to encourage individuals to produce more fully articulate accounts that can be challenged. For the voyeur, and the social scientists (if they are different), it offers an opportunity to observe the 'process of collective sense-making' – or how opinions are expressed, defended and modified in conversation. Social scientists (of a particular type) love to say things like 'thinking is a socially shared activity' and that ideas are almost never generated in splendid isolation. All very interesting stuff but for people in business what they really want to know is: how, what, when and why ordinary members of the public vote, purchase, complain, join, leave and generally make social and economic decisions. Precisely how they defend or rationalize their position is of far less relevance.

Focus groups can be cheap(ish), quick and easy to run. Reports are often interesting in the way a Sunday supplement is. People who run focus groups like to talk up the effort and expertise involved, spend time recruiting, briefing and debriefing participants, transcribing, planning the best possible way to lead the discussion. And then there is moderator mystique, which is often portrayed as a clinical skill not easily acquired. Some claim special quasi-therapeutic, neo-psychoanalytic, crypto-detective skills that make them particularly good at the task both of running the group and also decoding the transcript. Whilst some believe the former is little more skilful than livening up a cocktail party and the latter being a sub-editor on a newspaper, others claim great things of their favourite moderator.

Indeed, the word 'moderator' is interesting. Strictly, it means arbitrator or mediator or even presiding officer. However, most moderators need and claim more skills than judicious chairmanship. Most of the time they are more like secondary-school teachers shutting up garrulous attention seekers, whilst attempting to cajole those less uninhibited to say what they genuinely think.

But do they work? Do they provide, at the simplest level, reliable data? A recent paper by two economists based in Belfast and Newcastle set out to test some simple but important ideas. They noted that precisely because of the interaction processes producing the data (discussing the quotes), any findings from the discussion are not independent of these interactions. Put simply: do different groups with different moderators produce different answers even to the same issues? They ran eight focus groups and looked for convergence in conclusions. They also got independent observers to watch videotapes of the different groups and check inter-coder agreement (or whether they came to similar conclusions).

As one may predict, they found more convergence than divergence both between the analyses of different observers and also between the results of the different groups. The reliability goes up, if people in the group are given basic information beforehand so that we can be sure that there is a similar fundamental level of understanding and knowledge of a particular topic. And they were forced to conclude 'in order to gain any real credence within economics, unstructural analysis of focus groups is in most cases insufficient to generate worthwhile insight, providing an easy excuse to dismiss qualitative data out of hand as 'unobservant' and 'subjective''.

And there is the crunch. If things are not reliable, they cannot be valid – in other words, if you don't get a consistent finding using different groups, different occasions, different moderators, it is impossible to say whether their views are in any sense representative of anything.

There seems to be something of a reaction against focus groups. It is not certain exactly why. Certain decisions that have been based on them have been unpopular or shown to be mistaken. Perhaps they have been commissioned and used particularly by unpopular individuals. Often, however, decision makers seem unclear about what to do with their reports. It may be fun for social scientists but clearly not that helpful or cost-effective for decision makers.

Wouldn't it be fun to run a focus group with focus-group moderators or focus-group business users to get other views? That indeed would concentrate minds on the issue – or would it?

Going absent

Absenteeism is endemic to organizations. As long as people continue to suffer illness or discontent, they will take time off work. So as long as organizations continue to employ people – or until scientists devise a panacea – managers must face the problem of absenteeism.

However, it is almost impossible to come up with really accurate national or business figures on absenteeism. There are essentially three reasons for this. The first is that companies do not collect absenteeism data – they have no systems to do it, or the issue is too sensitive and hot from both a management and a union perspective. The second reason is that, whilst an organization may indeed collect these data regularly and accurately, they are, quite simply, too ashamed to publish or publicize it. The third reason is that there are too many definitions in the accident literature to agree on how to collect the data. We have authorized/certified vs. unauthorized/uncertified absence, contractual vs. non-contractual absence, sickness (injury) medical vs. non-sickness, non-injury/personal absence, etc. In other words, simple aggregated statistics are deeply misleading because they include different types of absenteeism.

There are abundant data on the sort of factors known to be related to levels of absenteeism. At the level of the *individual* worker, obvious factors include general health and resistance to illness, work-induced fatigue and shiftwork but also non-work-induced fatigue (like child care) and preferred hobbies (that sap energy or are dangerous).

Inevitably, *environmental* factors have an impact on absenteeism. Ambient flu and other viruses are important, as are fluctuations in atmospheric conditions. Jobs with well-known stresses like uncontrollable and excessive noise, powerful unpleasant odours and bright lights also affect illness behaviour.

Certainly, *administrative* factors relate closely to all aspects of absenteeism, particularly the index of absence used, the administrative categories used for the attribution of absence and the level of aggregation of absence data (particularly whether it is by the day, the week, the work group, the shift, the plant, etc).

But we do not know – despite various scare stories – that absenteeism still has a relatively low base rate. It is not that common a problem except in very specific sectors at particular periods of time. We also know that people underestimate their own absentee records but tend to inflate views about the absence of others. Self-evidently, managers and employees hold different standards about how much absenteeism is acceptable. Indeed, the very meaning of absence varies considerably among different groups. For some, it is a form of legitimate extra pay to compensate for perceived poor pay, extra stress or reduced holidays. For others, it is a way of getting even with colleagues who seem to take excessive time off work.

Certainly, supervisors' behaviours, values and modelling are crucial in shaping the attendance patterns of individual workers. Organizations themselves differ in how they measure and react to it.

It is difficult to assess the real cost of absence from work. But, to use old-fashioned terminology, it is true to say that there are various *stakeholders* in company absenteeism. For the *individual* workers, absenteeism can affect income and job security as well as reputation, which is related to the latter. Equally, failing to go absent (with legitimate sick leave) may have both acute and chronic effects on employees' health.

The *work group* itself has a considerable stake in absenteeism, particularly with respect to morale. People in work groups are very sensitive to equity – the ratio of inputs to outputs. If a group member takes excessive and perceived inappropriate absences without some equitable cost to the person (reduced wages, increased workload when present, reduced holidays), other group members are often affected. They may take revenge by going absent themselves, thus lowering the productivity of the group as a whole.

Inevitably, the *organization* as a whole has a serious stake in absenteeism. It is not difficult to see how both acute and chronic levels of absenteeism affect profit, staffing, customer relations and company reputation, which affects the share price. How organizations plan for dealing with unforeseen absences is indeed a fascinating index of their adaptability.

The *unions* are stakeholders in absenteeism. They negotiate over the causes and cures of problems and often have it as a major topic of dispute.

Every *worker's family* has a stake in absenteeism. Pressures at work, particularly with regard to retaining the job in periods of little job security, could lead to ill health that affects the whole family. Equally, pressures in the home can be a direct cause of absenteeism. Parental absenteeism patterns also provide a powerful model for young children and may influence either their readiness or reluctance to go absent. It has even been suggested that school truancy and phobia are clearly related to parental absence from work.

Of course, the *society as a whole* has a stake in absenteeism. Social values determine the value of work and leisure, illness and health, loyalty to family and employer. Albeit a crude measure of a society's health and happiness, absenteeism figures in the former Eastern bloc countries, though rarely reported, were certainly an amazing index of the inefficiency of socialism.

So what causes absenteeism? There are a bewildering number of explanations and theories. They are not contradictory but complementary, each emphasising a different cause. But perhaps they indicate best of all the complexity of the whole issue.

1. *Process and decision models.* This approach suggests absence is the result of many factors, especially personal attitudes to attendance, the perceptions of the company norms favouring attendance, perceived control over personal behaviour, and personal moral obligation to the organisation. This approach stresses that individuals make calculated and rational decisions to go absent.
2. *Withdrawal models.* The argument here is that job satisfaction is the best predictor of absenteeism, but is more related to frequency than to overall days lost. Commitment is less important but includes the extent to which people believe the organisation is committed to them. People go absent or withdraw as a reaction to job unhappiness with their work.

3. *Demographic models.* This lists all related factors that predict frequent absenteeism. Age is important (the graph is U-shaped), in that older and younger people are more prone to absenteeism. Gender is important but the results are equivocal. Women are usually absent more often than men, primarily due to childcare, but gender is confounded by many other factors (status, income). There is evidence of gender-absence cultures such that when stressed, men go on strike, women go absent.

4. *Medical models.* Sickness is the major cause of illness and is usually linked to smoking and drinking (quantity and chronicity), psychological illness (particularly neurosis) and pain. The extent to which lifestyle is modifiable and causes illness, which leads to absence, is most often debated.

5. *Stress models.* Stress causes absence and comes from many sources: the job (intrinsic and extrinsic factors), the home life, the personality of the individual. But it could be that those who are absent more exhibit less stress, owing to recuperative activities. In other words, absence relieves stress – the question is what is the optimum amount.

6. *Social and cultural models.* Departmental unit climate, or 'cultural', factors influence absenteeism powerfully. Normative perceptions are very important – thus, the simple rating of peer absence (how much absence colleagues take) is the best predictor of own frequency of illness. People are sensitive to levels of acceptable absence and culturally acceptable explanations/excuses for their absence.

7. *Conflict models.* These suggest that absenteeism is the manifestation of the unorganized conflict between management and labour (as opposed to strikes, which are usually organized). Absence is an index of industrial relations.

8. *Deviance models.* Absenteeism is deviant because of the negative consequences for organizational effectiveness and the violation of legal and psychological contracts. It can also be seen as a product of negative traits: malingering, disloyalty and laziness. Those who take this perspective maintain that (all) job absence is a sign of wickedness.

9. *Economic models.* Of course, these are rational economic explanations for absenteeism. Absenteeism and attendance are products

of labour supply. As wage rates increase, it is more attractive to sell leisure for work but, as income increases, people need time for consumer purposes. The cash-rich, time-poor workers are prone to absenteeism.

Absenteeism is a complex problem with multiple, interlinked causes that are only partly controllable by managers in companies. Like a lot of business problems, there remains no simple solution to cure it. But a good start is to begin to measure it reliably to get a better idea of the precise nature of the problem in one's own organization.

Help in a Crisis: the bystander effect

Over 40 years ago a young woman was murdered – by repeated stabbing – in New York. She took nearly 30 minutes to die and screamed, as one might, continuously and loudly throughout the attack. Police investigators later found over 70 people had heard her scream. Nobody did a thing.

This shocking and well-published event caused psychologists to investigate the phenomenon called the *bystander effect*. What the research showed is that, paradoxically, the more people who are present at the scene of an emergency (accident, murder, rape, attack) the less likely it is for anyone to intervene. The favourite explanation for this phenomenon is *diffusion of responsibility*.

It has been shown in many studies that when people are alone and notice an emergency they feel it their personal responsibility/duty to get involved but the more there are present and able to help, the fewer get involved.

Does the same apply to work? Why do you get more help and support in some organisations as opposed to others? Why do some people rally around in an emergency at work and others ignore you?

What the researchers of the bystander intervention phenomena found was that certain factors had a great effect on the likelihood of people offering help. These have important implications for those seeking help at work.

- *The ambiguity of the situation*
  How clear is it that people need help? We have all been embarrassed by having our offer of help refused because it was not
  really wanted. We misunderstood the situation. The more obvious it is that people require help, the more likely they are to
  receive it. The moral of the story is: don't hint, be explicit. When
  you want help either in an emergency or just on a day-to-day
  basis, make it clear what you need. Help others to help you and
  prevent their embarrassment or your helplessness.
- *Familiarity with the situation*
  The more familiar the bystander is with the emergency/situ-
  ation, the better they understand it, the more comfortable they
  feel in it and therefore the more likely they are to help. Where we
  are in a new and unfamiliar setting (foreign country, new to the
  organisation, in a strange branch/office) the less chance there is
  we intervene when we think others need help. Again, the moral
  for the victim is clarify the situation, particularly for the strangers
  who don't know the rules.
- *Cultural and organization norms*
  There are cultural norms and customs that determine helping.
  One used to give one's seat to old people, pregnant women, the
  disabled, etc. Certain categories of people are deemed worthy
  of help – the new recruit, the technophobic long-service
  employee – while others are not. Some organizations stress
  self-sufficiency, doing-it-alone, not needing others, while in
  others it is both normal and acceptable to ask for help from
  work colleagues.
- *The effect of models*
  Parents and managers, who are often *in loco parentis*, realize that to
  achieve certain (polite) behaviour they need to model it. See
  another (well-respected) person offer money, advice, support and
  others are more likely to follow. Senior managers have a responsibility to set a good example to others if they want supportive teams.
  Alas, many fall victim to the 'do as I say, not as I do' philosophy.
- *The characteristics of the victim*
  Many studies have shown that some people are more likely
  to be helped than others. Pregnant women, children, the
  disabled receive more help. But what occurs in the workplace?
  Demography makes a difference: men help women more than

men; the attractive more than the unattractive; the young more than the old. Victorians used to differentiate between the deserving and the undeserving poor. Most of us at work clearly differentiate between those deserving and those not deserving help.

* *Helping calculus*
There is often a cost to helping. It takes effort and time. It may involve money – or worse, the experience of being rejected. Do it once and one may be expected to do it again. So many people do their sums – their helping calculus – to determine if they are going to offer help or not. This means that in some instances we offer immediate help, but in others we hesitate because, quite simply, the cost is too high.

We are social animals. We live and work together. We help others and are helped by others. And we have the reciprocity deeply imbedded in our psyches. I buy you a drink, you buy me one. I invite you to dinner – later you reciprocate with a similar invitation. I send you a Christmas card: you reciprocate by return post. And, equally you reciprocate offers of help.

It is important to give and receive help at work. It builds cohesion and morale. It fosters teams, work and improves inter-departmental communication.

How to be a good client

There are dozens of books devoted to how to become good managers or leaders. There are many fewer on how to be a good follower or employee. There are now just a few tomes on how to be a good consultant but by that they nearly always mean a rich consultant.

But there is nothing at all on how to be a good client. Certainly the most important aspect is the nature of the relationship you have with the consultant. The good client, like the good patient, knows that the relationship is dependent on the consultant liking you and believing they can actually help both you and the business. So how about a few dos and don'ts?

1. *Do* attribute all of your success to your consultant and all failures to yourself or your boss.

2. *Do* gaze reverently into your consultant's eyes as he pontificates about the nature of the human condition, e-business, the future of the euro, etc.

3. *Do* occasionally confuse something that your consultant said with something that Tom Peters said.

4. *Do* complain about insensitive and judgemental bosses, colleagues, support staff, and especially prior consultants.

5. *Do* apologise profusely to your consultant for not showing faster improvement or organizational change.

6. *Do* casually inform your consultant that your department or organization is due some large sums of money in the near future.

7. *Do*, at random moments, say to the consultant, 'You *really care* about us, don't you?'

8. *Do* tell your consultant that you passed up a week in Barbados just so you wouldn't have to miss the team-building session.

9. *Do* tell your consultant that, when your organization gets into the top 100 companies, you will announce to the world that you owe it *all* to him.

10. *Do* tell your consultant that you're totally committed to sticking with the restructuring programme, even if it takes a decade.

11. *Don't* point out that your consultant and his colleagues constantly contradict themselves.

12. *Don't* embarrass your consultant by waking him up when he dozes off in the middle of your committee meetings that he says he wants to observe.

13. *Don't* tell your consultant that his mind is obviously on everything else in the world other than what you're saying.

14. *Don't* tell your consultant that his interpretations of your human resources problems are about as helpful as last year's horoscope.

15. *Don't* say to your consultant, 'So, tell me something I *didn't* know.'

16. *Don't* say to your consultant, 'For *this*, I'm paying you money?'

17. *Don't* say to your consultant, 'At least a plumber guarantees *his* work!'

18. *Don't* say to your consultant, 'What's the matter? Not smart enough to get into business school?'

19. *Don't* say to your consultant, 'Is doing consultancy the *only way* you can get your power needs met?'

20. *Don't ever* say to your consultant, 'But what should I *do* about my problem?'

Having the consultants in has numerous benefits. These include:

*   *Learning the buzzwords*
    You can excuse your incompetence behind meaningless quasi-diagnostic labels and business-speak. Thus, you are not simply an egocentric, illiterate manager but working in a non-re-engineered company with an outdated performance-management system and no share options.
*   *Use the consultant against your boss*
    When confronted by others for consultant-dependence, self-indulgence or overspending, you can quite simply say, 'Well, I am trying to maximize efficiency, plan ahead and save the business.' What you are doing is for the good of the company.
*   *Impress your friends*
    Having acquired the jargon, you can name-drop. Don't forget those magic letters and shorthand – KPMG, Arthur's, etc. Suggest that those consultants are now personal friends and they indeed are learning from you.

Being nice to consultants may preserve your job: being nasty may mean you soon find yourself 'let go' by the organization and all of a sudden one of those pathetic one-man bands of consultants in late middle age who have to try to re-invent themselves. The problem is that the consultant mafia may well remember your behaviour in the corporate world and gang up on you.

So be a good client, humour the gurus and learn the tricks so that you may avoid having to be one.

Humour at work

Political correctness (and its fellow-traveller, personal litigation) has almost killed off humour at work. It seems to be getting harder and harder to find jokes, puns and stories that do not offend someone who is prepared to complain to those in authority. Funny ha-ha is seen as somewhere between funny peculiar and funny pathetic – and it warrants punishment.

Humour can be a powerful weapon. But why do people differ so much in the jokes they tell and enjoy – and get offended by? Why do some people self-evidently enjoy aggressive or sexual humour, while others prefer intellectual or black humour? Is personality related to humour creation (e.g. telling jokes, making puns) and/or just appreciation of making jokes? Do people who make us laugh have quite different personality traits to those who do not or cannot?

Freud wrote a number of papers on humour and was clearly fascinated by its functions, as well as by the techniques/mechanics of making jokes. Jokes, like dreams, he thought provide an insight into the unconscious. They are important defence mechanisms, and suppressing them can lead to serious consequences. Freud divided jokes into two classes, namely the innocent/trivial and the tendentious. The latter served two major purposes – aggression (satire) or sex.

Thus, the purpose of the most interesting jokes is the expression of sexual or aggressive feelings that would otherwise be barred. Furthermore, the amount and timing of laughter correspond to the psychical energy saved by not having to repress. 'In jokes veritas!' Like dreams and many forms of art, Freud and his followers saw jokes as a socially accepted and socially shared mechanism of expressing what is normally forbidden.

Freud actually provided a number of interesting hypotheses about:

- Individuals finding aggressive jokes funniest will be those in whom aggression is normally repressed.
- Individuals finding sexual jokes funniest will be those whose sexuality is normally repressed. In this instance we can be more specific:
  (a) Anal jokes will appeal most to those fixated at the anal level (this is partly supported, in any case, by commonplace observation of primary-school humour).
  (b) Oral jokes will appeal to those fixated at the oral level. (To quote Bridget Brophy: in air-cunnilingus you meet a better class of fellatio.)
  (c) Homosexual and transvestite jokes will appeal to those with the relevant tastes.
- Those whose main defence mechanism is repression and who have a strong superego will be humourless (they will not laugh at jokes).

- Psychopaths should not find jokes amusing, for they have no need to lift repression in this way.
- Wits will be more neurotic than the normal population.
- Highly repressed individuals prefer jokes with complex joke-work to 'simple' jokes, and
- Joke deprivation should produce increased dreaming and/or direct expression of impulses, a hypothesis derived from both aspects of psychoanalytic theory.

It seems quite clear that different types of humour attract different types. Whether jokes or cartoons, it is possible to distinguish various types, such as *nonsense humour* (which depends on puns or incongruous combinations of elements), *satire* (which ridicules particular people, groups or institutions), *aggressive humour* (which may depict physical violence and brutality, outright insult, torture, even sadism) and *sexual humour* (from the suggestive to the downright crude and vulgar). Only nonsense humour seems acceptable at work, and then not always.

There are three main approaches to the psychology of humour. The *social* psychological approach concentrates on the social meaning of humour, the contexts or occasions for it, and the effects of humour on group facilitation. Social psychologists have always been interested in how humour can generate a sense of group solidarity/belongingness, provide a safety valve for dealing with group leisure, and help individuals cope with threatening, negative experiences. The *cognitive* psychologists are primarily interested in how and why people understand jokes. For instance, they have shown a curvilinear relationship between the difficulty of understanding a joke and its perceived funniness: too fast or too difficult is not that funny. Third, the *emotional* theorists suggest either that humour has arousal functions or that humour can be used by individuals to express effect. That means they use humour to stimulate themselves and others in social settings and they can express often-unacceptable emotions like anger or fear through humour.

Researchers have shown all sorts of curious personality correlates of humour. The *neurotic extrovert* likes humour to express aggression (in an acceptable way) and be accepted by the group. Short jokes, practical jokes and skits/comedy are apparently favoured. The *stable extrovert* supposedly enjoys jokes at their own expense, and approves of others who can laugh at themselves. The *neurotic introvert* enjoys satire, black humour and cartoons/written humour but is not, by definition, a very cheerful person. Finally, the *stable introvert* supposedly favours absurd or incongruous situations and the problem-solving process involved in decoding them.

Many professional humorists are notably introverted – serious people who are not prone much to laughter. Writers are more introverted than performers but even the latter tend to be unstable (neurotic), and characterized by anxiety, depression and low self-esteem. However, they find that their humour gives them power over others and an ability to compensate for their feelings of inferiority.

There are sex, age and intelligence correlates of humour – females more than males, adolescents more than adults, and more rather than less intelligent people, enjoy humour. The more recent research on humour production and appreciation is quite clear. Compared to introverts, extroverts are more cheerful, less serious and more able to produce more, if not funnier, punch lines and tend to appreciate jokes and cartoons. Neurotics (or, as the politically correct call them, those with negative affectivity) tend not to appreciate the possibilities of using humour as an antidote to negative effect.

And there is the rub. Many find humour an excellent defence mechanism and a means of coping with difficulties. It attacks and distorts reality; it makes things funny and therefore tolerable. It can be for many a coping strategy. Humour works best, particularly for the British with their love of irony, in adversity. Humour is dangerous, often because it helps cope with danger.

Humour can be therapeutic. But the sensitive flower may reduce the stressed stable extrovert to their own level. To outlaw, to disapprove of, or to punish humour at work is to increase stress and reduce coping mechanisms of many individuals. Paradoxically, it's rather funny, isn't it?

Intelligence at work

According to one psychologist, researchers in the controversial field of intelligence tend either to be *lumpers* or *splitters*. The former emphasizes that people who tend to do well on one sort of IQ test do well on practically all others. They talk of general intelligence (g) and see the IQ score (derived, of course, from a good test) as highly predictive of educational, business and life success.

Splitters, on the other hand, tend to be more impressed by different types of intelligences. They notice that while being equally bright, some (arts) students are good at words while others (science students) are good at numbers. Splitters have, of course, made very different distinctions; the most well-known perhaps is that of Gardner, who talks of seven multiple intelligences. He distinguished between language abilities, musical abilities, logical and mathematical reasoning, spatial reasoning, body-movement skills and social sensitivity. The lay person also likes to believe intelligence is multifaceted – despite evidence to the contrary.

However, since the turn of the century another distinction has been made between *fluid* and *crystallized* intelligence. The analogy is to water – fluid water can take any shape, whereas ice crystals are rigid. *Fluid intelligence* is effectively the power of reasoning, and processing information. It includes the ability to perceive relationships, deal with unfamiliar problems and gain new types of knowledge. *Crystallized intelligence* consists of acquired skills and specific knowledge in a person's experience. Crystallized intelligence thus includes the skills of an accountant, lawyer, as well as mechanic and salesperson.

Fluid intelligence peaks before 20 and remains constant, with some decline in later years. Crystallized intelligence, on the other hand, continues to increase as long as the person remains active. Thus, a schoolchild is quicker than an old-age pensioner at solving a problem that is unfamiliar to both of them, but even the most average OPA will excel at solving problems in his/her previous area of occupational specialization.

In some cases, people try to solve problems by thinking about them in familiar terms – that is by using crystallized intelligence. Most intelligence tests use both types of intelligence, though there is a clear preference for fluid intelligence tests. Thus, consider the following:

a.   Underline which of these numbers does not belong with the others:
     625, 361, 256, 193, 144
b.   Underline which of the following towns is the odd one out:
     Oslo, London, New York, Cairo, Bombay, Caracas, Madrid

The former is a measure of fluid, the latter of crystallized intelligence.

These two types of intelligence are highly correlated, although they are conceptually different. Usually what you have learned (crystallized intelligence) is determined by how well you learn (fluid intelligence). Inevitably, other factors, like personality, do play a part – introverts like to read, study and learn, while equally bright extroverts like to socialize, have fun and experiment. Introverts who like learning thus often do better at tests of crystallized intelligence. And, self-evidently, motivation is important – a highly motivated adult will learn more efficiently and effectively than an adult less interested in learning.

Thus, one good reason to have a measure of crystallized ability is that a tendency to work hard is a good measure of scholastic and business success – and hard work results in better scores in tests of crystallized ability. Another reason is that even short vocabulary tests give very reliable scores. To test fluid ability frequently requires rather long tests.

Quizzes in the media – *Mastermind* and *University Challenge* – were often tests of crystallized intelligence. This may account for the fact that the university-student contestants seemed, unlike policemen and the prime minister, to be getting older. It is simply harder to derive quick, varied and amusing tests of fluid intelligence for the media in a short time.

But with changing technology, the value of crystallized intelligence may be dropping. Crystallized intelligence comes with age and experience. It is a repository of knowledge. But, if that knowledge can be cheaply, accurately and efficiently stored and accessed by computers, by high fluid intelligence 'Young Turks', whence the usefulness of the years of experience?

Sceptics may argue that computers could also assist in fluid intelligence problems thus making that sort of intelligence equally less valuable. But, in the business world, it seems to be less and less the case.

It is business CEOs' fluid intelligence, personality and motivation that appear to be the key to success. In a different age, when education came through the apprenticeship system, the value of crystallized intelligence was particularly great. It still is in some sectors. Being a wine-buff, an antiques expert or a skilled musical performer all mean long hours of attempts to accumulate wisdom.

But, in the cut and thrust of a quick-changing business, crystallized intelligence is of less use, save, of course, a good memory for how things did not work out in the past. Tomorrow, it seems, belongs to the quick-witted, agile, fluid thinkers and less to the salty old stalactites and stalagmites, who cling to the cave walls gradually getting bigger. The future is fluid.

Job satisfaction

There are three pervasive and deeply misleading myths about job satisfaction. The first is that job satisfaction leads to, or somehow causes, productivity. The second is that job satisfaction is a function of particular facets of the job (not the person). The third is that there are two quite distinct types of job satisfaction: intrinsic and extrinsic, which have to be considered separately.

It is perfectly obvious to many managers that happy people are productive people. Make them happy and they will work well and will be highly productive. So there is an army of snake-oil salespeople who say that certain office features – furniture, lighting, technology – make workers happier and therefore more productive. Even the aromatherapists, the feng-shui mystics and the crystalteers have got in on the act. They will witter on about the 'harmony of the office environment' or the 'Tao of balance' which is simultaneously very important and efficiently controlled by their particular magic potion. Further, that the mysterious force impacts on productivity through employee job satisfaction.

There are various possibilities when considering the relationship between job satisfaction and productivity. It could be that these two things are quite unrelated and determined by different factors. Thus, it could be that money determines satisfaction but that productivity is determined by leadership style. A second possibility is that satisfaction produces (causes) productivity (which is what most people rather simplistically believe), while the third possibility is the precise reverse. Could productivity cause satisfaction?

Consider this counter-intuitive option – or is it? People who are well selected, talented and hard-working do well. Their productivity is rewarded by promotion and salary increase, which tend to make people happy and job satisfied. Equally, the unproductive individual tends not to receive praise, reward or promotion and hence becomes job dissatisfied and may leave. Thus, over time, you may get, if you are lucky, more and more satisfied and happy people.

There are also good reasons why satisfaction on its own may inhibit productivity. By concentrating on making staff happy and less pressurized, the manager may produce a dilatoriness in his or her staff that has an immediate effect on the customer, who, having to wait too long, withdraws his or her custom. An obvious example is to study job satisfaction and productivity pre- and post-privatization of a company such as a utility. Results suggest that job satisfaction goes down and productivity goes up. Over time, satisfaction recovers but reflects the fact that the successful stay and the failures go, or at least work harder. Thus, productivity and its concomitant rewards drive satisfaction.

There are two other possibilities concerning the relationship between productivity and job satisfaction. The first is called reciprocal causation and can lead to opposite effects – the vicious cycle and the virtuous cycle. The latter suggests that productivity leads to satisfaction, which increases productivity, which improves satisfaction, etc. The opposite may also just as easily occur. Poor productivity leads to low satisfaction, which depresses morale, incentive and energy and hence productivity.

Morale seems a function of success, not the other way around. The whole climate – a sort of corporate job satisfaction – improves when the profit figures and share price rise. However, morale probably drops back when the bad news is announced.

The final possibility is that the relationship between satisfaction and productivity is moderated by a third factor (or set of factors). To give an example from customer services: It is a fact that extroverts tend to be more happy (and job satisfied) than introverts, and also more productive (in a busy, noisy situation). Thus, what looks like a relationship between satisfaction and productivity is a function of the personality of the individual. It may equally be their age, intelligence or some background factors. Trying to improve productivity by concentrating on improving satisfaction is quite ineffective because there is no causal link.

The second myth (that it is job satisfaction that is a function of the job) was shattered by studies on identical twins separated at birth. These are used to determine to what extent a phenomenon like intelligence or personality is determined by nature or nurture. It is the preferred method of behaviour geneticists who want to understand the role of genes and environment in the make-up of behavioural patterns. One research team turned their attention to job satisfaction, and what they found astonished many who were convinced that job satisfaction, almost by definition, was a function of the job. Most employees still believe it is pay, conditions, opportunities for advancement, supervisory style, etc. that are the main drivers of satisfaction (and then productivity).

The researchers found, to everyone's surprise, that job satisfaction is in a large part heritable – it is a function of the person. We have all met employees who have been miserable, pissed off, unproductive in every job that they have been in. They are the sort of Typhus Mary of misery who carry around 'nyetness' and negativity wherever they go. Equally, there are those who seem to enjoy all the jobs they are in, irrespective of the very different conditions they encounter.

It's rather too simple to call them optimists and pessimists but that is the idea. And the positivity or negativity comes from within. It may be a function of many things – personality, intelligence, upbringing – but it is difficult to change, as all therapists will tell you. Redecorating the office or changing the job title of a pessimist prone to job dissatisfaction will have little long-term impact on either satisfaction or productivity.

So, if you want job satisfied people, select them carefully. Their personality and their work history are usually sufficient guides to whether they will be happy or unhappy.

For over 40 years, HR managers with a basic education in HR have preferred to distinguish between intrinsic and extrinsic satisfaction. Intrinsic comes from the pure love of doing the job; extrinsic means rewards for doing something that may not be that enjoyable to do. Some make the distinction between *hygiene* and *motivator* factors.

Hygiene needs were said to be satisfied by the level of certain conditions called 'hygiene factors' or 'dissatisifers': supervision, interpersonal relations, physical working conditions, salary, company policies and administrative practices, benefits and job security. These factors are all concerned with the context or environment in which the job has to be done. When these factors are unfavourable, job dissatisfaction results. Conversely, when hygiene factors are positive, such as when workers perceive that their pay is fair and that their working conditions are good, then barriers to job satisfaction are removed. However, the fulfilment of hygiene needs cannot in itself result in job satisfaction, but only in the reduction or elimination of dissatisfaction.

Unlike hygiene needs, motivator needs are fulfilled by motivator factors or satisfiers: achievement, recognition, work itself, responsibility and advancement. Whereas hygiene factors are related to the context of work, motivator factors are concerned with the nature of that work itself and the consequences of work. According to the theory, the factors that lead to job satisfaction are those that satisfy an individual's need for self-actualization (self-fulfilment) in their work, and it is only from the performance of the task that individuals can enjoy the rewards that will reinforce their aspirations. Compared to hygiene factors, which result in a 'neutral state' (neither satisfied nor dissatisfied) when present, positive motivator factors supposedly result in job satisfaction. When recognition, responsibility and other motivator factors are absent from a job, however, the result will not be dissatisfaction, as with the absence of hygiene factors, but rather the same neutral state associated with the presence of hygiene factors.

The theory (by Herzberg and his team) led to the widespread enthusiasm for job enrichment (rotating, enlarging jobs), defined as an attempt by management to design tasks in such a way as to build in the opportunity for personal achievement, recognition, challenge and individual growth. It provided workers with more responsibility and autonomy in carrying out a complete task, and with timely feed-back on performance.

Nice theory, pity about the data. Research in fact stopped in the 1970s on this theory because of little support. One problem was the classification of factors. For instance, are training opportunities a motivator or hygiene factor? It depends both on the training and the individual. Is performance-related pay a hygiene factor? It depends on whether it is seen as recognition for doing a good job, a type of feedback, or simply another appraisal system. Money – that is salary level – has always been seen as an extrinsic factor, but it too can be intrinsic.

The classification system is just too simple. If you are a manager eager, as all should be, to maximize staff productivity, don't waste time, effort and money on trying to beautify the working environment. Help the staff be productive through goal-setting and support, and reward them appropriately. Select people with a history of job satisfaction, positive outlook and enthusiasm, though realize this in itself won't ensure productivity. Third, don't kid yourself that what is intrinsically or extrinsically motivating and satisfying to you applies to your staff, or that they do not need to be rewarded for good work. All jobs need equitable rewards and can be satisfying.

Key result areas

In the old days it was called Management-by-Objectives (MBO). People supposedly had targets and objectives and it was the task of the manager to use carrots and sticks to achieve them. It is not clear why these ideas fall out of fashion – except, of course, like the clothing industry, management is very fashion conscious, happy to discard attractive, sensible and serviceable concepts for the promise of the new. However, it could be argued that the idea remains in fashion, except now under a new acronym, KRA or Key Result Areas.

MBO claimed it was a technique for increasing employee involvement in planning and controlling activities and that, through involvement and employee enrolment in the concept, performance would be optimum. There were slight variations in the systems but they supposedly had four steps.

1. Collectively formulate job objectives compatible with overall departmental objectives.
2. Collectively formulate an action plan, evaluating technique and schedule.
3. Implement the plan.
4. Monitor success as you are going along and take corrective action.

Researchers found that MBO had the promise of solving a number of intractable problems. These included the vagueness of performance targets: MBO theory said the boss and report should agree specific, explicit goals. MBOs overcame the uncertainty in work planning because with the goals clearly set they would lay out a clear and flexible plan for work procedures.

It was argued that programmes tended to work better under some circumstances rather than others. They tended to be more successful in the short term (under two years) than the long term; more successful in the private than the public sector; and more in organizations removed from direct contact with customers.

The MBO researchers found that systems failed if upper-level managers' commitment was half-hearted. If MBO was not integrated into the overall philosophy of management it failed because it was seen as little more than a gimmick to seduce employees into being more productive. And it seemed important that the goals of the employees had to be integrated into larger organizational goals for the whole thing to succeed.

The modern equivalent of MBO is *Performance Management Systems*. The idea is that the organization 'as a system' (across the whole organization) helps it to manage (optimize) the *performance* of everyone in the organization. Also, there are set rules and processes that allow mangers to set goals and targets that performance is assessed against. And these assessments of success determine pay, promotion, development and training.

A crucial part of this process for both the employer and employee, rater and ratee, assessor and assessed, is understanding the job and the most crucial features of it. Many organizations called those *Key Result Areas*, though they can also be known as Key Objectives, or Key Result Behaviours.

Understanding, describing and being able to evaluate *Key Result Areas* is a fundamentally important task for both manager and employees. These may or may not be set out in the job description. Job descriptions tend to be somewhat vague and often out of date. One way to begin to understand one's KRA's is to write – in no more than one paragraph – a job purpose statement. What is the purpose of the job? If you have difficulty with this task it is time to start searching for another.

It is a good idea to list the various important tasks/goals that one has. These may be about finance, or administration or maintenance or project management. If there is really only one very large goal, as may be the case with some finance, project management or R & D specialists, this needs to be split up into natural components.

Most people have between four and seven really important KRAs. They are areas where success should lead to recognition (possibly financial or promotion) but where failure could lead to termination. They should be fundamental to the job. And they may change in part from year to year as things change. They are the areas in which you can make a difference. They are a detailed, current, job description.

It is possible to specify key objectives for each KRA and an action plan for how to achieve them, but by far the most important and difficult part of this whole exercise is in specifying *success criteria.*

Many people argue that they (and their jobs) are somehow special – that unlike most other jobs, theirs (uniquely) cannot be measured. But ask them how promotion decisions are made and they tend not to mumble on about experience but quality (or quantity) of work, which can, of course, in principle be measured. Success criteria are agreed outcomes and it is always better to have several because any single criterion can lead to distorted behaviour.

It is easy to measure a saleman's success criteria: revenue, profit, sales calls, costs, targets reached, etc. Even dreary old dons are measured by money brought into research grants, publications (and citations) and student feedback. Traffic wardens are measured by pedometers that measure how far they walk on a daily basis, tickets issued, complaints and traffic flow.

There are, in essence, five typical types of success criteria. One of the most popular is *time:* deadlines reached, average time to do a job, down time, etc. The next most popular is *money:* it is easy to count, and is a simple comparator across a range of jobs. The problem with money, however, is that, like time, is a very simple outcome measure and one can easily trade off things like quality, morale or team-work to achieve money if indeed it is the only major outcome variable.

Quality and quantity are favourite criteria – the latter being easier to measure than the former. Quantity can be weighed, tallied – and nowadays electronically gathered. Quality is more difficult and may best be measured by when it goes wrong. 'Rejects', remainders and 'second best' are indices of quality. Most manufacturers when given an order for 10,000 widgets make a few hundred more, lest inspection fail a specific number. The fewer extra one makes, the better the production process, the better the quality.

The fifth useful method is *customer feedback*. More and more managers are experiencing the shock of 360-degree feedback, where they are being evaluated by their boss, but also by their peers (colleagues) reports (subordinates), customers (clients, patients, shareholders) as well as themselves. It is surprising how few service personnel jobs actually collect feedback. Some wait passively for letters of compliment or complaint, but for realistic feedback one needs to ask the customers to be proactive.

Hotels, restaurants and airlines actively seek feedback, and they determine their success and failure by it. To move an average rating from 4.15 to 4.35 (out of 5) is a sign of success, and a reasonable success criterion.

The best success criteria are literally that – criteria not a criterion. Success is often a trade-off between time, money and quality. Things that come quick and cheap tend to be shoddy, those that are quick but of high quality tend to be expensive. Set one or two criteria only and it is likely that one is sacrificing a third.

It is, quite frankly, pretty pointless writing KRAs or attempting MBOs without specifying in advance the success criteria that one is trying to achieve. It is the most difficult bit, and the major problem for all performance managers. It is true you can't manage what you don't measure.

Meetings

Lonely? Bored? No one paying any attention to you? Having trouble filling your day? Hate the responsibility of making decisions? Why not have a meeting, which is the practical alternative to work? In doing so, you will meet other people, feel important, get listened to and off-load many decision-making responsibilities.

Meetings remain the bane of most business people's lives. Despite the fact one almost always hates them, many feel upset if they are not invited. Indeed, one index of the usefulness of the meeting or the importance of the people attending is when they try too hard to avoid coming.

Many people are deeply frustrated and cynical about meetings. They argue that meetings rarely generate good ideas but have a propensity to kill them. Cynics also follow unwritten rules that paradoxically are self-fulfilling ways of ensuring the meeting can never work. These include never arriving on time (it shows you are both naïve and underworked), don't say anything until the meeting has nearly ended (it shows you are thoughtful and have considered what has been said), always be vague and talk in grandiose generalities (as it never offends anyone or makes enemies), if there is doubt or disagreement, suggest the forming of a subcommittee and be the first to suggest both postponement of tricky issues and also adjournment (as this will make you very popular).

Without doubt, the greatest mythology around meetings is that they are useful for generating new, good, innovative ideas. Traditionally, brainstorming groups follow set rules: be freewheeling, 'far out' in your suggestions, do not criticize others' ideas (verbally or nonverbally), consider piggy-backing by following and expanding on the thoughts of others.

But study after study has shown that brainstorming meetings produce fewer ideas, and fewer high quality ideas and suggestions, than individuals working on their own. Three reasons are given for this repeated finding, which have important implications for all meetings. They are *evaluation apprehension, production blocking,* and *social loafing*. The first means feeling anxious about suggesting something really radical or innovative. Too often, there is a conspiracy of silence in meetings, particularly if powerful individuals are present. Despite all the assurances about anonymity, honest answering, etc., nearly everyone has learnt to 'button up' at meetings. Hence, the useful-suggestion boxes where people can give feedback and provide innovative ideas anonymously and without threat of punishment. The trouble, of course, is that they are also free of reward, so rarely used.

The second problem is production blocking, which means you can't think while some neurotic, attention-seeking fool is babbling on. Thinking is often done best in silence. Ask any inventor when he got his best idea. The moral may be to have a silent period – a few minutes will do – in the middle of a meeting. It can have a salutary and powerful effect.

The third issue is social loafing, by far the most common feature of all meetings. What it means is that, while apparently working and paying attention, one is privately doing nothing. It is easy, for instance, in brainstorming groups to want to be the person who 'chalks up' the ideas. That menial but high-profile task apparently absolves one from thinking or really contributing in any way.

Apart from 'going round the room', the best way to prevent social loafing is to make the admission price of coming to the meeting written (e-mailed) evidence that one has thought through the problem beforehand.

However, we all know that the real reason for most meetings is diffusion of responsibility, so that all attendees are equally guilty because they were party to the decision, even if they remained silent. It is one's presence rather than contribution that is really at stake.

So how to remedy the situation. Below are a baker's dozen of suggestions.

Tips for a successful meeting:

- Be sure there is a clear, thoughtful, useful and comprehensive agenda, rank-ordered for importance, circulated some time ahead.
- Refuse to attend if there is no agenda. Even consider indicating the (rough) amount of time to be spent on any item. Often, with bad chairmanship, time spent is in inverse proportion to importance.
- Start on time; stipulate an ending time and stick to it.
- Have short (less than 30-minute) meetings standing up.
- Invite only salient people with a reputation for problem-solving not problem-creating. Remember that the length of a meeting rises with the square of the number of people present.
- Have a clear rationale for who attends and why.
- If the result of a meeting is mainly to schedule another, it should be taken as a sign of failure. Soon, the meetings become more of a problem than they were designed to solve in the first place.
- Delegate trustworthy but competent staff to attend less serious meetings.
- One-to-one meetings are often more productive than with many others present.
- Both chairperson and attendees should know what you want from a meeting before you start it.
- Where appropriate, make sure people have done their preparation/homework necessary before coming to a meeting.
- Get a rating of the meeting in terms of usefulness and time-well-spent after the meeting from all who attended, and learn from the feedback.
- Consider using e-meetings and video conferences.

Money and happiness

The question of the relationship between money and happiness used to be the most frequently debated in the pub and the pulpit. Inevitably, the answers were somewhat different. For the common drinker, it was abundantly self-evident that money was a source of happiness – or, at the very least, poverty was a source of unhappiness. And we know from movies that money and riches are desserts for a good life – though they must be spent wisely for the betterment of all.

From the pulpit one heard all of that stuff about the 'love of money being the root of all evil' – and parables and case histories of people who sacrifice love, happiness and kindness for money but find it no use to them. Hence, all they can do is give it away with the same fanaticism with which it was amassed in the first place.

But all the speculation and moralizing has had to bow to the data. Over the past 20 years or so, there have been numerous surveys in various countries, which have provided data on both individuals' and countries' wealth and happiness. The data fairly consistently show the following:

1. There is a small but positive relationship between income and self-reported happiness. This is true of all Western countries. However, we do not know which causes which – that happy people tend to make more money or that being wealthy makes you happy.
2. Other factors like marital and employment status are more closely linked to happiness than income.
3. In the West, there has been clear evidence that we have all become immeasurably richer. The trend is clear, linear and 'ever upward'. But the data on happiness are 'untrended'. The line is surprisingly flat. We are twice as rich as our parents, and four times as rich as our grandparents but about as happy as either. The two trends (natural wealth and general happiness) are unconnected.
4. Happiness over the life cycle is also untrended. Despite the fact that some people do so much better than others, they appear to be as happy in middle life and old age as they were in their youth.

Two academic disciplines that have had little to do with one another have been particularly interested in the question of wealth and happiness. Psychologists have turned from an obsession with depression and illness to a few tentative studies on happiness. One famous observation was that until recently in most psychology libraries there were 85 times as many books and papers on depression than on happiness. Economists have also turned their back on their image as the 'dismal science' to study happiness – particularly how economic factors like welfare spending, taxation, local democracy and, of course, growth can lead to happiness.

Most psychologists are not surprised by the weak relationship between wealth and happiness, because they claim the latter is determined by psychological variables. The economists are often more surprised, and often dismayed, because they assume that economic variables have a direct impact on individual and collective well-being. For the psychologists, the question is often 'Does being happy make you richer?', while for the economists the central issue is 'Does being richer make you happy?'

Wealth is weakly related to happiness. How does one explain it? The first academic game is to challenge the data. How good are the measures of happiness? It is indeed true that they are not very impressive. They often constitute little more than survey data or questions like 'How happy are you at present?', 'How satisfied are you with your life?' or, more dubiously, measures of unhappiness like mental illness.

Psychologists express considerable discomfort with these single-item measures, arguing that they are highly unreliable, invalid and grossly insensitive measures of such a complex thing such as happiness. They talk about social desirability, biased responding, non-equivalent translations – and other technical terms, which mean people cannot, do not, or will not answer the question(s) honestly. After all, some feel under pressure to say they are happier than they are (sunny side up), while others have a vested interest in reporting unhappiness and stress (like litigious victims).

So they advocate spending more time on better methods of assessment or even giving up subjective self-report measures in favour of objective methods. The search for credible 'objective' measures is far from simple, though many have been considered. These include consumption of medicines, visiting one's GP, going to the theatre, etc. As yet we have no clear set of behaviours that is an obviously culture-free index of happiness, even when combining many different factors.

Others have argued that the data show that wealth does affect happiness, but that other factors are more important. And through their calculations some economists have come up with 'happiness calculus'. This works a little like the way insurance companies cost the loss of a limb or the loss of an eye. Money brings happiness but not much. A good job and a happy marriage bring more. Thus, in happiness dollars, here are some astounding facts:

- To compensate for divorce, one would need $100,000 per annum
- To compensate an unemployed man for the social benefits of work, he would need $60,000 to attain equal levels of happiness

- To compensate the average American for being black would take $30,000 per annum.

Whether you believe the figures or not, they certainly sober one up. To talk in these terms may seem at first impossibly simple-minded and vulgar but they do bring to the table the clarity of numeric calculations, rather than comparative linguistic platitudes.

Economists and psychologists have also examined another factor, though the former tend to call it 'relative deprivation' and the latter 'social comparison'. What it means is this – to feel happy with my increasing wealth, I need to feel richer than others. Individual well-being decreases as others' income or consumption increases. Inequality-aversion leads to no happiness, inequality-loving to more happiness. The idea is that any notion of wealth is necessarily comparative – I either compare my current wealth to past wealth or the wealth of my comparison group.

The trouble is this – as you get richer, your aspirations change, as does your salient reference group. The richer you become the more you mix with the rich and so, compared to them, don't feel rich at all. Once certain expectations are met, they are easily jettisoned for greater things that others have. It is a real joy flying business class for the first time, but one soon discovers those in that cabin are enormously unhappy about not being in first class! It seems an element of *schadenfreude* is essential for happiness!

Related to social comparison is the issue of adaptation or habituation. What it means is that it does not take long to adapt to increasing wealth – even a sudden windfall, or loss. Thus, even if one is getting increasingly rich, one does not feel it. Like any powerful drug, one needs a greater strength of injection – all the time – to feel the benefit; otherwise, it goes away.

Psychologists have also been particularly impressed by the stability of happiness of individuals over time, even those who suffer or delight in massive changes. Studies on serious accident victims and lottery winners show predictable changes soon after the event, but that a few years later their natural dispositional level of happiness returns. Thus, the paraplegic and the millionaire may be equally happy once they have returned to their initial state of happiness.

Psychologists tend to focus on internal causes of happiness like personality factors, while economists focus on external factors like social status. Psychologists have repeatedly demonstrated that personality variables like extroversion and stability (the opposite of neuroticism) and self-esteem are three times more powerful factors in predicting happiness than wealth. And, as personality variables are largely inheritable, it has not been a dramatic step for some to claim that happiness is largely genetic. Some appear convinced that in a few years we shall have isolated the 'happy gene'.

Perhaps it is because psychologists through therapy, behaviour modification and other techniques have tried, mostly unsuccessfully, to change people that they believe in the immutability of happiness. Therapy works on those who want to change, and try hard – but not on the majority. It is self-evidently extremely difficult to change a pessimist into an optimist (and vice versa). A disposition to be optimistic, cheerful and look on the sunny side of life seems terribly stable and not easily open to modification by therapists or economic variables.

Economists seem horrified by the idea that happiness is not a function of economic, political and social conditions. After all, growth and welfare economists are in the business of finding policy-making decisions that lead to happiness. Hence, they have tried to show that political freedom is linked to happiness in cross-national studies. Or that certain tax or welfare arrangements in a country lead to optimal well-being of the citizens. Some have demonstrated the finding that citizens tend to be happiest when their own party is in power and that left-wing people care more about unemployment and right-wing people about inflation. But it remains fairly galling to note that economic growth does not make people happier, partly because it is undercut by proportionate growth in aspirations of the population.

What does all this number crunching and theory say to the ordinary citizen and the layman? Choose your parents and spouse well and get a good job. Pursue passions that might lead to happiness, not the latter itself. Don't be afraid of social inequality but try to manage expectations. Remind people where they have 'come from' as well as where they want to go to. But do not pin your hopes on economic growth to bring greater happiness to society.

It all does sound a bit like the views from the pulpit are the crux of the issue after all! But then the voice from the pub can still be heard. 'Whoever said money does not bring happiness didn't know where to shop.'

Nothing works: the wisdom of fatalism

Fatalism is not only out of fashion – it's considered to be seriously psychologically unhealthy. Indeed, fatalism and fatality are listed next to each other in the dictionary! Consultants of all shapes and sizes, be they personal trainers, therapists, self-helpers or business people, have tried to banish the idea that nothing works – after all, they are in the business of change – and making things work.

Fatalism is technically the doctrine that (all/some) people are powerless to change events, since the outcome is determined in advance – by biology, gurus, God, parents, teachers, managers, etc. Hence the most sensible attitude is one of resignation. Nearly all the great world religions' teachers preach the benefits of stoicism and fortitude in the face of adversity and setback.

Fortitude, one of the cardinal virtues, means moral strength and courage to endure physical, moral and psychological pain. Those with fortitude often persevere with the indifference of a stoic, whose philosophy is that it is a personal duty to accept his or her fate.

Religions also teach that adversity can lead to growth – that out of suffering can come salvation; that – in rather more modern parlance – no pain no gain. Believers of most religions pose the question about why God (the all-powerful and all loving) allows suffering. It's called the Problem of Evil. And the title of books like *Why Bad Things Happen to Good People* show how difficult a problem it is for the believer. There are 'set answers': suffering is the result of nature, our own sins, others' sins. But, we are told, God works through suffering: to test us and to teach us.

There is a famous scene in *Lawrence of Arabia* where the hero reacts badly to his Islamic colleagues who refuse to retrace their steps to help a lost companion. 'It is written', they said, suggesting that his misfortune is the working of pre-ordained fate. And after his heroic efforts with two child helpers, Lawrence disdainfully replies with sand-dried voice, 'Nothing is written'. It represents the triumph of courage, effort and activity over despair and despondency.

There is a difference between fortitude and stupidity, as St. Francis of Assisi knew well. His prayer, quoted famously by Baroness Thatcher on the day of the second successful election victory, asked the Almighty for *courage to change the things one can change*, the tolerance or *fortitude to accept those one cannot change* and most importantly, the *wisdom to know the difference*.

To endure uncontrollable suffering stoically is to have wise fortitude; to endure pain, poverty, humiliation that is preventable, reversible or stoppable is simply daft, stubborn or irrational. Being able to differentiate that which responds to treatment from that which doesn't is the trick. And alas, some things do not respond: nothing works and we have therefore to endure.

Fanatics, it is said, redouble their effort even though they may have forgotten their aim. We certainly know about addicted gamblers who gamble to regain money lost, only to lose more. We seem so unhappy to accept our fate, even rejecting the concept itself.

We seem to want to believe that everything is possible; that everything is changeable. One of the most common questions received after giving somebody personality test feedback is 'does our personality change' or rather 'can we change our personality'. Can introverts become extroverts, neurotics stable, the feckless conscientious? Personal experience, at observing others (ideally at reunions) if not ourselves, is frankly no.

Change is either too difficult, too expensive or involves too much effort. People do change after trauma, sometimes after therapy, occasionally after training. But they really need to want to. Sometimes things are pretty irreversible.

Declining markets for redundant technology are one such example. The long-playing record, the slide rule, the manual typewriter may retain a few maverick adherents but the product is effectively dead except for collectors. Things do change irrevocably.

Companies, like people, have terminal illnesses. No amount of effort, money or prayer will, alas, change that.

Three things appear to make us unwilling these days to accept the possibility of fate or the virtues of stoicism. The first, of course, is our sheer need to want to believe that cure, recovery, profit, expansion or whatever we seek is possible. Clinicians call it denial; the religions, hope; the cynics desperation.

The second factor is cultural values. In the latter part of the twentieth century, we were taught that everything is possible. There is no need to endure because through science and therapists all can be changed. Medicine can correct all nature's faults from buck-teeth and skin blemishes to total deafness. Psychologists can cure depression. Financial advisers can cure poverty.

Our culture sees fatalism as dysfunctional. Explaining things as an 'Act of God' can be found only in insurance company forms. We are encouraged in self-discovery and self-expression, not fortitude. Adversity is seen as unjust, and victimhood is not to be endured but to be used for compensation. Everyone else is to blamed rather than oneself.

The cultural values of previous ages made Scott of the Antarctic, Florence Nightingale, and Shackleton. They endured hardship, and the outcome of their endeavour was less important than the way they endured the hero's adversity. Phlegmatic and stoical in the face of danger and opposition, past generations' heroes stand in strong contrast to those of today.

The third factor that leads people to scorn fatalism is the change industry. There is an army of change management consultants who talk of transformation. Demand has resulted in supply. Dozens of people, from financial gurus to aroma therapists, all offer hope of change. Everything can be improved – we are promised.

But when subjected to rigorous test we find that few miraculous cures work. Many enjoy the benefits of a placebo, and any benefits accrued are short term. It's not that nothing works – but rather that few things work in highly specific situations to change things fundamentally.

Fatalism may not be healthy. But all the great world religions – mono- or polytheist – Eastern or Western – have understood the wisdom of fatalism. And the wisdom of knowing the difference between trying and accepting.

Organizational betrayal

The rise of interest in business ethics has, paradoxically, or perhaps causally, been accompanied by an awareness of corporate betrayal. Bookshops are filled with sanctimonious tomes on corporate ethics and social responsibility. At the same time, there has been a meteoric growth of private detective agencies working for organizations, which spy on employees thought to be up to no good.

Yet many people believe that people *betray* their country, *cheat on* their spouse but *get even with* their employer. The morality around, evidence of, and excuses for, organizational betrayal and theft is an important, if hidden, issue.

To betray means to deliver to an enemy things obtained by treachery, disloyalty or a violation of trust. Quislings and traitors are now called whistle-blowers, which is almost an acceptable behaviour. Some newspapers (e.g. *The Times Higher Educational Supplement*) actually have a weekly column where people are invited to whistle-blow on their colleagues or their administration, no doubt to ensure justice prevails. Bad-mouthing one's employer and attempting to wreck the reputation of a company seems fairly common place, though it may not go as far as selling company secrets.

How do people cheat on their company? They do so primarily in two different ways: theft and whistle-blowing. The former can take many forms: stealing time (through excessive and unwarranted absenteeism), stealing money (through embezzlement and other means) or stealing goods (which is the easiest). People can work in groups (syndicates, cells) within an organization to attempt theft on a

112

grand scale or more often quiet loners, with a full understanding of how things work, can quietly syphon off a fortune.

Absenteeism and petty theft tend to be more blue-collar activities, serious embezzlement a white-collar habit. The latter is mainly about trying to destroy the reputation of the company, which can have profound effects on the share price. Employees can imply or explicitly state that the company or some of its employees are acting illegally, immorally, irresponsibly or just unkindly. So we see accusations of racism, illegal underpayment, nepotism, bribery, exploitation of Third World employees and ruination of the environment.

It is very difficult to get accurate figures on such things as employee theft. The American Management Association estimated that $10-$12 billion is stolen every year. Companies do not keep good records, do not know the extent of the problem, or are simply too embarrassed to own up. Ignorance and shame hide these statistics as much as they do incest or alcoholism.

Psychologists explain employee theft in terms of distributive justice and equity theory. Employees have a clear notion of fairness about how they are treated in the workplace. Equitably stealing is a way of redressing grievances, seeking revenge on a company when the equitable or fair situation has changed to become inequitable. When employees feel underbenefited, unbalanced or short-changed in, say, not receiving appropriate pay and recognition, they try to 're-establish distributive justice' in their exchange relationships with their employer by stealing.

Theft can be both restitutional and retaliative. The former is about 'evening the score' for being treated unfairly, while the latter is about reciprocity. Employees feel entitled to steal because of the way they are treated, but this link can be ameliorated by the way they are treated. Thus, in one study, researchers found that when told their pay had to be cut, those who were given an inadequate explanation stole twice as much in 'restitution' as those who were given adequate explanation. The extent to which the employees display social sensitivity is also important. The combined effects of treating people inequitably (pay below market rates) and without dignity lead them to retaliate with typical 'reciprocal deviance'. In other words, it is not only the magnitude of perceived injustice that makes a difference but also the way inequity is presented to the workforce.

There is a lot of disagreement about what constitutes company theft and why it occurs. Part of the problem is definitional. In the USA, the National Council on Crime and Delinquency defined it thus: 'A rational crime of opportunity, done as an intentional act that involves a breach of trust, resulting in a direct economic benefit to the actor against the employing organization, within varying degrees of localized tolerance.' Note the last phase: the escape clause – the grey area between legitimate and legal, the criminal and wrong.

At work, stealing is in the eye of the beholder. People are happy to talk about *taking things* from the shop – a value-neutral word – but not *stealing things* – that is clearly wrong. Thus, the disagreement often lies not in whether people did it, but whether the act was legitimate.

In every such situation, there are factors called driving and encouraging forces that seem to encourage theft and whistle-blowing. Equally, there are, or should be, restraining or inhibiting forces that hopefully prevent it. The image may be taken from physics or warfare or, more aptly, scales of justice. The forces of good may overpower the evil empire but equally, as we all know, it is not a just world and sometimes bad deeds go unpunished. Good things happen to bad organizations and vice versa.

Further, these forces happen at four quite different levels and help to account for the complexity of the whole issue. First, the *individual level*: are some people more prone to steal? And, if so, is it because of their personality, their morality or the pressures they are under? There is considerable evidence that personality is related to crime. Criminals are more likely to be extroverts who are characterized by risk-taking, impulsiveness, as well as by a lack of reflection and responsibility. They also tend to be tough-minded, cold, aggressive, manipulative and eager to assert their masculinity. Forensic psych-iatry is replete with evidence of those types who steal for kicks.

Second, individuals also steal because of *vice-based pressure*. Gambling debts, addictions to expensive substances, or financial pressure due to divorce or bad investments can all lead individuals to be desperate and to steal to alleviate pressure.

And, of course, there is what we called *moral imbecility* in the nineteenth century and now called a psychopath or sociopath or the antisocial personality. Children need to be taught about self-control, self-restraint. They need to develop a super-ego or conscience and this is usually done through instilling feelings of guilt or through fear of consequence. Poor parenting leads to failure of self-control mechanisms, that in turn lead to antisocial people.

It is curious how people of low moral fibre excuse and explain away their criminal and immoral behaviour. Some try *minimization*: 'the company can easily afford it', others *externalization*: 'the boss let/made me do it', some *normalize*: 'we all do that around here', and quite often *superordination*: 'I took it because they owed me'. They simply don't care.

And where do you find extroverted, tough-minded people who may be prone to vice-based pressures? Not on the shop floor but on the trading floor. The fast-moving world of sales, marketing and advertising has its own share of rogues. Creatives often share characteristics with psychopaths and can have a very tenuous grasp on moral issues. No wonder, then, that 'creative accounting' is a middle-class term for everything from tax evasion to usury!

One's *work group* often has well-specified social rules about stealing: the amounts of various items (wine, stationery) considered acceptable to steal, the conditions under which theft is acceptable (the weekend, when certain people are not there), and how to do it without being caught. Certainly, the power of these informal rules may be much stronger than the formal regulations. Gerald Mars, the anthropologist, divided fiddlers into four groups, depending on how much authority people have in their job and how strong their group is. *Hawks* are expedient, corner-cutting, ethical entrepreneurs. *Donkeys* tend to be in isolated subordinated jobs that are not very group-conscious, while *wolves* fiddle in packs. Rubbish collection workers are such a group. Finally, *vultures* need group support but have much autonomy. Driver/deliverers are good examples of the latter. There are massive institutionalized fiddles in some sections of society.

Curiously, there are forces operating at the organizational level that encourage theft. Theft may be part of an invisible wage structure, where supervisors reward workers with stolen goods or time off because they have no other powers at their discretion. 'Side payments' are thought to be quicker, cheaper and more convenient than pay rises, official promotions or changing taxable salaries. Some supervisors encourage stealing to punish their boss, some for excitement, but many because they have legitimate authority or methods to genuinely reward the good work of those who directly report to them.

Of course, most organizations try to inhibit theft and they do so by various means. Some try to model ethical and moral leadership, believing that honesty and dishonesty starts at the top. Most try to specify formal practices and codes of ethics. And they try all sorts of ways, many of which work quite well. They know if you genuinely treat people with dignity and respect, it helps. We all know it is more difficult to steal from a friend than from someone who doesn't care about you.

Others wisely get all their employees involved in formally defining theft. Yes, the dreaded focus groups or brainstorming sessions can help because people feel more committed to decisions they were part of. If you agree that a certain act is theft, which is wrong, it is harder to rationalize it away. Another quite effective method is to tell the whole organization the total costs of stealing and how that money could otherwise be usefully employed – for instance, in raising all salaries. This encourages staff to reject the 'they can easily afford it' line and even whistle-blow on each other because they know that others' stealing costs them directly.

Some organizations use corporate hotlines, which can work quite well. Others skilfully rotate group membership to break up work-group norms condoning theft. Comparatively few organizations ever think in their recruitment and selection policies that they should look out for and, of course, reject people who are predisposed to steal.

And, finally, there are cultural/national differences in how we react to ethical problems. And whether disloyalty to family overrides loyalty to the organization, which overrides loyalty to the government. That is why cross-national business and negotiations are so interesting and tricky. And it also explains why organizational theft and betrayal may be such a big issue in one country and thought of as relatively normal and unimportant in others.

Organizational surveys

Old hands at the climate-survey business will usually know the results long before the questionnaire is devised and the data crunched. This is not due to their perspicacious consultancy insights or the results of deeply meaningful focus groups. The answer is much more simple than that.

Essentially, all climate surveys yield the same basic results. And the reason for this is that they usually reflect the three basic and probably false beliefs that all employees seem to hold. What all surveys show is that the workforce is concerned really with three issues: *communication, morale* and *remuneration.*

Nearly all employees believe that their boss knows a secret that directly affects them and which that they are not willing to divulge. It may be about restructuring, moving, merging, training or outsourcing – all pretty terrifying concepts. Most employees believe that their immediate boss won't or can't tell them these secrets. Curiously, this phenomenon happens at all levels. The troops believe supervisors have secrets, supervisors believe junior managers harbour crucial non-impartable information, junior managers are convinced those middle managers they meet have access to plans that involve them, while those remaining middle managers know the directors, in secret, plan for the future, which is also their future.

It is not only the paranoid who believe in the 'secret theory'. Many have various conspiracy explanations as to why they are not told things, which range from the mundane to the fantastical. Hence, they become convinced that there is a *communication problem* in the organization. Try to find one climate survey that does not highlight this!

The naïve manager, new to survey data, often calls meetings to communicate and solve the problem. They are often genuinely surprised by the results and have invested in 'in-house' papers, magazines, even radio and television programmes, to ensure there is full, up-to-date, communication at all levels. Most do not know what staff could possibly want to know that is not readily available – especially on the intranet. So they hold meetings and try to find out what staff want to know. Because the staff do not know what they do not know, they can't ask. So the meeting exacerbates the problem rather than solving it. And the myth continues: there is a communication problem in the organization.

The second belief that seems endemic in companies resolves around *morale*. Ask people how current morale is in the organization as a whole and they will happily rabbit on about stress, depression, sickness, gloom and despair. There are three extremely common beliefs about morale: first, it has never been at a lower ebb and, second, logically, that things were better in the past. The theory is about the steady, relatively rapid drop in morale from some mythical, halcyon past to the current low.

But the third feature of the morale myth is quite curious. Ask people about morale in their section (department), they will tell you they are fine. Ask them about other departments and you get the opposite story: 'We are OK but in the organization as a whole, things are grim.'

Psychologists call this an 'attribution error' and it may have multiple causes and functions. But it means that it remains extremely unwise to ask people about company morale. Ask them about morale in their group and you usually get 'fine'; ask them about others and all you hear is 'terrible'. And because surveys often ask people about company morale, they come up with pretty grim findings.

The third utterly predictable result from the survey is about *pay*. People believe that they are underpaid both by comparable market-forces standards and also in terms of the effort they personally put in. They also believe the differentials are wrong, in that the gap between levels is too great. So the whole pay issue is a source of whingeing – and it was ever thus.

Even when the whole thing is broadened out to the wider issue of 'total package' remuneration, the same cry is heard: 'We are essentially underpaid.' Most people have no idea of market value, benchmark rates, though they can tell you about newspaper articles or a chat in the pub that led them to believe they are ultimately poorly dealt with.

What is curious about this belief is that it exists quite independently of how much people are actually paid or, indeed, how hard they work. If you ask them why they don't leave, they tell you about the small group and their loyalty to them, which reflects on the morale issue.

Some will talk about shareholder greed, others about directors being out of touch. Few talk about market forces. But, increasingly, many are worried about their job and are prepared to accept a lower salary for job security.

The three myths lead to utterly predictable survey results. Surveys usually divide up questions into certain sections – teamwork, innovation, training, etc. And there is 'good news'. Staff report delivering superlative customer service; they believe they are innovative and claim they are good at teamwork.

The issue of training yields variable answers, depending on whether the company believes training to be a reward or a punishment. Equally, questions about structure and conflict management can go either way.

But you can be pretty sure about the results in the three areas specified above: communication, morale and pay problems. Some managers go so far as to exclude questions about pay from the survey because they know the results before bothering with expensive survey work. But they are nearly always happy to leave in the stuff about communication and morale.

The moral of the story is this: Don't be alarmed or dispirited about your survey results unnecessarily. Everyone believes they are not fully and fairly communicated with, are poorly paid and in a company with low morale. Phrase the question differently and sensitively and you will probably get a different and more realistic picture of what people actually think and feel.

Over- and understaffing: big company, small company

What is the difference in working for a big or a small company? And to use the old and now politically incorrect jargon, what difference does it make if one is in an over- vs. undermanned environment?

A friend asks for advice because they have been offered two similar and exciting jobs. Your friend is a late 20s MBA with about as much confidence as he lacks in material experience, having never really had a proper job, but surprisingly he seeks your good counsel.

The only real difference between the two organizations is in size. One has a London office of 60 in total, including support staff; the other has over 3000. Both are well-known, serious players. Both are blue chip, both multinational, both highly profitable. So what do you advise? The major difference seems to be size.

This issue is often about what we used to call 'over- and undermanning', though now we talk about staffing levels. Of course, optimal staffing may change. The number of people in any situation is clearly going to affect the quality and quantity of the interaction in that situation. This is particularly true of work situations, where inappropriate manning levels can cause industrial and political disputes about manning and job specification in certain job situations.

Research has pretty unequivocally shown that occupants in undermanned settings:

1. work harder and longer to support the setting and its function
2. get involved in more difficult and important tasks
3. participate in a greater diversity of tasks and roles
4. become less sensitive to differences between people
5. have a lower level of maximal or best performance
6. have a greater functional importance as individuals within the setting
7. become more responsible in the sense that the setting and what others gain from it depend on the individual occupant
8. view themselves and others more in terms of task-related than socio-emotional characteristics
9. set lower standards and fewer tests for admission into a setting
10. have greater insecurity about the eventual maintenance of the setting
11. have more frequent occurrences of success and failure, depending upon the outcome of the setting's functions.

Some researchers have shown that members of small churches contributed more money, attended Sunday worship more frequently, spent more time in church settings and were more approving of high levels of support for church activities, than members of a large church.

Later work made a number of important distinctions in this area. The traditional index of degree of manning of an organization was replaced by a more precise measure, which takes account of the capacity and the number of applications for organizational settings. Second, a more complex specification of the degrees of manning: in terms of two mutually exclusive sets of organizational setting occupants (performers and non-performers) and the minimum/maximum capacity for maintenance of a organizational setting.

So, like all things, there is a trade-off between being over- or understaffed. To answer the question of the young friend, however, it seems good advice to join the new, small, but growing, company. In big, overstaffed organizations (these two terms are not synonymous, however) the induction period may be long but there may be years of menial work before skills are developed. Even MBAs will note that for months they do filing, photocopying and coffee making, until seri-

ous work is found for them. On the other hand, the new person join-
ing the understaffed organization is greeted with joy and relief and
literally put to work immediately. The newcomer in the understaffed
organization learns more quickly – the learning curve is steep. They
have to have a go at practically everything – there is nobody else to
do the various jobs.

For the manager/owner of an organization, the understaffed
organization, of course, means a lower payroll, which is good. The
trade-off can be seen above in points 5, 9 and 10: the work is often
not as good and the staff feel more stressed and insecure. So the
answer is the *via media*: the optimally staffed organization. Easily said,
not so easily done. According to whose definition is optimal – just so?
What happens if the work is 'lumpy', characterized by 'boom' and
'bust' – by periods of great pressure and nothing to do.

There are some old familiar concepts from the world of bureaucracy like 'chain of command', and 'specialization of labour' that
might help inform decision-making about optimal staffing, but often
it is a matter of trial and error. It can also be a matter of preference
and a matter of corporate culture. The lean-and-mean company is a
byword for understaffing; the bloated bureaucracy the opposite.

Place-dropping

As I said to the Queen, 'I have always loathed name-droppers.' To perfect successful name-dropping demands the learning of two criteria. The first criterion is, of course, fame, though in certain circles notoriety may be preferable. Thus, it may be better to know a Great Train Robber than the Chancellor of the Exchequer (if, of course, they are distinguishable). The more generally famous the name-dropped person is, the better, but this may depend on to whom and where the name is dropped. To a group of academic entomologists, the most impressive name to drop may be quite unknown (and therefore worthless) to a gathering of the Women's Institute in Slough. To drop a name of a fish in a small pond is not as impressive as dropping the name of the biggest fish in a universal pond.

The second criterion is the nature of the relationship with the name one drops. To sit next to a famous person at dinner is better than seeing him or her in the street, but not nearly as impressive as being a friend and invited to parties at his/her home (no doubt stately). It is not clear that 'being at school with' or 'being in the same platoon as' a famous person is particularly meritworthy unless, of course, one has a particularly revealing story about the famous person's unusual habits, driving ambition or general nastiness. The most important feature is that the name-dropped person has chosen you as a friend, colleague, consultant, etc.

The essence of successful name-dropping, then, is to mention the name (preferably nick- or shortened, as in Larry Olivier) of a person known to and admired by one's audience and whom one knows as a friend or colleague.

Place-dropping, though a newer art form, operates in much the same way. Place-dropping is also a form of impression management and reveals those most crucially important features about oneself – taste and wealth. In the colonies, there were two types of place drop- pers: the *Whenwes* and the *Bintus*. The Whenwes were by far the most prestigious. Place-dropping for these old colonials involved the requis- ite prefix to a story – 'When we were in Tanganyika' or 'When we were in Borneo'. The crucial feature was the place mentioned. There was a pecking order to the colonies. In the Central African Federation (what is now Zambia, Zimbabwe and Malawi), Northern Rhodesia was considered superior to Nyasaland, which was prefer- able to Southern Rhodesia. Singapore was several social rungs above Borneo. There was general agreement about which colonies one should have administered (or at least visited), based on their facilities (country club, racecourse), climate (temperate) and wealth (as much as possible). 'When we were in...' was a venerable prefix like 'Let us pray' or 'According to scripture' and was a most important way of disclosing one's experience of Empire.

The Bintus, on the other hand, were definitely the lower orders, whose experiences were essentially derivative. Apropos the charm of Simla or some other hill station, a Bintu will say, 'Oh, I've been to India.' Any mention of current events is a prompt for the Bintu, as in, 'Hong Kong? I've been to Hong Kong.' Household items collected on travels also serve: 'These spoons came from Zanzibar. Have you been to Zanzibar?' Empire has ended, yet more and more people are able to travel abroad on holiday and hence are in the position to place-drop.

Modern place-dropping, like name-dropping, is distinguished by two characteristics. The first is the exclusivity of the place dropped. The exclusiveness may be obtained in many ways but the most usual is by wealth. Most of the best places to drop are far away and hence expensive to get to. Some do not have any form of regular transport so must be organized with great expense and difficulty. Occasionally, a place may be out-of-bounds, privately owned or exceptionally remote and hence very exclusive. But exclusivity is not enough.

The second crucial factor is authenticity. The experience must be authentic in that things are done as a native, not as a tourist. It is essential to refrain from pseudo-events, contrived experiences and artificial products of tourist activity. Authenticity may relate to people you meet – usually peasants and natives – who have not come into contact with tourists and maintain their original quaint ways. In this sense, visitors may become latter-day anthropologists with their 'own people' and exclusive insights into their behaviour and ideas. Sadly, this means the natives probably won't have souvenirs or trinkets to sell – a problem because these, frequently garish, objects, displayed like trophies in the living room or study, offer the ideal opportunity to place-drop. The availability of commercially produced souvenirs is inversely related to the authenticity of place. Another feature of authenticity is activity – where and what you eat, where you stay, what you visit. In ever-popular (and hence non-place-droppable) Greece, it is essential to stay in small taverna high in the mountains (definitely not on the beach) and spend time in a little-known chapel with superlative fourteenth-century frescoes (not sunbathing).

The essence of authenticity then is to meet, interact with, behave as, and gain a deep insight into, the natives. When in Rome, do as the Romans do, go where the Romans go, eat what and where the Romans eat. This is a very cheap and effective means of emphasizing authenticity in the place-dropping routine. That is why the highest compliment that can be paid to a foreigner is to be stopped in the street and asked the way by a native.

Travel experiences, like any other consumer product, are used to demonstrate one's status and perceived worth. These experiences are the stuff of place-dropping. To be a successful place-dropper, then, is to mention a place that is exclusive and authentic. A week in Rangoon, which featured a trip on a cargo boat up the Irrawaddy or a sailing holiday around the Maldives to the British Indian Ocean territory, preferably in native craft, for example: certainly exclusive, probably authentic. At the opposite extreme, a package holiday to the Holiday Inn in Majorca is definitely not the stuff of name-dropping. Beware of being exclusive but not authentic – perhaps a week in Raffles Hotel, Singapore – or non-exclusive but authentic such as picking grapes in the south of France. Even non-exclusive, non-authentic places can be rescued. For instance, if one went to Minorca to stay with Robert Graves (by invitation), the impressive name-dropping could easily compensate for the relatively down-market place-dropping.

The great problem with place-dropping – and, to a lesser extent name-dropping – is that places, like people, go out of fashion. It is now too late to go to Cape Town, even Phnom Pénh – it being neither authentic nor exclusive, though ten years ago it was high on both. Places go in and out of fashion depending on wars, dictators, tour operators and the like. A week in Beirut or Tehran over Christmas is pretty impressive, if for nothing other than its stupidity.

Because place-dropping shows values and status, there is considerable disagreement as to what is name-drop worthy. Perhaps the equivalent in business is organization-dropping, which follows all the above rules.

Playing your cards right

These days, Christmas cards are big business. The custom of exchanging cards at Christmas is a major source of income for various companies, charities and the Post Office. Last year alone, Oxfam sold over 30,000,000 cards, the total cost of which exceeded £3,000,000. Christmas cards, with the enclosed family newsletter, also play an important part in the way people maintain contact with one another. Indeed, it's often the only time of year when people write to each other.

It is interesting to note that the iconography of the very first commercially printed card caused a problem. The card, printed by Cole and Horsley in 1846, depicted members of a family group cheerfully drinking wine and was strongly condemned by the temperance movement. At a time when crinolines, gas lamps, top-hatted gentlemen and horse-drawn carriages were an everyday sight, Christmas cards usually depicted cosy indoor family scenes. One wonders if, by the middle of the twenty-first century, nostalgic cards with pictures of glass office blocks and merry stockbrokers wearing red braces will be the norm.

But what do Christmas cards tell us about the senders? Why do we choose to send some cards rather than others? Whom do we send cards to and why? How and why do we display our cards?

Some people go through their address book, noting the names of friends and acquaintances with whom they would like to resume contact after a period of lapsed communication. Others get out last year's cards and religiously repay their debts. Some do it more haphazardly, preparing a shopping list while there is still time, or simply tit-for-tatting as cards arrive. These lists tell us quite a lot about the senders – such as their class, social aspirations and values.

Christmas-card exchange is clearly about class. On the whole, the exchange of Christmas cards has been a lower middle-class pastime. Working-class people rely more extensively on tightly knit family networks for their friendships. Also, they still tend to be less geographically mobile and to live and die in the same town or city. It seems fairly pointless to working-class people to waste money on posting cards to family, friends and work associates whom they will probably see on Christmas Day. Alternatively, some may actually *deliver* cards themselves, thus conforming to the middle-class habit of card exchange, but by a working-class contact pattern.

A good measure of social, rather than geographic, mobility may be seen in the exchange of cards. This is illustrated most clearly in the disparity between the number of cards sent and the number received. As with buying drinks, there exists a reciprocity norm – the expectation that *both* parties will exchange cards.

However, this reciprocity principle does not always work and, indeed, there is clearly always some disparity between the number of cards sent and those received. This is not accidental. If one sorts out the cards one receives from people to whom one sent cards and received none from, and those from whom one received cards but did not bother to reciprocate, from those where the exchange was on an equal footing, one discovers an interesting difference – that of social status or standing. People to whom you sent cards and did not receive cards from in return are likely to be above you in the social ladder, and be those who you might want to cultivate. Those from whom you received cards and did not reciprocate are, by the same token, likely to be attempting to ingratiate themselves with or gain favours from you. Of course, this is more exaggerated in individuals who are upwardly socially mobile.

What do cards tell us about the senders? There are many types of cards are available, conveying hidden messages that are contained in the varied iconography; messages about the values, personality and self-concept of the receiver, as well as the sender. Consider the range of cards available: home-made, privately printed, institutional, charity, political, commercial, reconditioned.

A person choosing to send a *home-made card* may be sending along with it a whole string of messages. They may be showing that they are wealthy and leisured and hence have the time to spend preparing each card by hand. On the other hand, they may be showing off their artistic ability (or lack of it) in an acceptable self-advertisement. They might be showing how much they care by personalizing every card with an especially appropriate (even poetic) message just for *you*. In time, they might even become well known for their cards and have a theme for the past year, or the year to come in almost oracular fashion.

A person sending a *Green card* is making a statement about themselves. This type of card is invariably printed on recycled paper and will feature a large-eyed seal, a winsome baby elephant, a whale leaping out of the sea, or some similar type of endangered species. The greeting inside will often be written in several languages, none of which the recipient is likely to understand. The intention is to emphasize the sender's deep concern with the environment and all things ecological and to make the recipient feel cheap and uncaring for sending a card with a mouse in a stocking on the front.

By contrast, a *privately printed card* speaks of money and wealth, being usually very expensive. Yet it may have other messages as well. It may indicate to the receiver how busy the sender is on other important (money-making?) matters – too busy in fact to bother wasting hours signing cards. These cards, like personalized car number-plates, are often unique to the particular sender. Some may even, viceregally, use the family crest. Gold is a popular colour and embossed lettering essential.

There is another variant of the printed card – the *photograph card*. These may be family shots, a picture of the new house, or pictures from abroad, all calculated to announce in pictures an important fact such as an addition to the family, where we spent our summer holiday or how big our house is.

Many organizations print the *institutional card*: hospitals, universities, military establishments and the like. These usually sober cards may simply have a crest or an outline of the more attractive buildings of the institution on the outside and a simple, restricted goodwill message on the inside. Institutions housed in outstandingly ugly buildings may have to resort to using a thick covering of snow to hide the fact. Others reflect the white-heat technology they use by computer graphics of futuristic designs. In choosing these cards, the sender may be choosing to identify himself or herself with the institution and what it stands for. This has much the same function as people who wear allegiance ties, cuff links, blazer badges or some other form of insignia, stating publicly their identification with the values and aims of an institution.

Increasingly popular is the *charity card*. Choosing to buy and send a charity card enables the sender to do a number of things: advertise their generosity by choosing one charity rather than another (compare the RSPCA and Oxfam) and not to discriminate between recipients. The charity card may also be seen as attempting to communicate that most illusory of concepts – 'the true spirit or meaning of Christmas': goodwill, brotherhood, peace and generosity. Because these cards enable one to do so many things simultaneously, they are rapidly becoming the most popular.

More recently, we have seen the rise of the *political card*. This may be the CND card or cards with political jokes. *Private Eye* is a good source of the socially aware card. Once again, these cards allow the self-disclosure of social and political beliefs and are probably likely to be extensively reciprocated among small groups.

The true spirit of Christmas often disappears beneath the status-driven dementia of a small percentage of the population, who lock themselves away at the beginning of December and comb their address books for the names of favoured friends and family. These people send large, opulent cards with a proliferation of gold embossed 'art' on the front (bells or holly for preference) to work superiors and rich relations, mock-Dickensian scenes to peers and close family, and cheap, thin cards depicting mice peeping out of Christmas stockings to their secretaries and poor relations.

But what of the *commercial card*, sold everywhere, from newsagents to supermarkets? These cards nearly always contain pictures of idealized Dickensian Christmases (gas lamps, crinolines, snow scenes, coach and four), occasionally featuring mythical figures (Santa Claus) or Europeanized Biblical scenes. Snow at Christmas is rare in Britain, yet many cards depict snow scenes. Another popular theme is fluffy, anthropomorphized animals. The words on the inside often reflect the picture on the outside – idyllic and twee. These cards are found worldwide. But they are particularly inappropriate in the Southern Hemisphere, where Christmas occurs in midsummer. One advantage of these cards is that there is not a great likelihood of more than one of people getting the same design.

There is a vast range of commercial cards, from the amusing to the religious, the extremely cheap to the very expensive. Some are noticeably larger than the average card, others well under half the size of the standard envelope. Satirical magazines now have advertisements for *pagan cards* – a golden opportunity for the rugged individualist who wishes to escape from snow scenes and Victorian gentlemen in top hats.

Right at the bottom of the heap are *musical cards*. These are the Trabants of the Christmas card world. Their tinny warblings can only be stopped by violent means and to, make things worse, the picture will either be of a fluffy animal or a badly drawn snow scene. Sever all relations with people who send these cards. There is no hope for them.

Finally, for those who have no desire to remember what Christmas is really about, there is the *cartoon card*. With the addition of a red envelope and a Yuletide theme, everyday cartoons and line drawings can be turned into Christmas cards. Most are fairly amusing and are ideal to send to work peers with a good sense of humour. Ironically, they are the only kind of cards featuring animals that it is socially acceptable to send, as the little creatures will have been well and truly invested with human characteristics, and will probably be wearing harlequin glasses into the bargain.

There are other forms of cards. The ecologically minded send cards that have been *reconditioned* by a variety of methods, nearly all of them messy. This involves collecting used cards and scoring out previous handwritten messages so that they may be used again. The most zealous even produce their own envelopes from old newspapers. Businesses now regularly send cards, the opulence (or lack of it) reflecting profits in the preceding financial year.

What one writes on a Christmas card is a useful indicator of intention. A long, handwritten message asking after the health and happiness of the recipient is often sent by someone trying to impress. Little jokes can be read as a desperate attempt to make the recipient forget that it has been some time since they last wrote. Conversely, a simple signature is usually the sign of a busy person with no time or need to impress anyone. These are nearly always found on the privately printed card.

There is one other aspect to the exchange of Christmas cards that should not be overlooked: the way they are displayed. These displays vary enormously; some people throw cards that have been read into a pile, others prop them up around the room on any available space. Some string them across the room, carefully placing identical cards at opposite ends, while others use them to decorate the tree. For some, the display of cards is an advertisement of their popularity, a way of showing others the sheer number of friends and acquaintances they have.

For others, it is an excuse to exercise artistic flair in choosing how to display them – almost a species of flower arranging. Some people actually feel obliged to display more prominently cards of people who are likely to call and want to see their cards in places of honour. A hundred years ago, such people would have left a little pile of calling cards bearing the names of rich and titled folk in their hall for all to see and marvel at. These days, such tokens of favour are lovingly displayed as near to the front door as possible, where no visitor can miss them.

Just like the decisions we make about whom to vote for, whom to marry, and what to wear (things we think of as purely rational, individual matters), the decisions to send which Christmas cards to whom may, in fact, say a lot more about us than we would care to admit.

Pleasing parents at work?

Most people are Freudians (or is it Jesuits?), in the sense that they often acknowledge the importance of early and middle childhood in development of adult personality. Yet very rarely, and to their cost, do they question the upbringing of potential employees in selection interviews. Perhaps they believe it will lead to accusations of being an amateur psychologist. Or it may be that they do not know which questions to ask or how to interpret the answers.

Indeed, even those books of smart questions to ask interviewees or their rejoinders, smart questions to reply to smart-arse interviewees seem to neglect the role of parental expectations and their influence on the later business life of their children.

All parents have hopes, longings and fears for their children, which they communicate implicitly or explicitly. Asked what they hope for their children and all parents give the obvious bland answers about health and happiness. But most feel more inhibited about saying: 'I would like him to be an accountant' or, more unacceptable: 'I would like her to marry someone of her own race.'

In the long, complex and difficult process of socializing children, parents very clearly communicate their values: the importance of honesty or success, the role of competitiveness, the value of education, etc. Through constant reinforcement by all sorts of things like pocket money regimes, as well as specific rewards and punishments for school and sports achievement and failure (as well as rule-breaking) parents try to inculcate moral codes, values and, by definition, aspirations for personal job achievement.

By the time they are adults, and definitely after they themselves have children, most grown-ups can reflect relatively accurately and extensively on the sort of 'expectation messages' they received from their parents. Middle-aged professional women are particularly interesting in this regard because they often explain their unusual success in a man's world in terms of parents who disregard the sex-role expectations and beliefs of their era and encouraged their daughters to take up occupations and professions not usual or 'proper' for women to follow.

The example of parents living out their thwarted hopes through their children is well known. Parents who could not afford to go to university often communicate early the importance of education. The B-rate or amateur actor may often encourage his or her children to succeed on the stage where they did not. Others long to have a professional in the family – a doctor, an actuary, a professor or a lawyer – something stable and respectable. Probably the minority send the message that money is unimportant, though patently some send the opposite message.

One study interviewed adults about the 'money messages' they got from their parents. People said:

- My mother said only poor people went to heaven.
- My father said only criminals were wealthy.
- My parents warned me not to let anyone know we had money or they would jinx us.
- My parents said I was a popular kid because they were rich enough to have a house with a tennis court. They told me, quite plainly, that if one were without money, one would be without friends.
- My father always said a man should never let a woman know he has money or she'll find a way to take it away from him.
- My parents said there was a 'secret' to making money but that no one in our family knew what it was. Making lots of money was something of which only 'other people' were capable.

- My parents, who were quite well off, never let me spend a penny without my begging and pleading. They said I must never forget that we could 'wake up poor in the morning'. Sometimes I would lie awake at bedtime, afraid to close my eyes for fear I would wake up hungry and cold.

Interestingly, entrepreneurial, self-made people who want their children to follow their example insist that they are left no money or have to struggle to make it. They argue that one appreciates the worth of things more if one has to pay for them.

Assuming that most people are, or were, aware of their parents' expectations, the consequences can be most important. Of course, one has to acknowledge that some parents send conflicting messages – either the same parent at different times or different parents sending different messages. Self-contradicting parents like this were once thought of as possibly generating mental illness in their children. But it is simply more likely to lead the children in later life to dither and procrastinate in making up their minds regarding vocational choice. It is possible that some children are too ignorant or unsubtle to pick up the signals. But most people can talk extensively about parental expectations at dinner parties, to chat-show hosts – and to psychotherapists.

Some children appear to understand and fulfil the expectations of their parents. They 'got the message' and by hard work, ability and/or luck, did what their parents hoped. But there are two other scenarios that are much more interesting: the child who doesn't fulfil or live up to the expectations of parents and both know it, and those who overfill the expectations of parents with modest hopes and want them (the parents) to understand their success.

It is not uncommon to meet the person who self-confessedly did not achieve what their parents wanted – who did not have the grades to go to university, the raw talent on the playing field or under the spotlights, the temperament for scientific or selling work. Some children attempt, often with parental consent, to exploit nepotistic arrangements to further their career, despite their obvious lack of talent. In this sense, they fulfil their parents' hopes but exclusively with parental help. Some sink into mild, free-floating depression – ending up ultimately self-fulfilling prophecies of underachievement.

But there are a number of curious compensators: those who try to do much better in a field than their parents did not really want them to go into. This is frequently the case among very successful salesmen. Let's face it – no parent wants their son or daughter to be or marry a salesperson, an estate agent, a used-car dealer or a politician and the like. But those with a gift for the cut and thrust of business, of persuasion, negotiation, risk-taking, courage, etc. may become both rich and powerful in these less-than-respectable occupations. The question is whether their success, in the eyes of themselves and their parents, is sufficient compensation for the 'respectability' they hope for. The less they feel it is, the more they are driven to greater and greater success, until somehow the equation is rectified.

Others feel pressured to take the 'good works' route: the potential doctor who becomes a social worker, the hopeful professor who teaches in a Third World high school, the prospective lawyer who works in the voluntary sector. It would be as much folly to believe that all the above professionals are somehow choosing this job in reaction to 'underexpectation' as to pretend it never happens.

Therapists will tell of the depressed multi-millionaire who feels a failure because they sell insurance rather than practise dentistry. They often downgrade their achievements, even cause their own downfall, because they have not themselves valued what they do. To start up a successful chain of shops, to employ hundreds of people, to become a vice-president of a multinational is still not, in the eyes of some parents, a worthwhile and respectable activity. They cannot explain to their friends what their children do, often feeling they (rightly) have rather insecure careers and are dubious about their professional status and qualifications.

It is, paradoxically, equally a problem for children of parents with few or low expectations. Often, the problem revolves around getting the parents to understand the extent of one's success. There are, of course, many reasons why parents have relatively low expectations of their children's job career. They may themselves come from modest backgrounds, believe little in the possibility of upward social mobility, don't appreciate or encourage talent in their children or think that the costs of business success are not worth it!

Very often, parental expectations of this sort get fulfilled. That is, mediocre expectations lead to mediocre careers. But, occasionally, children with considerable talent do extremely well vocationally – to their parents' surprise. Or else the children become profoundly influenced by a teacher, a peer group or feedback on their ability and go on to achieve great success. The somewhat bizarre actions of middle-aged people can sometimes be perfectly understood in terms of their perceptions of parental expectations.

Consider first the case of the successful business consultant who spent large sums of money on his family car so that it was always top of the range and the latest model. The frequent changes made little economic sense, particularly given he was relatively little interested in cars and their increasingly sophisticated gadgetry. The answer lay in the man's modest childhood where his car-mad father owned a small, barely successful garage. The father, it seemed, would only understand his son's success in terms of the car he drove. So, as the son got richer, the only way he could clearly demonstrate this to his dad was by the car-buying.

A second example is of the academic with endless degrees. One young professor earned three doctorates with hard effort. It turned out his mother, a nurse, did not marry a doctor so wished her son to become one. He did not like it but kept on getting doctorates. He was in the proper sense a real doctor – but not in the eyes of his mother.

Measuring ability and personality for a selector is not particularly a problem. But measuring the third arm of triumvirate motivation is. Many people find it difficult to describe (or admit) what really motivates them.

One easy way into the issue is to talk about parental expectations of them and how/whether they have been fulfilled. Parental vocational expectations are not the only motivational force, of course, but a significantly neglected one. And the parental voices from the past can often explain the powerful motivational forces of people in business.

Pluralistic ignorance

Have you ever thought that you alone believe the boss is rather dim or his boss is basically corrupt? Have you secretly supposed that the whole restructuring initiative was a disastrous waste of time and money? Do you think that others share your opinions but dare not mention them, or that you uniquely have these rather critical and subversive views?

The psycho-jargon for this is *pluralistic ignorance*. It is easily illustrated in the following example. Three or four couples decide to go to dinner and a show to celebrate some event. 'Doing diaries' is a nightmare: some go abroad a lot, others need babysitters, one couple has a long way to travel. It takes a little careful enquiring as to the preferred food and entertainment of the disparate individuals involved. After a few false starts, both restaurant and theatre are booked at some cost.

And the evening is a disappointment. The restaurant and the food are between 'so-so' and mediocre. It is a pre-show, tourist rip-off menu, of Alzheimer's memorability. The service is surly, the wine thin and massively marked up and the food from the ready-steady heat-up school of cookery. Alas, the show was not much better, a sort of Eurovision song musical, with end-of-the-pier faded stars belting out eminently forgettable ditties.

And so ended an expensive evening everyone looked forward to. And, after the show, nearly everyone felt the need to improve morale through social dissembling. Many said how much they had enjoyed the dinner and others remarked on how much they had enjoyed the show. The fact that they talked more of the theatre building than the show, and the length of the wine list rather than the food, was neither here nor there.

To an onlooker, it seemed as if the evening had been an enormous success rather than a significant letdown. Indeed, to members of the group themselves it appeared they had all had a really good time. Well, they all said so. But going back in the car each couple expressed their real views and disappointment. What they had said publicly was the opposite of what they thought. They had done so to try to help the group.

Yet, as they secretly confided to one another their real views, how could they know what the others really thought? They were either telling the truth or not. How was one to know? We are all aware of different tastes in both food and entertainment. It is quite possible they did enjoy the food and the show. They may even have enjoyed it as much as they said.

And that is pluralistic ignorance. It means holding back in publicly stating a view because they believe others feel differently. Hence, the lack of shared information sustains a false impression. One example is shown in an early study on attitudes toward defence and disarmament among a national sample of voters. They found that *personally* 70 per cent of these respondents favoured disarmament, even if it meant loss of income. However, only 38 per cent of them thought that *others* felt that way. Therefore, the dominant view supported disarmament but was not perceived as such.

A more recent example concerns what people said they intend to do with money received from income tax cuts in the United States. The poll conducted by telephone asked a national sample: 'If you received a tax cut, would you spend most of it or save most of it?' They were also asked: 'Do you think most people would spend more than they would save or save more than they would spend?' The comparison of results by per centage is as follows:

	Self	Other people
Save more	53	22
Spend more	33	66
Both equally	8	4
Don't know	6	8

Evidently, individuals intended to save their money in a considerably higher proportion than they believed others would. But, if those others are like themselves, the belief is greatly mistaken.

Indeed, the surprise failure of Neil Kinnock to be elected may have been in part a result of pluralistic ignorance. *All* the polls said he would win relatively comfortably but nice Mr Major was elected. Glennis Kinnock later reported that a few days before the election you could 'see it in voters' eyes'; despite what they said, they were not going to vote for Labour.

It seemed the public felt the need to say they were going to vote Labour but did not like or trust the Welsh windbag and his shadow cabinet. So in public they told the pollsters fact to face or telephonically (often in earshot of others) they were voting Labour, but actually felt safer with the Tories.

How does pluralistic ignorance operate in the office? Most of us feel constrained by a number of forces, from political correctness to threat of dismissal, in not saying what we think about a whole range of issues. Indeed, we are often compelled to say the opposite, thus ensuring pluralistic ignorance.

The results of climate surveys and 360-degree feedback *can* break the circle of ignorance. If, and only if, the respondent feels completely secure that their response *really* is anonymous do they feel confident enough to say what they think. Hence the shock for senior managers who, after years of biased feedback, get the truth of how others see them. The usual way of getting feedback through open appraisals and the like can encourage pluralistic ignorance. This is more frequently the case in secretive, non-communicative organizations where employees really have no idea what their colleagues really think.

Of course, the shrewd manager can really exploit this phenomenon. If no one dares say they feel underpaid, neglected, abused, badly managed and the like, a new (or even long-standing) employee may feel they are the odd one out, they have strange perceptions, they are not normal. These managers may have discovered that any survey or attempt to find out (and dare publish) what the workforce really think opens up a can of worms. It empowers staff, unites them and builds a sense of community – often against the bad boss. So pluralistic ignorance is bliss.

The psychology of change

The trouble with both the idea and practice of organizational change is that it is, at the same time, both dull and anxiety provoking. The topic is boring because it is so frequently mentioned but it is frightening because it is difficult, almost unnatural, to change.

Learning new skills, or how to treat staff and customers differently, or how to face the ruthlessness of market forces, naturally induces anxiety. It also causes problems for those who have to, or choose to, bring about change. 'Adapt or die: change or decay' is not a simple rallying cry for the senior manager. It is a reality. The question is how to bring about successful change to maximize effectiveness and minimize pain.

Rapid changes in technology, markets and the world economy have meant that organizations have been forced to change dramatically, not only in what they do but in how they do it. A major task for all organizations is effectively managing change. The targets of change are frequently the organizational structure, the technology and the people.

There are often both internal and external pressures for change. Organizations must have the *courage* to change the things they can change, the *tolerance* and adaptability to leave unchanged the things they cannot change, and the *wisdom* to know the difference. Many hope to be adaptive and flexible. One objective is often to eliminate the typical structure in favour of an ever-changing network of teams, alliances and coalitions, which supposedly adapt appropriately to internal and external forces. This maybe true for young, bright, ambitious and very well-motivated (and rewarded) staff like management consultants – but not for most people. Organizations cannot change everything. They can, with difficulty, persistence and determination, change their goals and strategies, technology, structure and people. None is easy to change. It is a much more difficult task changing people – look at poor Woody Allen – 30 years in therapy and still not better.

Curiously, there are both changophiles and changophobes. Some like the idea of changing people or systems. They are counsellors and consultants who make a lot of money with their promises of change. On the other hand are those who have heard of it all before and do their best to resist change, change agents, new technology, etc. They are the dinosaurs of the modern age.

Perhaps the four most common pressures of change are:

- *Globalization*: there is an increasing global market for products but, in order to compete effectively in it, many organizations have to change their culture, structure and operations. Globalization in IT means that people with the lowest per capita income in countries, like India or the Philippines, can be easily employed at a fraction of the cost of Westerners.
- *Changing technology*: the rapid expansion of information-systems technology, computer-integrated manufacturing, virtual-reality technology and robots, and the speed, power and cost of various operations has changed remarkably. It is difficult to keep up, even if you are a literate or bright young person, let alone if you are a wrinkly. Anything that can be automated will be, and this will destroy many jobs, organizations and processes.
- *Rapid product obsolescence*: the shortened life cycle of products occurs because of innovations, and thus leads to the necessity to shorten production lead times. Hence, organizations have to adapt quickly

and constantly to new information and facilitate transitions to new forms of operations.

- *Changing nature of the workforce*: depending on the demographic nature of the country, there are many important and noticeable changes. In the West, the workforce is ageing; in underdeveloped countries, it is possible to have two-thirds of the workforce under 20.

Change is both ubiquitous and constant. It can be planned or not planned and, as such, some organizations are *proactive* and others *re-active*. Forces for change can also come from the inside or the outside, or usually both.

Change involves the unfreezing of old ways, changes established, and the refreezing into a new normative pattern. When does change occur and when not? Whether or not the organizational change will be made depends on members' beliefs regarding the relative benefits and costs of making change.

Organizational factors for and against change:

For change

- repealed or revised laws or regulations (often government based) that lead to new opportunities, markets or ways of operating
- rapidly changing environment (geographic, market, political situation) that makes old methods, processes or products redundant
- improved technology, or technology that can do things faster, cheaper and more reliably
- new product development or selection by consumers
- changed workforce (for example, more educated, more women) with different demands and skills
- more technically trained management, who appreciate the possibilities of, and need for, the new technology
- organizational crisis (for example, impending bankruptcy, purchase) that requires change of necessity
- reduced productivity, product quality that, of necessity, leads to a change
- reduced satisfaction, commitment by staff, which ultimately forces a crisis of morale and reduced productivity
- increased turnover, absenteeism and other signs of organizational stress.

Against change

- individual distrust of change agents, be they consultants, new managers or technocrats
- individual fear of change, especially fear of the unknown or fear that personal or occupational security will be challenged
- individual desires for maintaining power in the present structure
- individual complacency and believing all is well
- lack of resources to support change so that early efforts collapse
- conflict between individual and organizational goals
- organizational inertia against changing the status quo.

Change tactics can be described on various levels: quick versus slow, unilateral versus participative, planned versus evolving, and aiming to eliminate resistance versus pacification. The choice of strategy inevitably depends on many things, including the importance of the required change, the distribution of power in the organization, the management culture and style, as well as the perceived strength and source of the resistant forces.

Individuals don't change themselves; they are changed by others. They tend to be more accepting of change when:

- it is understood
- it does not threaten security
- those affected have helped to create it
- it follows other successful changes
- it genuinely reduces a work burden
- the outcome is reasonably certain
- the implementation has been mutually planned
- top management support is strongly evident.

As anyone will tell you, it is rare to find all the above points in any management change initiative. Hence the fact that change pro-grammes frequently fail! Individuals and groups, like organizations as a whole, need to experience different things during the process of change. Old beliefs and behaviours need to be challenged, rejected, unfrozen and the new pattern established.

But what strategies do managers and organizations use to ensure that change occurs? There are a number of quite different options.

1. *The Fellowship Strategy*: This relies heavily on interpersonal relations and uses seminars, dinners and open meetings to announce and discuss what needs to be changed and how. People at all levels are listened to, and supposedly treated equally, and conflicting opinions are expressed. This 'warm and fuzzy' approach emphasizes personal commitment over strategy; so tough decision-making strategy and the change process may have serious problems getting going as a consequence. But, being conflict averse, this strategy actually ducks crucial issues and flounders; it even wastes time conspicuously. Many non-fellowship types leave the organization out of frustration.

2. *The Political Strategy*: This approach targets the real power structure in the organization. The strategy seeks to identify and persuade those in the organization who are most respected and who have large constituencies. Political strategists flatter, bargain and compromise to achieve their ends. But this strategy destabilizes the organization because of the ongoing shift in people's political stances. It can also have problems maintaining credibility because it is so obviously devious and managers who choose this approach often have great difficulty with questions of values, ethics and loyalty, given all the resulting conspiracies. It can even give politics a bad name.

3. *The Economic Strategy*: The economist, of course, believes that money is the best persuader: He who controls the purse strings can buy or change anything – or so they believe. Everybody has their price. 'Buying people off' can be both costly and too dependent on economic motives. It is also very short term. People adapt to money changes too fast for them to be truly effective in the long term. This strategy also suppresses and ignores all questions that are not answerable in bottom-line profit or loss terms. All emotional issues are ignored to the ultimate cost of the organization as a whole.

4. *The Academic Strategy*: This approach assumes that, if you present people with enough information and the correct facts, they will accept the need to change and will actually do so. The academic strategist commissions studies and reports, with employees,

experts and consultants to do the research. They value this detached, disinterested, analytic approach. But it is extremely difficult, after the analysis phase, to mobilize energy and resources to do anything. Analysis paralysis often results because the study phase lasts too long and the results recommended are often out of date when they are published. Change tends to become an academic question.

5. *The Engineering Strategy*: This is the technocratic, mainly IT, approach, which assumes that if the physical nature of the job is changed (by using new equipment in a different layout) enough people will be forced to change. The strong emphasis on the structural aspects of problems leads to a sensitivity to the working environment, which is particularly helpful in unstable situations. The concern with channels of communication is also helpful. The trouble is that most people don't like being treated as machine oper-ators and hence do not feel committed to changes. They have to adopt technology that may not be designed to meet their many and varied needs. Structural or environmental change can also produce unexpected results by breaking up happy and efficient teams. Only really high-level managers can conceive what it is all about. The approach is far too impersonal and ignores the most important question for all those being changed: what is in this for me?

6. *The Military Strategy*: This approach is reliant on brute force, is not the exclusive preserve of the military or paramilitary organizations such as the police but of radical groups such as anti-hunt demonstrators, animal-rights groups and extremist political parties. Physical strength, agility and scrupulous following of the plan are rewarded. Those who refuse change are removed. The discipline of the military approach excels when the maintenance of order is required. But a drawback of this strategy is that the enforcer of change can never relax, otherwise the imposed change will disappear. Furthermore, force is met by force and the result is an ever-escalating cycle of violence, whistle-blowing and Ludditism.

7. *The Confrontational Strategy*: This high-risk emotional strategy reckons that if you can arouse and then mobilize anger in people to confront a problem, they will change as a result. Much depends on the strategist's ability to argue the points, as well as direct and control the stirred-up anger without resorting to violence. This

approach even encourages people to confront problems they would prefer not to address and to bring things out into the open. However, all this realized anger tends to focus too much on the problem and not enough on the solution. Anger and conflict also tend to polarize people and can cause a major backlash. The British, in particular, find this approach to change, with its display of highly charged emotions, extremely uncomfortable.

So which to choose? Well, as the academics say, that depends. Each strategy has something going for it. But managers usually have their own preferred method, which is as much a function of their personality and experience as of the problem confronting them.

Questionnaires

'Would you mind answering a few straightforward questions about your experience in this shopping centre?' The questioners holding the questionnaires are, like traffic wardens, becoming ubiquitous.

In hotels, or airlines, in restaurants – indeed everywhere in the service business, the questionnaire is used as a way of benchmarking customer satisfaction. Some are administered over the phone by the cold calling – the intensely annoying, after-hours, at-home method. Others are administered face to face by the intrusive interviewer. And some are given to you with a free pen to complete.

They can be very long. Most people have probably experienced the in-air questionnaire administered soon after take off. Certain seat numbers have been randomly targeted and by virtue of the fact that you are sitting in 18b or 46c you are asked politely to complete the form to keep marketing happy. And on long-haul it can help you pass the time.

The questionnaires are meant to help organizations get data on client experiences. They are used to track satisfaction, to test re-actions to changes, they help understand psychographic and demographic differences in the whole experience.

Most people assume that it's a pretty simple common-sensical business to construct a straightforward questionnaire. They are wrong, as many have found out. Questionnaires can be full of leading questions, double negatives, impossible rating scales.

But they can be both useful and important, particularly surveys of staff and customers. Over a dozen arguments can be made for designing, administering and scoring a sensitive, well-constructed questionnaire survey. They are:

To separate fact from opinion

A survey provides quantifiable information. Many managers, salesmen and others claim to know what customers and employees want, think and need. Often the only way to fight such ingrained opinion is to present factual survey information that goes beyond the 'gut feeling' beliefs of staff who may not always be in touch with client or peer opinions. The quality of plans and objectives of the professional depends to a large extent on the quality of the information upon which these plans are made. All decisions and plans should require factual input, and this can include systematic feedback from survey respondents. Professionally conducted surveys can be expected to provide hard empirical data upon which solid, workable plans can be based.

To obtain unbiased information

A report written from the evidence collected from a good survey or questionnaire, with present facts rather than value judgements, can show how preconceived notions on the part of many people are not necessarily objective truths. It is common for management to see the way things are done through their own 'rose-coloured spectacles', ignoring or misinterpreting the ideas, beliefs and experiences of staff and clients.

A survey provides an upward flow of information towards management, whereas usually the flow of information is downwards from management.

To know if the organization is meeting its objectives or is at risk

A survey or questionnaire can provide vital information to an organization to determine if it is fulfilling its objectives as perceived by the customer. This can be not only in terms of meeting planned targets but also whether or not the organization is meeting its legal and contractual obligations. This reduces the possibility of customer complaints, staff complaints and expensive lawsuits. Whereas 'objective' criteria on certain factors may be collected (e.g. time delays) these criteria may not accord with customer or staff perceptions of them.

To identify opportunities for growth, change and improvement

Surveys can be used to question a particular method, procedure or technique so that its effectiveness can be evaluated. A survey can therefore challenge the status quo in the light of changing circumstances.

Surveys have also identified staff dissatisfaction with appraisal systems, allowing them to be altered and improved to make them more equitable and understandable.

To improve the morale and motivation of the respondents
A survey or questionnaire enables all the respondents to express a viewpoint. This improvement in communication can improve morale and motivation at all levels directly as a result of balloting respondents for their opinions. Equally, of course, surveys can raise expectations and, if not acted upon, may lower morale and motivation. The idea that a survey is a vote of confidence or an upward feedback mechanism can work well to improve the morale of respondents, provided the results of the survey are acted on in a timely way.

To assess respondents' needs
A survey can produce a comprehensive assessment of staff training needs or new customer needs. A survey can also provide an assessment of an individual's self-perceived effectiveness at his or her job. This type of survey can provide valuable extra information to the more traditional appraisal process. This is especially valuable in cases where managers dislike the feeling that they are sitting in judgement or have concerns that personal feelings may cloud the issue and render their judgements less than accurate.

To assess the status and capability of equipment and buildings, etc.
A survey can be used to assess the status and capability of equipment or buildings within the organization by assessing physical condition, maintenance requirements, repair and fault history, as well as the need for modified equipment to perform new procedures. A survey can show the effectiveness of preventive maintenance or condition monitoring systems and assess whether or not, in the light of technological advances and competitors' activities, the equipment wastes resources (such as floor space or energy). Surveys can also determine users' attitudes towards equipment and buildings, whether state-of-the-art or old-fashioned.

To provide insight into recruitment and selection
By selecting (or rejecting) people with specific preferences, values and potentialities, it is possible both to maintain and to change a corporate

culture. Some organizations are very careful to select employees from a particular background, knowing that they share common beliefs, attitudes and values. Surveys can be used in 'exit interviews' or to assess the selection experience of those accepted and rejected by the organization. Some questionnaires, on the other hand, are used in the selection process itself, for example to measure personality, values or expectations.

To measure the culture of the organization

Surveys of staff show the values of a department or organization as a whole. Based on a culture survey, a manager may wish to change corporate culture and identity by recruiting a different group who do not share the same beliefs and values. Culture or climate questionnaires can be very useful as an index of 'before' and 'after' radical change within an organization. They can also be used to explain patterns of friction within an organization and why certain groups respond in the way they do.

To provide an insight into customers' backgrounds

Organizations draw their clients from cultural, class and geographical locations. Surveys of customer/client backgrounds provide information to the professional so that resources can be more accurately allocated where they are needed most.

To assist the assessment of staff training

It is often difficult to determine whether training courses are worthwhile investments. A survey or questionnaire can provide useful information about training for the personnel who participate. These surveys yield information about who has been trained on what, their reactions to courses, and any perceived further training needs. One can also take a look at attitudes, beliefs and knowledge before and after a course, as well as some time later when they can be related to actual changes in workplace practice.

To show potential fit and misfit in mergers, acquisitions and partnerships

In the search for the best-value return on investment, many organizations throughout the world are being subjected to increasing scrutiny and change. Surveys are used to guide policy and strategic development. Surveys are also used to determine the level of difficulty organizations, departments, trusts, etc., would have if they were to merge. By surveying aspects of two organizations before the merger, it is possible to determine the nature, extent and implications of a merger between them.

To show the quality of work and staff during 'quality audits'

Public and private organizations are increasingly accountable to commissions, inspectorates and other bodies for their behaviour and the quality of their work. Surveys can be used to present direct and unbiased evidence of the quality of work and quality of staff.

One can very easily be over-surveyed. And it is particularly annoying if you give freely of your time in being surveyed and it appears the results are ignored.

But, well-designed and judiciously used, they can be very useful for anyone managing staff and listening to clients.

Rating scales

It is not difficult to convince people of the logic and benefits of, as well as necessity for, a performance management system. The philosophy of such systems stresses fairness and feedback and the idea that performance, in order to be managed, must be measured and equitably rewarded. People are developed, promoted, rewarded and trained not on their service record, their relationship with the CEO, or their networks, but on their performance.

And yet so many performance management systems fail. Introduced with a high profile launch, they may be quietly disposed of a few years later. The appraisal process that they insist on seems to generate more aggravation than they are worth. And so the poor HR director has to accept some fudge where people are not properly rated on their true performance.

Performance management systems stall, fail or have serious problems mainly for three reasons. The first is that the organization is not good at, or used to, measuring performance. It is indeed true – you can't manage what you don't measure. Many organizations – particularly bureaucratic ones in the public sector – often claim that although the philosophy of performance management systems are valid, even 'right-on', they do not apply to *them*. Their argument, which is totally facetious, is that you can't really measure *their* performance. Somehow the quality and quantity of performance in their job and their sector escapes any sort of measurement.

The best way to confront this defensive nonsense is to enquire about the criteria upon which it is decided to promote, train and sack people. The response will be that it is on the quality of performance.

And how is that judged or measured? Exactly! What exists, exists in some quantity (and quality) and can, in principle, be measured.

To set specific, attainable and measurable goals is the first and obvious task. The job of the manager is to get the best out of the staff: to challenge them to achieve the optimum, and setting targets is precisely that process.

The second reason why the systems fail lies in the differentiation in the reward. The philosophy of performance measurement systems is that there should be a direct and equitable link between input and output – performance and money. If your work is evaluated, measured or rated at three times as good as average you should equitably receive three times the reward. This often causes great envy among those who get little or no performance-related pay.

So the organization ensures that the difference between the top and bottom performers is minimized and may be as little as a few hundred pounds anually. That strategy may placate the mediocre but is hardly motivating for the best staff. The whole system then looks like a massive paper chase to acquire a few hundred pounds.

The third reason is the most common, and concerns the nature of the ratings. There are two quite distinct problems, which all lead to the same accusation that the system is essentially inaccurate and unfair. The issues are these:

Who does the rating?
The objections here are either that the boss (nearly always the only rater) is either unfair or does not know enough about the person. People are clearly aware that some bosses are softies and others bastards. The former set low standards, are easily fobbed off with excuses and give universally high ratings, while the latter are the precise opposite. The objection then is that the rating is a function of the rater not the ratee.

There are two, not mutually exclusive, solutions to this problem. The first is rater training. That is, people can be taught to give reliable judgements. Tea tasters, dog judges, wine buyers can all be taught how to judge reliably. That is, *different* raters of dogs, tea or wine give the same ratings. With a little training managers could be taught likewise.

A second solution is to increase the number of judges. Thus one could be rated by a boss, a boss's boss, colleagues (peers), subordinates, clients and customers. In this sense, 360-degree feedback can be used for ratings. This approach ensures both that maverick raters (those one has a 'personality clash' with) are both exposed and watered down by others. One's rating then is the average of all those one works with and for. This system nearly always helps the problem considerably.

On what scale is one rated?
When the rater make behaviour judgements on teamwork, leadership innovation, etc., they do so on a scale. This is often a five-point scale going from unacceptable or poor through to excellent or well above average. What organizations soon discover is that in fact the five-point scale is actually a three-point scale. Nobody dares rate as 1 or 2 for fear of upsetting their staff.

There are some very important, yet very simple recommendations that one can make regarding rating scales in order to make them effective.

1. Make the scale wide
    Use 8 or 10 or 20-point scales. This will ensure much greater differentiation. One Oxford don pointed out how a simple alpha, beta, gamma scale soon has pluses and minuses attached. First you could get a beta double plus, better than a beta plus/minus or a beta double minus. So a three-point scale became a nine-point scale. Even that was not enough. A further plus and minus was added. This allowed one to differentiate between an Alpha double plus minus, from an Alpha plus double minus. The three-point scale had become nearly a 30-point scale.
    Scale width helps differentiation. This is good for two reasons. It allows the manager to make finer differentiations between and within individuals. That is, one can give a much better picture of both strengths and weaknesses (sorry, developmental opportunities) reflecting the degree of these. Next it allows the reward package to be applied much more sensitively.
2. Don't have a mid-point
    What does three on a five-point scale mean? Neither one nor the other; strictly average. Mid-points are for fence sitters; for the uncommitted. A six-point (better 10 or 12-point) scale ensures that one comes down on one side or the other.

3. Don't insist on verbal descriptives.

    The reason why so many organizations have five-point scales is
    the lack of adjectives to describe performance. It could go from
    un-acceptable, poor, below average, average, good, very good,
    excellent, superb. That is eight, but the question remains as to
    whether the difference between unacceptable and poor is the
    same as between good and very good. The issue is essentially that
    verbal and numeric scales have very different properties. The
    difference between partly acceptable and moderately acceptable
    may not be the same as between moderately acceptable and
    highly acceptable. In the jargon, we have two systems: nominal
    and interval, which are not the same.

From a rating point of view it is best to have a wide scale
anchored by only two adjectives.

Unacceptable performance   Excellent performance

1   2   3   4   5   6   7   8   9   10

1 is very bad, 10 is very good. Now rate. At this point someone
says he/she can't do this because they do not know the difference
between a 5 and 6 if there are no words. The answer is '1'.

Resist, at all costs, having verbal labels across your wide scale. It
is a road to ruin.

It is not impossible to achieve reliable differentiating rating in a
performance management system. It takes courage to resist all the
nonsense thrown at one by the obsessional resisters . But stick to your
goals on this issue and most problems will be minimalized.

Research

Research, observed a somewhat cynical academic, is a bit like praying.
It is an activity that is private, respectable, but pointless. Ask someone
what they are doing, and if they say 'praying' you enquire no further –
being embarrassed, in awe, sympathetic. One can achieve the same
effect in the ivory tower by saying one is doing research.

And many people have picked up the jargon. They say, 'I am
researching the problem' which is respectable and a worthy thing to
do. Not everyone is convinced. Cynics think that basic research is the

process of going up dark alleys to see if they are blind. They also note the self-perpetuating nature of research, believing that the most common outcome is to have two questions where there was one before. After all, re-search is to search again. Researchers know that a successful research outcome means that less, rather than more research needs to be done. No experiment is a failure: it is just as useful as an example of how not to do an experiment. Others think that if an experiment works something has clearly gone wrong.

Sceptics argue that if you research enough you will find evidence in support of your theory. It tends to make you dissatisfied with the answers you currently have. Further, it can be seen as copying or plagiarizing the ideas of many different people at the same time.

R & D is often 'blue sky' research. It is a 'blind date' with knowledge. It means going into the unknown; thinking the unthinkable. It can mean going into the unknown without a map. Hypothesis testing is one form of research – making really new discoveries another.

Do businesses have to do research? Some argue it's essential: cheap if you want to stay in business, expensive if you do not. Others don't mind copying the innovator. The Japanese are supposed to be masters at perfecting good ideas while the British are famous for not exploiting their inventions. Part of the problem is the culture and values of the typical R & D department – and the type of people they attract.

Consider the typical departmental culture in R & D. It is a high-risk, slow feedback existence. For some it is rather like a form of slow-drip water torture. Managers here – ex-boffins as a rule – are ponderous and decisions are slow. They tend to be consultative and can have cash-flow problems, being neither entrepreneurial nor good accountants.

R & D specialists are not people-people. High on IQ; low on EQ. Research is a hobby, a refuge, even a hiding place. Many are big boys with expensive toys. And they are deeply committed to the science. Many are otherworldly academic types who may long for the long-past quiet life in academia. Many are not interested in business at all.

At the end of the scale is the typical marketing department with its work hard, play hard philosophy. Marketeers tend to be open, friendly, carousing extroverts who prefer to measure quantity rather than quality. They are famous for their short attention spans and their dislike of detailed paperwork.

The high-octane marketing person is not a long-term planner. They reward persistence and are very customer-sensitive. The rites and rituals of marketeers revolve around energetic games, contests and conferences. They thrive on quick, tangible feedback and love awards.

Imagine the differences between the two. R & D people call customers 'users' and find them an interfering nuisance. Marketeers want a product now, and that people buy in large numbers irrespective of its fancy gadgetry.

Researchers complain that they are not understood; marketeers that they cannot sell dull products.

Things might be changing, particularly at the senior level. But research can remain, in all but the pharmaceutical and high-tech computer world, a dirty word for wasted money – not a respectable activity.

Self-esteem: too much and too little

The self-esteem industry is big business. Half the self-help books on the shelves attempt to teach or improve self-esteem. Therapists, counsellors, priests and salespeople all rabbit on about understanding and valuing the self as leading to health, happiness and success. And they are certainly partly right.

But the manifestation of too much, as well as too little, self-esteem can be both a cause and a consequence of management failure. The Americans have long believed in the power and importance of self-esteem, which partly explains their self-confidence and assertiveness. It is often surprising to see, particularly, young people of very average ability look so manifestly confident. They appear all to have passed 'Assertiveness 101' but failed 'Charm 101', telling you openly and frankly about their beliefs, problems, wishes and values, as if they deserve automatic respect or are fascinating on the topic.

The norm of reciprocity – the idea that we have to respond in like measure makes it all rather too much for the cowering British, who are taught that humility and discretion are virtues. To get or even fabricate skeletons in the cupboard and expect sympathy, forgiveness and empathy for our victim status is not really terribly British. We rather admire humility in all our public figures and particularly those who have a lot to be humble about.

Of course, one should clearly distinguish between the genuine and the fake article. There are those who are genuinely humble and meek, believing that their ability and contribution are somehow pretty average, even unworthy. The trouble with humility is that one can easily be abused by those with hubris, and be trodden upon.

When the 'yes-man' meets the abominable 'no-man' the latter wins. There is, however, deep within Anglo-Saxon culture a respect for the amateur, self-effacing person who with sheer talent wins through. It's the story of the hare and the tortoise, David and Goliath and the victory of the humble and meek, who shall inherit the earth. Part of the appeal of the film *Chariots of Fire* depicted just such an alliance.

There is a rather sinister fake version of this seen in such places as the Hampstead dinner party, the academic seminar and the political debating chamber. It is the false humility that is a sort of attention-getting technique. It is deeply unattractive but difficult to sustain and therefore easily discovered.

The manager with low esteem is not necessarily the manager with humility. One can be confident about oneself, but humble. The low self-esteem person, on the other hand, is probably a handicap to his/her family, self, work group and organization. Lacking in confidence and self-respect, they may be overcautious when required to take a risk, dithering when one really needs to be decisive, pusillanimous when one needs to be brave. Low self-esteem is associated with anxiety, depression, hypochondria and business failure. Hence, the myriad books that attempt to bolster blame elsewhere and celebrate victimhood.

But people with low self-esteem seldom get into positions of power. Low self-esteem prevents risk-taking, bold decision-making, opportunism and openness to excitement and challenges, which are the stuff of success in business. We all need enough narcissism for healthy day-to-day functioning. We need to be sufficiently interested in ourselves to function well in the cut and thrust of business life.

It is those with seeming limitless self-esteem and concomitant hubris that are the real problem. But extreme narcissists are a real hazard and not that uncommon among our captains of industry. They are often people completely preoccupied with being superior, unique or special. They shamelessly exaggerate their talents and indulge in addictively boastful and pretentious self-aggrandizement. They are often mildly amusing, even pathetic, but narcissists often possess extremely vindictive characteristics.

The psychological interpretation of unnaturally high levels of narcissism is essentially compensatory. Many business narcissists believe they have been fundamentally wronged in the past and that they are 'owed'. Their feelings of internal insecurity can be satisfied by only regular adulation, affirmation and recognition. They yearn for a strong positive self-image to combat their real feelings of helplessness and low self-esteem. A certain foreign storeowner seems to fit the description.

One of the most frequently observed characteristics of the narcissist is capriciousness – inconsistent, erratic, unpredictable behaviour. Naturally, most psychologists see the origins of narcissistic behaviour in early childhood. The inconsistent parent (caregiver) who was attentive to all outward, public signs of achievement and success but blind to and ignorant of (or, worse, disapproving of) the child's personal feelings.

This inconsistency often leads to the young adult being confused and never developing a clear sense of who they are or establishing a coherent value system. They are, as our soul brothers have been known to remark, 'not comfortable in their own skin'. This can and does result in a lifelong compensatory quest for full self-regard and self-assertion. The wells of the origin of the problem are both deep and murky, and passions they engender seem remorseless.

The narcissist is quite plainly dysfunctional. He or she fails to understand or appreciate others, be they colleagues, subordinates or clients. They often see people as sort of possessions whose major function is as an accessory to their pursuit of fame and glory. People are used to reflect glory. Do any of our current or past great business figures spring to mind at this point?

Personal and work relationships for narcissists are particularly interesting. If the narcissist's 'other half' is prepared to offer continual, unconditional, even escalatory admiration, all is well. But they have to direct all their efforts, all the time, to minister to the needs of their master to overcome the inner emptiness and worthlessness he/she is experiencing. Naturally, narcissists search them out because they are rare, probably equally dysfunctional, people labelled appropriately as 'complementary narcissists'. They are complementary in both senses of the word.

But it is more likely that people just 'go along' collusively with those bullying, business narcissists. Some could be called dependent – products of overanxious parents or with a history of sickness – who need to express their unreserved devotion. The narcissist needs the mirror-hungry soul characterized by excessive neediness and submissiveness. They are self-deprecators who find acting independently difficult. They like to attach themselves to those who give them direction and they are prepared to pay a great price for supposed closeness. Terrified of being deserted by a powerful hero, they can make extraordinary self-sacrificing acts to stay in with the narcissist. Supposedly, this reminds them of the real, but more likely imagined, perfect relationship with the all-powerful parents.

But there are nearly always tears before bedtime. Even the best-fitting collusive relationships fail. Some narcissists begin to feel angry and trapped by their fawning, doting supplicants. The narcissist may become angry, aggressive and dismissive but, of course, the victim enjoys the martyrdom. And so the persecutor and the victim remain entwined.

There are two big paradoxes in all this. First, given a modicum of ability, drive and style, the narcissist often becomes successful in business. Many of their pathologies – toughness with staff, apparent immense self-confidence, the search for and obtaining of recognition and rewards – initially stand them in good stead. This is often useful at the beginning of their careers.

But nearly all drink too deeply from the cup of heavily scented narcissistic brew. They believe their own propaganda and their critical decision-making fails. The odd collusive and dysfunctional relationship entered into by powerful narcissists does not result in a talented, balanced management team. It is the critical-thinking failures that cost most. Organizations led by genuine narcissists often have management boards that suffer from 'groupthink'. They make bold and dramatic decisions and may even flout the law. Many of the latter are to be found to have partaken in a number of illegal acts.

The second paradox is that both hubris and humility are driven by the same engine of low self-esteem and regard. The need to feel an authentic, loveworthy and competent individual can be a lifelong quest for many. It is indeed the best gift from a parent to his/her child. Hence all the books and therapists working on the topic.

Serious selection

Remember the joke of the bride at the wedding thinking, 'Aisle, Altar, Hymn,' or more likely, 'I'll alter him' only to discover sometime later that changing people (reforming husbands) is far from simple. Better to pick the ideal mate not necessarily requiring much change.

Some organizations spend more effort on selection than on training, believing it is a better strategy. Their philosophy, which is certainly supported by the training literature, is that unless one has people of a certain calibre and temperament no amount or type of training will be effective.

But what to look for in the selection procedure? There are various arguments on the benefits and drawbacks of various methods: assessment centres, biodata, interviews, personality tests – even graphological analysis. It is often a vituperative but sterile argument. The real point should be how to get the most salient and sensitive information about a candidate so as to make an informed judgement.

Psychologists have distinguished between three types of data: *self-report data* (obtained from questionnaires and interviews), *observational data* (obtained from assessment centres and references) and *test data* (obtained by ability and personality tests as well as biodata). Each type of data has advantages and disadvantages; so it is best to have all three sets of data.

The following is the way one organization goes about its recruitment and selection process. It means that, when the final selection committee meets, it has an impressive document that contains all sorts of data on the individual. Further, it should be noted that there is a member of this committee who does not belong to the organization. He or she takes full part in the final decision but has the multiple task of having to see fair play, brings an outside perspective and sometimes uses his or her own background and skills to interpret the candidate profiles.

The procedure goes like this: Short-listed candidates are interviewed for about two hours by a middle-ranking HR specialist. This interview is fully written up: the questions asked, the answers given and an interpretation. It runs to about 10 pages (4,000 words). If this interviewer is happy, the candidate goes into an assessment centre. This is time-consuming and costly but, because of the range of exercises used, the final report is rich in detail. It contains comparative statistics but also expert judgements of professional raters.

Once again, if the candidate does well at this hurdle, he or she is interviewed once more, this time by a senior HR interviewer who has read the first interview. Again, the interview lasts about two hours and is written up in full.

The following step, all being well, is to contact five (at least) referees who know the candidate in a variety of settings. Some of these may be nominated by the candidate, others approached directly. Also, and where they allow it, appraisal data from the candidate's previous employers are requested.

Thus, when the final selection committee of three or four very senior people from different departments (plus the outsider) meets, they have a very impressive document to consider. It contains a lengthy application form with some open-ended questions about achievements and failures, as well as fairly standard questions. It also contains the details of the two interviews, the assessment centre's report and the five to seven reference letters. It takes about two hours to read this report thoroughly, which may be 50 to 80 pages long.

The final selection committee meets about two hours before the candidate arrives. Each has been requested to make a pre-interview rating on about 20 dimensions (or competences) relevant to the job before coming to the meeting. They share their perceptions and concerns. Their task is to plan fully the final interview: what questions to ask that tap into the fundamental concerns the committee has elicited. They consider what possible answers they may get, what they might mean, and what further questions to ask. They plan who asks the questions and in which order.

Thus, before the interview begins, they have a clear and thoughtful agenda. The interview is much like any other. It lasts about 1½ hours and candidates are invited to ask questions at the end.

After the interview, each member of the committee makes a private independent rating on the dimensions specified earlier. Thereafter, each is discussed one at a time. The chairperson, whose job it is to write a final, decisive report, attempts to understand, reconcile and integrate views, but is not obliged to find consensus if there is disagreement.

There is a final decision about accepting or rejecting, which is, of course, the culmination of the exercise. But, although the committee makes a recommendation, it has to be approved by the head of HR or some other senior person familiar with selection issues.

What does this all cost? In 'man-hours', there are the two initial interviews and the writeups. There is the final selection committee preparation and interview. And there is quite a lot of support-staff work in chasing up references and co-ordinating interviews and preparing documents. Assessment centres are very expensive (it is difficult to put a figure on it, but somewhere between £5,000 and £10,000).

It is worth it? Do we need to be that thorough? Even most CEOs of blue-chip companies whose profile might make or break the company hardly ever get selected so carefully. The answer lies predominantly in the cost of making an error in selection. The long- and short-term costs of making a poor selection decision easily outweigh the costs and effort of putting in time at the front end. Serious selection should be a 'must' for serious jobs.

Service recovery

It used to be called 'customer complaints'. It was often the smallest department in the biggest of organisations, and only side-lined people worked there. Now it is called 'service recovery'. And it is sexy. Thanks to the service – profit chain, which is a business model, it is seen as a crucial function and serious money is often invested in it.

There appear to be three phases in the service recovery business history. Until the 1980s customer complaints were relatively few and judged to be more a nuisance than anything else. For 30 years after the Second World War one saw more protectionism and more state owned monopolies. Service was often poor but complaints were ineffectual. And, more importantly, there was no real option. Faced with those great bureaucratic monoliths like British Telecom, British Rail, British Gas, one had to like it or lump it. There was no real alternative.

The complaints department often dealt exclusively with complaint letters. Some were courageous enough to deal with telephone calls, but that was often simply too difficult. Letters of compliment, if they existed, may also have been sent to that department. It might have been called the 'customer feedback department', but it was not. It was seen as important enough to deal with – albeit painfully bureaucratically – but not important enough to be proactive. The general idea was to resolve problems as cheaply as possible and deal with the general nuisance of the 'complaining type'.

The rise in litigation has meant that most companies in the service business have seen a steady linear rise in the number of complaints that they receive. The holiday business is a good example and this may be in part due to the over zealous and unrealistic marketing. People in all forms of transportation – airlines, rail, coaches, too are noticing the trend. Now we read of the army, the NHS, universities all being sued for not fulfilling customer needs, desires and expectations.

There are at least three different views on this phenomenon. The *cynical* position is this: most customers who complain are not genuine. They have read about preposterous compensation that others receive and provide 'cock-and-bull' stories to try to get money. They treat a customer complaint a little like a lottery ticket.

Cynics believe that there is a small number of either deviant malcontents with nothing better to do and impossible to satisfy, or else they are essentially dishonest looking for, exaggerating, or causing problems to complain about. The cynical management therefore turns the customer complaint department into a mini-form of the CID. Their job is to challenge to get at the truth. Many assume one is guilty until proven innocent – not the other way round.

The cynics delay, bamboozle, deny. One has to be prepared to play the long game to get justice from the cynic. Remember, they are trained in counter-espionage. They don't believe you; don't want to say sorry; won't recompense you. That is their aim based on their philosophy.

It is no accident that there are all those television programmes that are dedicated to hounding organizations that refuse to admit liability. Note how rare it is for the programme to take the side of the company. Nearly all support the customer. This, of course, only increases the paranoia of the cynic – and the 'blood-lust' of the complainer.

The second approach may be titled the *modified expectation* position. Some companies think the rise in complaints is a function primarily of the rise of (unfulfillable) expectations on the part of the public. They expect everything to run like clockwork. They want everything to be a bargain. They expect every holiday resort to be paradise. And when it isn't, they complain.

There are two responses of companies who believe in the expectation explanation. The first is the small print method. As we all know 'what the big print giveth, the small print taketh away'. This is a quasi-legalistic method of saying, 'I told you so in the first place'. The second response is to have a word with the marketing department to get them to focus on aspects of the service/product that receive least, not most, complaints. Thus, airlines focus on food, not seats; on the destination, not departure time.

The unfulfillable expectations organization is despondent. It can't control the expectations of the public rising, and blames other 'irresponsible advertisers', the education system, the web, America, etc. for this inexorable rise. But they take the issue semi-seriously, as they know the value of the customer. Their favoured response is the grovelling letter rather than the fat cheque. They know that the speed and the time of the response can quickly mollify: not everyone, but enough people to hold this very severe problem at bay.

The third group see the complaint as an *opportunity* rather than seeing the complainant as an *opportunist*. Often their philosophy is based on two things. The first is called the service–profit chain. Stated simply, this is a business model (boxes with arrows) that shows what-causes-what. The question is what produces profit, and the answer is the most direct cause, which (for most businesses) is customer loyalty, which is due to customer satisfaction, which is primarily due to staff performance, which is caused by their satisfaction, which is a function of how they are managed. This group constantly underlines the concept of customer loyalty because they see it as a primary cause of profit.

The second factor is that they accept that 'cock-ups' happen: service failure is inevitable. The central question is how one deals with it. What the service recovery people argue is that, paradoxically, people can be induced to being more loyal *after* a cock-up if it is well dealt with. Spill a drop of red wine on a business class customer and offer him a bottle of champagne and you will increase loyalty.

The service recovery people are also eager to do their sums, and they do it like this. Think of how much a premium customer pays you per annum when using your product. It may be pizzas or airline seats; it may be clothes or telecommunications. Let us say a business traveller prefers your airline, choosing to fly business class across the pond eight times a year. Maybe that is worth £4000 in profit. Now consider the 'life-time' of this person who may stay in that position with that company for five years. So over five years this traveller will generate £20,000 profit at current rates.

Now let us imagine this customer complains: he ordered a vegetarian meal and never got it; his luggage went to Atlanta when he went to New York; his complimentary limo arrives late and he missed the flight. What should you do?

The service recovery philosophy says you are staring at a possible loss of £20,000. There is plenty of choice in airlines across the pond. So you have to act quickly, subtly and equitably. Get the facts, apologise, explain and if necessary compensate. Two tickets to Paris, a complimentary case of champagne, a first class ticket to New York. Remember always the £20,000.

Customers are divided into various categories depending on their experiences and positions of loyalty. Disciples spread the word on your behalf, being almost illogically loyal. Terrorists do the opposite, broadcasting your terrible service. The one acts as free advertising, the other like the opposition. But most are indifferent – one aeroplane interior, one freshly delivered pizza, one pair of underwear, looks much like another. So you need to hook them – to improve your loyalty. And this can be done with service recovery as well as routine delivery.

Is the complaining customer a wingeing litigant, a person with unreal expectations, or (for the most part) an opportunity to ensure loyalty? How your organization deals with customer feedback soon tells you its underlying philosophy.

Spiritual intelligence

For at least half of the last century, there was fairly good agreement that intelligence was a coherent entity. Bright people tended to be good at most things, and vice versa. While sceptics argued that intelligence is only what intelligence tests measure, it seemed apparent to most people that those who were good at the arithmetic problems were also good at the vocabulary tests. Clever people were quick, logical and had a good memory and sound judgement.

This view has been called that of the *lumpers*, who see intelligence as being global so that one IQ test score should suffice to describe it accurately. On the other side are the *splitters*, who insist that intelligence is made up of a number of specific mental facilities so that one might be intelligent in one but not another.

The early splitters talked about specific abilities: *mathematical, spatial* and *verbal*. Later, a distinction was made between *fluid* intelligence like problem-solving and reasoning, which declines with age, and *crystallized* intelligence, which was about general knowledge and kept growing as long as you live.

However, the splitters of the 1980s really took the splitting business seriously. The foremost advocate of the area is Howard Gardner, whose book on multiple intelligence became enormously popular with educators, even if the academics gave it a polite 'thumbs-down'.

In the early 1990s, he proposed seven different types of intelligence. They were: *verbal* or linguistic intelligence (the ability to use words), *logical* or mathematical intelligence (the ability to reason logically, solve number problems), *spatial* intelligence (the ability to find your way around the environment, and form mental images), *musical* intelligence (the ability to perceive and create pitch and rhythm patterns), *body-kinetic* intelligence (the ability to carry out motor movement, e.g. being a surgeon or a dancer), *interpersonal* intelligence (the ability to understand other people), and *intrapersonal* intelligence (the ability to understand yourself and develop a sense of your own identity).

But it was Goleman's popularization of the concept of Emotional Intelligence that really took the world by storm. Goleman was a 'bifurcating splitter'. He said precious little about orthodox intelligence but claimed that understanding and controlling one's own and others emotions was a form of intelligence. Further, emotional intelligence was said to be a better predictor of success at work than 'regular' intelligence.

Again, the academics rejected much of the theory for being a populist ragbag of old, sometimes disproven, often unproven, ideas and concepts. By ring-fencing these very varying behaviours and skills, the critics claimed EQ confounds and obfuscates much more than it enlightens.

But a new sport had been created – hunt the new intelligence. Not to be outdone by all the hype, Gardner has just brought out a new book in which he considers the possibility of three new intelligences, which makes 10 in all.

In his latest book, Gardner defines intelligence as a 'biographical potential to process information that can be activated in a cultural setting to solve problems or create products that are of value in a culture' (pp. 38-44). In it, he introduces three possible new intelligences, though he notes: 'The strength of the evidence for these varies, and whether or not to declare a certain human capacity another type of intelligence is certainly a judgement call' (p. 47). His new intelligences are *naturalist* intelligence, which is 'expertise in the recognition and classification of the numerous species – the flora and fauna – of his or her environment' (p. 43). It is the capacity of taxonomization: to recognize members of a group, to distinguish among members of a species and to chart out the relations, formally or informally, among several species. *Spiritual intelligence* is another, which is the ability to master a set of diffuse and abstract concepts about being, but also mastering the craft of altering one's consciousness in attaining a certain state of being. It is an 'intelligence that explores the nature of existence in its multifarious guises' (p. 60). *Existential* intelligence is yet more difficult to define: 'the capacity to locate oneself with respect to the furthest reaches of the cosmos – the infinite and infinitesimal - and the related capacity to locate oneself with respect to such existential features of the human condition as the significance of life, the meaning of death, the ultimate fate of the physical and psychological worlds and such profound experiences as love of another person or total immersion in a work of art' (p. 61).

However, on further reflection, Gardner concludes: 'My review process indicates that the naturalists' intelligence clearly merits addition to the list of the original seven intelligences,' (p. 52) and later, 'despite the attractiveness of a ninth intelligence, however, I am not adding existential intelligence to the list. I find the phenomenon perplexing enough and the distance from the other intelligences vast enough to dictate prudence – at least for now. At most, I am willing, Fellini-style, to joke about 8½ intelligences' (p. 66).

But already spiritual intelligence (SI) is taking hold of the popular imagination. Quite why is uncertain. Perhaps because we live in a post-Christian, post-materialist world that has long turned its back on spiritual issues. Perhaps it is that many of us have strong unfulfilled spiritual yearnings, which we see satisfied in those who have rejected the rat race. Perhaps it's all part of the disillusionment with science and progress. Who knows? But what is certain is that we are bound to hear more about SQ and EQ than IQ!

Sweatshop to virtual organization

The world of work is changing. It is quite possible that your grandfather *slaved* in a Victorian *workshop*, your father *laboured* in a standard *post-war office*, you *work* in an *open-planned office* and your children *explore* in a *virtual organization*.

On observing the bombed House of Commons, Churchill said that we shape our buildings but afterwards they shape us. He argued, as environmental psychologists have been able to demonstrate, that the physical factors associated with work can and do have a major impact on work style. But so do corporate culture and the theories of managers and consultants.

Over 30 years ago, a guru called McGregor suggested that managers held either of two, mutually contradictory, theories about workers. Those who believed in *theory X* believe all workers don't like work, avoid it, have little ambition, try to avoid responsibility and need firm direction, control and coercion. Workers are lazy, feckless, impossible to change and hence require tough management techniques. Those who subscribe to *theory Y* maintain that, under the right conditions, people not only work conscientiously but seek commitment, challenge (blah blah) and reach their potential. They believe that (all) jobs can be intrinsically satisfying and that people can be encouraged to be both productive and happy at work. The bosses who believed that workers avoided work were commonplace for our grandfathers. Hopefully, our children will enjoy a world where *theory Y* is supreme.

In the good old days of mass production, there was command-and-control management. There were few suppliers, a relatively stable market and very low labour flexibility. Fashions for centralization and decentralization came and went with periods of integration and disintegration.

A period of lean-management production started in the 1990s. There were those dreaded ideas of de-layered management, process redesign and horizontal integration. And now we have what is called *agile* production with all employees having a self-employment mindset with carefully selected and updated core competences, with many alliances all over the world.

It is possible that every generation experiences work quite differently as a function of management theories and the demands of current technology. Consider the six examples in Table 1. They are speculative and possibly something of a caricature. But the real question is whether the columns represent progress. Is the world of work tomorrow going to be better than that of today?

Futurology is a dangerous pursuit. Despite the fact that there are more and better economic, demographic, technological (and

Table 1: Sweatshop to virtual organization

	Grandfather's workshop 1920s	*Father's office 1950s*	*Your open-planned work environment 2000*	*Your child's virtual organization 2020*
The Boss's Office	The foreman has a functional office with tea-making facilities, personnel files and all the valuable equipment	A dark-panelled sober office dominated by a high desk, which has executive toys and an ashtray on it	The boss's glass-panelled enclosure has a door that is always open. A coffee table dominates	Nobody has an office. But the building has 'meeting stations' for stand-up meetings and mass-visual display areas
Incentive Systems	Knowing that after 40 years of dedicated service you were least likely to be laid off.	Meet your pre-set goals (management by objectives) and you keep your job.	Training courses to 'upskill' yourself and performance-related pay	Equity in the company. Total freedom to plan own career; go part-time, etc.
Appraisal Systems	If your boss never shouted at you or demanded you to see him in his office, you were OK	Annual, staff department driven by bureaucratic process of no consequence	Mandatory, three times a year progress reviews that bosses have been trained to give	360° feedback data, fed into development- and assessment-centre data and biannual 20-page report delivered
Skills Valued	Manual and engineering skills	Knowledge of systems	Computing	Knowledge and know-how at the cutting edge of bio-technology
Career Opportunities	None, unless you married the boss's daughter	In the service-based system loyalty was rewarded by the 'Buggins turn' system	Performance-based but liable to erratic but enthusiastic restructuring, downsizing and re-appraising	The word 'career' went out of fashion. Workers each carry and compose portfolios of work experience and skills
Working hours	0700–1800 with a short dinner break and the odd tea break	0800–1700 with fixed, negotiated breaks	Half an hour before the boss; an hour after he/she leaves. Sandwich or desk lunch	Personal circadian rhythms dictate flexitime pattern chosen

even meteorological) forecasts, futurology is no science. It may be the product of analysis and judgement but inevitably contains considerable conjecture. Try playing the stock market, if you don't agree.

It is both amusing and salutary to review 'serious' forecasts over the past century to see how wrong they can be. Famous examples include Lord Kelvin, President of the Royal Society, who noted in 1895 that 'heavier than air flying machines are impossible' or the British Astronomer Royal declaring in 1956 that space travel is 'utter bilge'. Prediction of the spread of computers was equally bad: The Chairman of IBM in 1943 predicted a world market of 'maybe five computers', while the founder-president of Digital Equipment Corporation said as late as 1977 that 'there is no reason for any individuals to have a computer in their home'.

In 1998 the Henley Centre – a dedicated forecasting centre – made predictions about work. Their predictions concerned a number of specified work-related issues and, being more recent and more data-based, are probably more useful.

• Working hours: They believe people will have a shorter working day (5 hours to 25 hours per week) but that many businesses will be open 24 hours per day. People will work 3–4-day weeks; the remaining time will be 'absorbed by leisure and community work'.
• Travel: Their vision is one of rail renaissance and privatized automated roads: 'we might go to work in our solar-powered, eco-friendly, self-driving car along privatized roads employing automated highway systems, which control the speed and direction of the car. Congestion should be a thing of the past as the on-board global positioning system automatically redirects and navigates – The longest commuter journey will be just under two hours, mainly for the very wealthy using the space shuttle (to travel outside the world's atmosphere, and back again) to Sydney or San Francisco' (p.12–13). If only!
• Communication: Personal computers will become all the more powerful 'virtual glasses receiving wireless digital video will enable us to talk and see anybody in the world whilst still on the move' (p. 13). Yet they do not believe there will be information overload. Again: is this naïve optimism?

- Home working: They argue that a quarter of all people will work from home and that 10 per cent of top companies will be virtual companies, which will be very flat organizations.
- Careers: they acknowledge little job tenure, and therefore the necessity of precautionary saving for no-work periods. 'There will also be vast armies of self-employed, stimulated by the online world and the ease with which the next generation internet-matches the supply and demand for funds to start up businesses' (p. 12).

They argue that the most likely scenario for the year 2020, specifically in Great Britain, will be characterized by some fluctuation in economic cycles. They believe real incomes will have increased by over 40 per cent but that those disposable-income gains are absorbed by 'personal welfare' costs that cover health, education and pensions. Globalization may undermine the national tax base because of 'footloose companies' and electronic commerce. On a more negative note, they speculate about permanent labour market uncertainty, strains on social cohesion and a widening skills imbalance based on education and high unemployment. They also believe that widening income distribution may force an electoral backlash and a limited increase in higher tax rates.

It seems a truism that there is a radical change in the way (most) individuals and organizations work and that those many changing patterns are inflicting considerable pressure on nearly all individuals and organizations. Pressures facing individuals relate to careers, knowledge and skills. Lifelong employment for many is no longer possible and the emphasis has changed from being employed to being employable. Individuals are required to take responsibility for their own career planning, development, pension and training. It has been suggested by many that human knowledge and technical skills are becoming obsolete faster now than at any time in human history. Employees, in all sectors, need to refresh, expand and broaden their skills. This may be desirable if you are young, talented and educated – but it may equally be a nightmare for the older, unskilled worker.

There has been a clear movement from mass production, through decentralized production, lean production, to agile production with high labour flexibility. Workforces tend to be more temporary, yet those in work require more skills. Some companies talk of fewer but more able and flexible core employees as well as well-managed and often outsourced non-core employees. There are, it seems, two sorts of 'haves' and 'have-nots': those with and those without a job, and those genuinely between jobs versus those who will probably be 'resting' for a very long time.

Those who portend, presage and prophesy the future clearly fall into two groups: *Naïve, enthusiastic optimists* paint a glowing picture of the future where technology liberates one from drudgery. Many dirty, dangerous, degrading jobs, they argue, will be done by machines, which will increase the possibility of more intrinsic job satisfaction for many workers.

More cautious and considered optimists see a cost to the change in jobs. The cost is twofold: first the good life will be available only to those in wealthy, developed countries, and second it will often be at the cost of social factors: a less cohesive society, an increase in loneliness etc.

Sceptical, cynical pessimists see technology as alienating and perceive the speed of change as unnecessary. They see a trade-off between speed and quality and a growing schism in previously coherent societies between the 'haves' (with skills, knowledge, jobs) and the 'have-nots' (without all of the above). They feel the virtual organization of teleworkers is a poor substitute for the camaraderie of office gossip, contact with staff and the opportunity to use one's talents.

Optimism, not pessimism, sells. One has only to look at the business section of bookshops to see this. They are full of 'one-minute manager secrets of highly successful people techniques'. They maintain that human behaviour (of employees) is easily changeable and that good managers have ability to control it. They stress the power of technology and techniques that have an immediate short-term pay-off.

Enthusiasts are engineering technocrats. They believe that they invent technology, but it often invents us. The invention of technology created the suburbs, computers the possibility of virtual companies. We cannot always see the result of the technology, but optimistic soothsayers think they can.

But pessimists stress the costs of change and those who will not benefit from it. They know that human behaviour and human needs have not changed much over the millennia and do not see how smart computers make much difference. They are often social scientists and humanists who know how difficult it is to change people.

Take the issue of teleworking in the electrical cottage and the virtual workplace. Enthusiasts say it is perfect for employee *and* employer. Employees don't have to commute, which saves time and the environment. Teleworkers have incredible flexibility and can structure their work around personal commitments and timetables. They can work in their preferred place, in their casual clothes, at the time of day that suits them best, free of interruption. The employers can have intercontinental teams and access at all times. They don't have to pay for buildings consultants. They can even make the teleworker self-employed and save even more.

But the pessimist sees problems. Teleworkers are difficult to monitor. Not all have the space at home. Do customers like teleworkers? More importantly, does the satellite tele-collage satisfy the needs of the worker? They have no co-workers for casual gossip. An organized job gives a sense of identity and loyalty. They need to be self-disciplined, conscientious introverts without much ambition, because they are easily forgotten. They are the colonial people away from head office, centre of empire, where people do come in.

So the optimists and pessimists remain in mortal combat about all innovations at work. Pessimists accuse optimists of having little or no learning experience. They know good judgement comes from experience, which comes from bad judgement. They see cheerful naïvety as blissful unawareness of the nightmare ahead. On the other hand, optimists can't abide the doleful negativity of the pessimist who, on smelling flowers, looks around for the coffin.

Inevitably, both optimists and pessimists are likely to have some of their predictions come true. There will be things about the sweatshop that people will miss – all the old certainties; and there will be things about the new order that will benefit everyone.

The toxic boss

Results from studies on the origin of delinquency and criminality make depressing reading. As does coming across young children in a clearly toxic family; one feels they really have so little chance of growing up as healthy, responsible, adaptable individuals. The anti-social personality has often had a miserable upbringing which, alas, he or she often perpetuates, producing a cycle of misfortune, neglect, unhappiness and crime.

Reading the list of typical characteristics of the dysfunctional parent in the toxic family, it is not difficult to see why children from these families end up as they do. Moody, egocentric, uneducated, immoral 'care-givers' give little care. Instead of providing the loving, stable environment, they do the opposite, which can have a disastrous long-term effect on the child.

And the same can happen at work. Dysfunctional managers create toxic offices. They manage, often in a brief period of time, to create mayhem, distrust and disaffection. And even in stable adults this can have long-term consequences. That perfidious issue of 'stress at work' and its more serious cousin the nervous breakdown are often caused by the dysfunctional manager.

To many, especially young people, a manager is *in loco parentis*. They can have considerable influence over one's health, happiness and future. They can create an environment that allows employees to give of their best. They can stretch staff by setting reachable but challenging goals and they can give them support in doing so. They can be helpful and encouraging and consistent – or not.

But there are some seriously poor managers who create a working environment at the precise opposite end of the spectrum.

What are the symptoms of the dysfunctional manager? Check this list:

- *Inconsistency and unpredictability*: This is often the hallmark of the type. They are unpredictable to staff, to clients and customers – even their family. You can never be sure about what they will say or do. They are fickle and capricious. The job of a parent and manager is often to create stability in a world of chaos, a sense of security in an insecure world, not the opposite. A dysfunctional manager is often more than inconsistent in that they give contradictory and mixed messages that are very difficult to interpret.
- *Low tolerance of provocation and emotional sensitivity*: Dysfunctional managers easily fly off the handle. They are known for their moodiness. One has quite literally to tread around them very gently. Jokes backfire – unless, of course, they make them. They take offence, harbour grudges and can show great mood swings, especially when stressed.
- *Hedonism and self-indulgence*: The dysfunctional manager is no puritan: they like pleasure. The golf round on a Friday afternoon, those expensive meals, that overpriced office furniture are all ways of a dysfunctional manager pleasing himself or herself. And they are often deeply selfish about them. There can be real problems if their pleasures are addictive, which so often they can be. The hedonistic, addictive personality is a real nightmare not only from a financial point of view.
- *Nowness and no long-term planning*: The dysfunctional parent and dysfunctional manager live everyday as it comes – not for religious reasons, but because they can't or won't plan for the future. They never understood postponement of gratification. Hence, they experience serious setbacks when unexpected things happen. Saving for a rainy day is not part of that reputation. They can't or won't plan for future eventualities.
- *Restlessness and excitement seeking*: The dysfunctional manager is always on the go. They get bored easily, can't pay attention. They look as if they have an adult form of ADHD. They look as if they need thrills and variety to keep them going. And, inevitably, they

find themselves in situations that are commercially, even physically, dangerous. They chop and change all the time. They can't sit
still and rarely pay attention to others.

*   *Learning problems*: Dysfunctional managers don't learn from their
    mistakes. In fact, they don't like learning at all. The skill-based
    seminar is not for them. Outward bound perhaps, but not the
    conference centre. Many have few educational qualifications.
    They don't value them in their staff or themselves. Hence, they do
    not encourage learning of any sort, often pooh-poohing the
    educated staff member.

*   *Poor emotional control: let feelings hang out*: Dysfunctional managers are
    the opposite of the stereotypic reserved and controlled English-
    men. They shout and weep, sulk and gush with little embarrass-
    ment or control. This is not the result of some California-based
    therapy: in fact, they have poor self-control. They become well
    known for their outbursts.

*   *Placing little value on skill attainment*: The dysfunctional manager does
    not have an MBA. They despise attempts of their staff to upgrade
    their skills. They talk about gut feelings, experience or, worse still,
    luck. They are loath to invest in training on the job.

*   *Perpetual low-grade physical illness*: Dysfunctional bosses always seem
    to be ill. They get coughs, colds, chills – whatever is going around.
    They certainly are not health conscious, and are very liable to
    absenteeism.

The dysfunctional boss, like the delinquent child, may have come from
a dysfunctional home or socialized in a dysfunctional organization.
Management consultants often talk about management practices they
have come across that are little short of startling. They cause unhappiness and reduce productivity and morale, which, over time, can lead to
the breakdown of the staff.

It has been observed by the business guru Manfred Kets de Vries
that whole organizations can become toxic because of the character
of senior managers. Toxic senior managers see the world in a particular way, which influences their selection, self-perception and style.

The workplace can become psychologically as well as physically
toxic. The dysfunctional manager is a sort of Typhus Mary of stress
and incompetence, taking the disease around with them wherever
they go. Worse, they model dysfunctionality to young staff, who may

consider their behaviour normal. The cure, alas, is often not worth the candle. Dysfunctional managers need more than counselling: they really need cancelling.

The trauma of retirement

A surprising number of people, and men in particular, find retirement traumatic. Hemingway in his 50s wrote: 'Retirement is the ugliest word in the language.' People are retiring younger and younger. Most people in the City aim to retire in their early 40s; people in the Foreign Office and some companies retire at 55. It is now becoming the exception to retire at 65. The pensions industry and the Government are very interested in the age of retirement, less so how one adapts to it.

Some people hate the idea of retirement at all. The American comedian, still performing at 90, said, in his view, 'Retirement at 65 is ridiculous. When I was 65, I still had pimples.' Others are happier to acknowledge the benefits both of old age and retirement, which are certainly more attractive than the alternative.

The demographic changes because of the post-war baby boom have led to many developed countries having a plethora of retirees and a paucity of job entrants. This has a significant effect on the economies of those countries, which has attracted researchers.

Research in the area has produced some fairly consistent findings:

- Most workers look forward to retirement and have a positive attitude towards it.
- Those with positive attitudes towards retirement tend to be: younger, with higher education, having had fewer episodes of unemployment, have a higher expected retirement income and tend to be in better health.
- The relationship of retirement attitudes to occupational status appears curvilinear, in that those at both ends of the spectrum (As and Es) have more negative attitudes.
- Neither work commitment nor job satisfaction appear to have a major association with attitude towards retirement.
- The transition from before to after retirement is not associated with any immediate reliable major health-status changes.

- There seems a slight tendency for unskilled workers to show a mild improvement in health status and for the other groups to show a mild decline soon after retiring.
- Comparisons of retirees with those continuing to work showed that in both groups a little over 40 per cent were classified as 'no change'; among those changing, there was a slight excess of decrements in health among those continuing to work.

A lot, but not all, of this is common sense. Nearly 250 years ago, Samuel Johnson said: 'The love of retirement has, in all ages, adhered closely to those minds which have been most enlarged by knowledge, or elevated by genius.'

A review of British research has attempted to find the best predictor of retirement satisfaction.

1. *Health* (both physical and mental) has been found to predict satisfaction in all studies, although the effect is modest. It is pretty obvious that it must make some difference.
2. *Finance* is a predictor in most studies but it is not linear, that the more money, the happier you are. There is a ceiling; once this point is reached, increases make little difference.
3. *Purpose in life* (life interests and self-esteem) was the strongest predictor in a study of retired British managers. That is, having self-confidence and some sense of purpose is really important.
4. *Having strong interests,* old or new, is important, such as belonging to educational, leisure or other organizations. The main predictors of satisfaction are the amount of social interaction and the number of different activities, not the use of skills.
5. *Education and social class* do predict satisfaction in retirement. Although middle-class people are giving up more interesting jobs, they have resources and leisure interests with which to replace work. Managers find it difficult to accept the loss of responsibility but professionals can keep up their skills and interests more easily, often by volunteer work.
6. *Satisfaction* can be best predicted when retirement is voluntary and planned. However, the effects of pre-retirement courses are found to be negligible. They provide interesting facts but there is little evidence that they help with adjustment.
7. *Married women* have the least difficulty in adjusting to retirement.

It is difficult to underestimate attitudes to, and expectations of, retirement. The more people plan for continuities in their lifestyle, the better. Surprisingly, job satisfaction and work commitment are not very relevant or powerful predictors of retirement satisfaction. This may be because personality factors play an important role in job satisfaction and retirement satisfaction – thus, being dissatisfied and disenchanted at work may easily spill over into retirement. Some people are just habitually happy or 'pissed off' at or after work

Some people just retire unhappily. Studies on those with a heavy dose of the work ethic show they also tend to resist early retirement and opt for delayed retirement. They tend, if possible, to continue working at the same job and find alternative employment, if available. Those with the work ethic report lower retirement satisfaction if unable to work and adapt to a new lifestyle, particularly in terms of timekeeping, closely akin to that of working people.

Most cope quite well with retirement because, for all intents and purposes, they continue to work, even if not paid to do so.

What the retiree discovers are the latent, non-obvious benefits of work – the things they take for granted! It is only after they retire that they realize the functions they fulfilled. Work provides many features that are psychologically very important. Five in particular are worth noting:

- *Work structures time*: Work structures the day, the week and even longer periods. The loss of a time structure can be very disorientating. Retired people are less organized and less purposeful in their use of time and often report depressive symptoms. A predictable pattern of activity with well-planned 'rhythms' is what most people seek. Hence the work-like routine that many retired people soon get into, even if it is walking the dog at a regular time.
- *Work provides regularly shared experiences*: Regular contact with non-nuclear family members provides an important source of social interaction. Social isolation is related to disturbed mental states. Social support from family and friends buffers the major causes of stress and increases coping ability, so reducing illness. If one's primary source of friends and contacts is work colleagues, then the benefits of social support are denied precisely when they are

most needed. One of the most frequently cited sources of job satisfaction is contact with other people. The retiree is, in short, lonely and bored – and suffers stress as a result.

- *Work provides experience of creativity, mastery, and a sense of purpose.* Both the organization and the production of work imply the interdependence of human beings. Take away some sense of relying on others, and they on you, and the retiree is left with a sense of uselessness. Work, even not particularly satisfying work, gives some sense of mastery or achievement. Creative activities stimulate people and provide a sense of satisfaction. A person's contribution to producing goods or providing services forges a link between the individual and the society of which he or she is a part. Work roles are not the only roles that offer the individual the opportunity of being useful and contributing to the community but, for the majority, they are the most central roles and consequently people deprived of the opportunity to work often feel useless and report that they lack a sense of purpose. Often, the more service-oriented the job he or she left, the more the retiree struggles with this issue.

- *Work is a source of personal status and identity*: A person's job is an important indicator of personal status in society – hence the often amusing debates over job titles. Furthermore, it is not only at work that jobs give a certain status, but also to their families. Retired people have lost their employment status and hence identity. Not unnaturally, there is a marked drop in self-esteem during the first phases of unemployment. That is why some professionals cling on to titles: e.g. Major (retd.), Emeritus Professor. You are what you do: when you stop doing it, you are nobody.

- *Work is a source of activity*: All work involves some expenditure of physical or mental effort. Whereas too much activity may induce fatigue and stress, too little activity results in boredom and restlessness, particularly among extroverts. People seek to maximize the amount of activity that suits them by choosing particular jobs or tasks that fulfil their needs. The retired, however, are not provided with this possibility and have to provide stimulation consistently to keep them active.

The role of the retired person is essentially no longer to have one. This can be difficult for both ex-breadwinner and homemaker, as they say in America, because retirement means twice as much husband and half as much money.

In the new era, when we now realize there will be no such thing as a job for life, people will no doubt have fallow periods between jobs. They will also be encouraged very early on to think clearly about retirement, pensions, downshifting and the like. These experiences are bound to make the trauma of retirement far less serious than it is for some today.

Underperformers and how to manage them

Managing the demotivated, uncooperative, negative, irritable, frequently absent employee is, what is called on training courses, a challenge. To have only conscientious, motivated talented peers and reports is as joyful as it is rare. It is, therefore, in training-speak, a developmental opportunity to learn how to manage the underperformer.

The ability to 'deal with' and cope with let alone 'cure' the underperformer is a major management skill. The sour, demotivated person can poison their peers. They tend to get 'dug in' and deeply resistant to all management attempts to improve their performance. In some jobs, whose outcome measures are clearly specifiable, it can be relatively straightforward to deal with the underperformer. It is easier to persuade a poor performer to leave or improve, if you have the data.

In some call centres these days, everyone is electronically monitored (number of calls per day, revenue per call, etc.). Some even have their chairs monitored (by heat or weight) – you can't be selling unless you are at your desk (with the headphones on). In this sense, one can challenge poor output on a daily basis, if you have proof, but most of us, alas, do not.

The fault of most managers is that they look for solutions before they understand the cause. Many are brought up with the 'fix it' mentality of the action man. They think of training courses, sabbaticals, even personal counselling. Some try to redeploy problem underperformers in another part of the organization – send them to the stores, HR or catering management. One CEO had the brilliant idea of herding them all together in a prestigious-sounding subsidiary and then selling it off.

What are the classic signs of underperformance? They tend to relate to timekeeping, mood states and focus. Underperformers suffer from both absenteeism and presenteeism. They like to escape as much as possible, and equate being present with doing work. They are also moody, irritable, critical, quick to fly off the handle and passive-aggressive. They have almost nothing positive to say about others and live in a world of sniping at the happy, contented and productive worker.

Most of all, they lose their enthusiasm and focus. They somehow remove their heart and brain before starting work, only to relocate and re-activate them after work. They represent the 'quit-but-stay' old dogs of the organization.

So how does one diagnose the cause of the problem? The answer is no different from that of your GP. Imagine a person going to a doctor complaining of a headache. Traditionally, the GP asks a series of set questions: When did it first occur? How long did it last? What pattern did it take? Had it ever occurred before? Essentially, they are questions about duration, frequency, intensity and unusualness of the given the medical condition of the person. By doing so, they may be able to determine whether the cause was anything as varied as stress, a brain tumour or hidden alcoholism.

Symptoms lead to questions, which lead to diagnosis and thence attempts to find a solution. Solutions may be as varied as warnings and sackings to offers of counselling or training.

Jobs change, they become more complex and the technology that needs to be mastered is forever being upgraded. People have to be bright *enough* for a job. Too bright and they get bored, but not bright enough and they become stressed, change-averse and unco-operative. It is not a favourable diagnosis but an important one – some people underperform because they are not bright enough to learn to adapt quickly enough.

And there are no easy solutions to this problem. Training courses don't make people more intelligent. In fact, they serve to expose those who are not bright enough. Those who, through lack of ability, can't hack the job need to be 'let go' – not passed on to personnel where they can do more damage. Demotion, early retire-ment or a lesser part-time job are the best solutions. They need to be helped not to lose face, but they need work more compatible with their abilities.

People underperform because they have not been trained to do it. The training has been absent, poor, too quick, too long ago and/or not supported in the workplace. It is a common problem, particularly where there is a change in structure, equipment, customer needs or the like. Underperformance can be fairly easily cured, if a judicious choice of courses is chosen and supported. In some organizations, training is seen as a reward – a jolly time at a nice hotel. In others, it is a punishment and the mark of Cain to peers. It should not, and need not, be either. Skills need to be acquired and practised in a changing world. More importantly, the organization needs to reward skills acquisition not punish it, which leads to deep cynicism about the whole enterprise.

There are three other important causes of underperformance, alongside lack of ability and training. The first is distraction – people have things going on in their lives that mean they take their eye off the ball. It may be an affair, sickness in the family or, more worryingly, some form of addiction – alcohol, drugs or gambling. The symptoms are secrecy (lots of phone calls), poor timekeeping, moodiness and increasing absenteeism. And the solution? Support first, deadlines second. That is, people often need help – time off, counselling, etc., but they need to be told there is a deadline by which time, if things are not going well, further steps will need to be taken.

Another problem is simply personality. People selected for a particular trait may soon be shown to have too much of it. The bold and confident young man might be hiding his narcissism. The diligent, careful, meticulous worker chosen for her conscientiousness may soon expose herself as a total neurotic compulsive. The agreeable and compliant person may turn out to be totally dependent. The clever sceptic may turn out to be paranoid, just as the creative turns out to be utterly unreliable and totally impractical. The excitable, amazing and enthusiastic creative may soon reveal that those traits are simply driven by powerful underlying neuroticism.

The quietly reserved person may later reveal themselves as indifferent and deeply uncommunicative. Equally, the easygoing may simply reveal themselves to be passive-aggressive. The problem is that people present the best side of their personality at interview. Often, one can have 'too much of a good thing', which leads to problems.

Therapy for difficult staff members may be too costly. Again, the best solution is to terminate the contract. People with non-optimal traits can be 'managed back' to being production workers but don't kid yourself that it is easy.

There is a fifth and final cause of underperformance, and that may be the way in which the person has been managed in the past. The corporate culture management style can and does have a massive impact on employee motivation and performance. Management is about challenge and support: bosses need to set clear, attainable but stretching goals for employees and then help them attain them. Goal-setting is often done badly – people are not set them, or they are impossible to achieve. Both situations are deeply stressful and lead to underperformance. Equally, one may have a very supportive and kind boss who does not push one to achieve; so little is done.

When a person has worked in one organization all their lives, they believe that what they are experiencing is normality. Those who change jobs become painfully and immediately aware of issues like corporate culture and all sorts of subtle norms about dress, timekeeping and expected productivity. Those going from public to private sector or from organizational to self-employment often have a great surprise. They then, and often only then, become aware of how the management style in their previous organization impacted on their and their colleagues' behaviour.

Normal, healthy, well-chosen and enthusiastic staff can become alienated, uncommitted underperformers through the way in which they are managed. These underperformers need 're-enthusing'. They need clear goals, lots of support and positive colleagues. They can, as Mao believed, be re-educated for the new order!

In other words, the source of the underperformance lies not in the employee but in the way in which they are managed. The fault, therefore, dear manager, may lie not in your employees but in yourself!

The uptake of innovation

Some people believe that Asians in general, and the Japanese in particular, are not creative but very good and astute copiers of others' bright ideas. This may or may not be true. But it does seem that in the Dragon Economies of Asia there is a rapid uptake of new technology.

Many businesspeople are often baffled and bewildered by the range and quality of new equipment they are offered. High-tech equipment, once the preserve of the rich, is everywhere: in the kitchen, the living room, the car and certainly the office. Statistics on the number of home computers, CD players, microwave ovens and the like show interesting differences within Asia that are not simply attributable to GNP. What determines the uptake of innovations? Which type of person gets in first and why, and who are those souls dragged kicking and screaming into the twenty-first century?

More importantly, how do manufacturers or legislators encourage technology uptake? How do they encourage the reticent on the one hand, but also satisfy the thirst for new products on the other? If there are genuine differences between countries, the impact on a company's marketing and sales strategy could be profound.

We all know about the S-shaped learning curve. The diffusion curve is much the same. That is, initial uptake is slow and done by a few. Then there is a noticeable, fast, steep increase as the idea or product takes off. It flattens again when the market becomes saturated.

The diffusion curve seems to contain five clear types of individuals. The first are the *innovators*. These are individuals who are always seeking to try out new ideas or equipment. They come in many shapes or forms: the eccentric, genius inventor, childlike adults who enjoy the electronic toys of their youth, socially inadequate technophiles who prefer computers to people. They may scour the pages of specialist magazines for new equipment or may even try building it themselves. They had CDs, computers, microwaves and faxes long before most people even knew what they were. They prefer to surf the Internet rather than play in the surf. Some can be innovation junkies who go for anything new and different regardless of its quality, usefulness or design. Others like to improve on current ideas and techniques.

The next group are the *early adopters*. These people take little or no persuasion, and are among the first of the population, to take on the innovation. They are at the beginning of the steep climb of the S-curve. All they have to be told is that there is new equipment that is faster, smarter or more elegant than theirs and they want it. Early adopters are ideal types for the advertiser because one mention of the product is sufficient to spur them to buy.

As the diffusion of innovation occurs and the new phenomenon becomes recognized, the *early majority* begin to take an interest. They need to be sold the idea, persuaded to buy. A little sceptical and a little cautious, the early majority are good candidates to adopt innovation but need some convincing. This is the midpoint on the diffusion curve and includes the bulk of the population. The product or the idea appears in the media and in shops more widely than before and the new 'thing' seems to be everywhere.

The *late majority* need the hard sell. Scepticism turns to cynicism, when they are faced with an innovation, and they frequently demand that its benefits are proved to them. Like all of us, they have probably bought some new idea or product that proved to be pretty useless or cumbersome, and they have not forgotten it. For them, the cupboard of unused gizmos (the toasted-sandwich maker, the slow cooker, the exercise bicycle) is an unwelcome reminder of previous purchasing imprudence. Some argue that the later one adopts an innovation, the cheaper it is and the more reliable. The pocket calculator is one example among many, and this also persuades the late majority to be cautious – perhaps rather too cautious for the advertiser.

Finally, at the top of the curve is the *laggard*. Like innovators, laggards come in very different forms but share a common reaction to innovation. There is the technophobe, terrified of anything not simple and mechanical. How many adults have to ask their children to programme the video? Then there are the change-averse, who hate learning anything new. They all share a fear of, and hostility to, innovation. For employers and legislators, the only way to make them comply is to change the rules. You have to ban or physically remove old equipment or make laws (for instance about seat belts or gas appliances) to achieve compliance. There are few easy ways to persuade the laggard, and advertising of product benefits is a waste of time for this group.

The problem of the diffusion of innovation for the manufacturer is threefold. First, they have to segment their market and be able to identify the demographic, geographic and psychographic correlates of the five different types mentioned above. Next, they have either to change their marketing strategy as the population moves up the S-curve or target it quite specifically to the different groups. But the third problem is the greatest of all: what to do when even the laggards have adopted the innovation? The only solution is to find a new product, a new idea, a new approach and start all over again. And, of course, companies, like their customers, can also be classified by the same fivefold scheme described above.

In the workplace, too, managers benefit from understanding the attitudes of their workforce, to innovation and adapting training programmes accordingly. This is particularly important for overseas subsidiaries run by ex-patriot mangers, who may assume that all cultures' attitudes to technology are like their own.

Values at work

Is it appropriate for a boss to enquire about a subordinate's private life? Is it ever a good thing to be a whistle-blower? Should affairs in the office simply be outlawed? Is performance-related pay essentially divisive, setting work colleagues against each other?

The answers to the above and other business ethics questions are powerfully influenced by a limited number of very basic convictions you hold about what is right and wrong, good or bad, desirable or not. These convictions or values are relatively stable and enduring throughout life, and guide and influence many attitudes and business decisions.

For those who enjoy quasi-legalistic, psychobabble definitions try this. 'A value is an enduring belief that a specific mode of conduct or end-state of existence; it is both personally and socially preferable to an opposite or converse mode of conduct or end-state of existence'.

Organisations talk 'a good game' about values. These may be enshrined (a very appropriate word) in their mission and vision statements. Whether they talk about it or not, by their behaviour it is clear that organizations, departments and teams have their own values. People often become aware of values only when there is a clear clash between their personal values and those around them at work.

One can experience value shock as poignantly as one can experience culture shock: anger, indignation, surprise, even disgust when confronted by a group with different values. The gift becomes the bribe; the family concern becomes the nepotistic organization.

Consider some Asian values:

Face-saving and avoidance of criticism

In many Asian countries, in order not to be criticized, messages have to be delivered privately and in-code. This is certainly not the Western style and can lead to both hurt and misinterpretation. It is easy to read lack of open disagreement or challenge as unanimous consent. It is also easy for second-rate ideas to be put into action.

Reciprocity that is not bound by time or distance

A favour given is remembered and must be repaid. This can and must be done whether it is four days, four months, four years or 40 years later. Further, it must be done when the people are in different organizations or even countries. The idea of reciprocating help (or perhaps its opposite) is a very powerful value.

In collectivist Asia, a good job is defined as prestigious and comfortable with internal harmony, equal distribution of rewards, and an opportunity to serve the organization which, in turn, is seen to contribute to society. In the industrial West, people value individual responsibility, freedom and control, equitable/performance-related rewards, and democratic and consultative management.

In the West we are pretty used to ethical debates. We all know where we stand on the 'right to life' vs 'right to choose' on 'life imprisonment' vs 'capital punishment' and on legalizing certain drugs.

But at work, values are not often debated – except where it's safe to do so.

Researchers on the topic of social values have conceived of them as a system of beliefs concerned with such issues as competence and morality, and which are derived in large from societal demands. These value systems are organized summaries of experience that capture the focal, abstracted qualities of past encounters; have an 'oughtness' (specifying prescribed and proscribed behaviours) quality about them, and which function as criteria or a framework against which present experience can be tested. Also, it is argued that these act as general motives.

Once a value is internalized, it consciously or unconsciously becomes a standard criterion for guiding action: for developing and maintaining attitudes towards relevant objects and situations, for justifying one's own and others' actions and attitudes, for morally judging self and others, and for comparing oneself with others.

Value systems are systematically linked to culture of origin, religion, chosen university discipline, political persuasion, generations within a family, age, sex, personality and educational background. These values in time may determine vocational choice and occupational behaviour. Social attitudes precede values, which emerge as abstractions from personal experience of one's own and others' behaviour. These values in time become organized into coherent value systems, which serve as frames of reference that guide beliefs and behaviour in many situations, such as work.

Personal values can be reflected in the values at work, which may be categorized into two facets. The first is whether the work value concerns an outcome of work (e.g. recognition, pay) or a resource that one shares merely by being associated with the work organization (e.g. working conditions, company reputation). The second facet categorizes work outcomes into instrumental (e.g. benefits), affective (e.g. relationship with co-workers) and cognitive (e.g. achievement, contribution to society). Some values are associated with the work ethic – achievement and hard working – whereas others are related to interpersonal relationships at work.

Employees who score highly on these work values focus on the content of their work. They are intinsically motivated , achievement-orientated and hardworking, striving to move upwards, and seek challenges. They usually have higher education and occupy senior positions in organizations and tend to be higher in organizational commitment.

There are values that are associated with the context of work: high salary, job security, pleasant physical working environment and many fringe benefits. These are more related to a person's basic survival needs than are the content-orientated values. People who have strong context-orientated, and thus extrinsic, work values ascribe much more importance to social status, comfort, salary and benefits. They view work not as much as an end in itself, but as a means to attain other, more desirable, ends. It is quite possible that a fairly large proportion of workers in developing countries are context-orientated, as they strive to better the livelihood of themselves and their families: work is primarily a chance for them to move up the social ladder. Employees who hold these values are often lower in organizational commitment than other employees.

Virtual teams at virtual work

More and more people have a virtual company in a virtual office. It's often a large carrier bag of papers in the spare bedroom. The company might have three virtual offices – a brother's spare-bedroom in America and the parents' loft in Australia. And they (the relatives) are directors of the company. It literally has no assets – and not many clients.

'Virtual' has two meanings: first, something being in essence or effect though not formally recognized or admitted; second something that is apparent rather than real. Many virtual companies are both.

But what is virtual work? Some people work in virtual teams. A virtual team is quite unlike its opposite – a real team. To be a real team means certain criteria have to be met.

- Members must be able to influence each other's beliefs and behaviours.
- They share common goals, objectives and targets.
- They have a relatively stable group structure, like social rules and roles that endure over time.
- They have clear patterns of affect – liking and disliking.
- They recognize themselves to be part of a team.

It is business babble folklore that teams go through quite specific developmental phases. They are called forming, storming, norming, performing and adjourning. This is all about getting to know each other.

But what about a virtual team? Virtual teams are most likely to be individuals who come together to solve a very particular problem. They are certainly task oriented, a sort of international task-force.

In all probability the virtual team never meets, but is hooked up to the web. Depending on where they are in the world, they might not even interact 'live' but merely send and receive messages. Imagine having a team member in New Zealand, 12 hours ahead of us. They check in as we clock off unless, of course, one is temporarily odd.

Thus, you may never meet (see) or talk to members of your team. The interaction is exclusively on screen. And this can cause problems, as we all know, with stories of e-mail madness. It is too easy to be brusque or unclear on the web.

So often, unlike pen pals, people who meet after a longish business e-mail relationship are surprised by how little they know about each other – and how their impressions were wrong.

When we do business we know there is a 'task-oriented bit' and a 'social bit'. In Western culture we celebrate after work. The Japanese do the opposite. They like to get to know you, trust you – find out about your values and lifestyle – and then do business.

Teamwork does not come easily to us Anglo-Saxon individualists. That is why we have to go on courses where semi-sadistic ex-corporals make you cold, wet, frightened and miserable, to teach you about real interdependence in a team. You have to learn to like, trust and feel secure with individuals by seeing them in a number of different situations.

None of this happens in virtual teams. Indeed, meetings may be more like casual sex encounters than one may dare to admit. There is little affect among team members. Little feeling of camaraderie; little passion except perhaps e-mail rage and frustration.

Virtual teams in virtual organizations are virtually automata.

There is nothing wrong with having an electronic meeting. But to pretend that people will co-operate and thrive in virtual teams is a virtual hope, sustained by a virtual myth.

Wastebasketry, shredding and recycling

The paperless office, the promise of the PC gurus, is a sad joke. We use more, rather than less, paper these days. And as a result, many contend with the littered desk and in-tray malaise. The sheer amount of paper that arrives on the desk through internal memoranda or external mail grows at a frightening pace. And the number of people who print e-mails grows ever greater.

Wastebasketryphobia is an important new syndrome. It is the inability to throw things away. But it is a healthy habit and a useful skill. The size, shape and position of your bin and basket are crucial indices of your status. Big basket, big person? A person who receives a lot of communication may or may not be important. Often, the chief writes, the others read; the chief communicates, the others receive the tablets.

But junk mail is no respecter of power, rank and status. In fact, junk mail received at home may be a very good function of status and income, because companies buy address lists of 'high spenders': people who fly first class, buy cases of champagne regularly and drive top-end-of-the-market cars.

The question is how, when and why to keep, vs. discard, papers at work. We have all experienced the problem of having thrown away crucial papers. We may have another problem, which is not being able to access papers easily in a morass of poorly filed papers that we refuse to throw away.

Attitudes to wastebasketry fall into three clear clusters:

1. *Obsessional hoarders* are unwilling and seemingly unable to throw
    things away. Everything is an obvious, crucial 'must-keep' either
    for sentimental or record-keeping reasons. Some joyfully cata-
    logue all in-tray materials; others pile it up rather haphazardly.
    They believe, when thinking of throwing things away, 'If you hesi-
    tate in your decision, then procrastinate the throwing away.' They
    keep reports, items 'with a future', evidence reference material –
    but everything else as well.
2. *Adjusted sorters* know the difference between the useful and the
    useless, the important and the unimportant. They are stable,
    rational people who do not become anxious in the business of
    making decisions about paper – given reasonable time and guide-
    lines, most are confident and able to differentiate between filing
    and flinging on a day-to-day basis.
3. *Reckless flingers* have been taught 'when in doubt, fling it out'. Their
    motto is 'use it and discard', which may apply even to books: once
    read, they are discarded. They are phobic about unnecessary bulk
    and irrelevant material, believing that the contents of all letters
    and memos are probably recorded elsewhere and therefore need
    not be kept. They may enjoy the austerity of the bare surround-
    ings, or feel weighed down so much by any paper that they need to
    fling it.

Naturally, Sigmund Freud had something to say on this issue, albeit
tangential. In an essay entitled *Character and Anal Eroticism* Freud (1908)
argued that character traits originate in the warding-off of certain
primitive biological impulses. In this essay, he first drew attention to
the relationship between adult attitudes to money as a product of anal
eroticism. Freud identified one of three main traits associated with
people who had fixated at the anal stage: orderliness, parsimony and
obstinacy, with associated qualities of cleanliness, conscientiousness,
trustworthiness, defiance and revengefulness. Obsessional hoarders
are clearly anal – but so are reckless flingers.

The child's first interest in his faeces turns to such things as mud,
sand, stones, thence to all man-made objects that can be collected,
like paper, and then to money. Children all experience pleasure in
the elimination of faeces. At an early age (around 2 years), parents
toilet-train their children – some showing enthusiasm and praise

(positive reinforcement) for defecation, others threatening and punishing a child when it refuses to do so (negative reinforcement). Potty or toilet training occurs at the same stage (so the theory goes) that the child is striving to achieve autonomy and a sense of worth.

Often, toilet training becomes a source of conflict between parents and children over whether the child is in control of his sphincter, or the parental rewards and coercion compel submission to their will. Furthermore, the child is fascinated by, and fantasizes over, his faeces, which are, after all, a creation of his own body. The child's confusion is made all the worse by the ambiguous reactions of parents who, on the one hand, treat the faeces as gifts and highly valued, and then behave as if they are dirty, untouchable and in need of immediate disposal.

If the child is traumatized by the experience of toilet-training, he or she tends to retain ways of coping and behaving learned during this phase for the rest of his or her life. The way in which a miser hoards money and paper is seen as symbolic of the child's refusal to eliminate faeces in the face of parental demands. The spendthrift, on the other hand, recalls the approval and affection that resulted from submission to parental authority to defecate. Thus, some people equate elimination/spending with receiving affection and hence feel more inclined to spend when feeling insecure, unloved or in need of affection.

The anal eliminators love to get rid of things: they feel purged, satisfied and lovable when things are thrown away. They are the reckless flingers. On the other hand, the anal retentives feel secure and powerful and even lovable only when holding on to things. This makes them obviously obsessional hoarders.

Precisely how someone disposes of waste (paper) may also tell you something about the moral value of the person. Is it correct to throw waste into other's baskets? Is a clever way of disposing of waste giving it (cc-ing) to a colleague? Or is that merely duplicating it! This is a double coup because you both get rid of it and feel you are being helpful and considerate. And what of the holier-than-thou recyclers who insist, in the authoritarian style of 'greenies', that certain papers are recycled. This tries to turn wastebasketry into a moral cause, though it implies that, boomerang-like, the paper you fling comes round again to get you.

Finally, does your wastebasket make you vulnerable to spies? These are becoming less of a joke as the James Bond, industrial espionage world is clearly with us. Shredding paper may be a requirement in some organizations. And there is something very satisfying in shredding the carefully prepared documents of bureaucrats. But, because information is power, one has to be very careful indeed with how even the shredded paper is disposed of, as the Americans discovered in Vietnam.

This means that wastebasketry may be a lost art. The new disposal may be akin to what boy scouts learned to do to used tin cans: bash, burn, bury.

What is OB?

Anyone who has experienced management education, be it a week-long seminar, a diploma or even an MBA, will have met 'Organizational Behaviour' or 'OB'. It is the behavioural science of business.

But what is OB: a bastard, non-discipline that receives the epithet 'studies' or an important, integrative, practical science? There is no doubt that OB mixes a number of the social sciences – primarily, sociology and psychology with a reasonable dose of anthropology, economics and political science. Is this exotic cocktail a good idea?

Any disinterested critic of OB may be forgiven for finding it pretentious, painfully obvious, turgid humbug. Some have suggested that OB specialists are not bright enough to become psychologists, or know enough to be sociologists. So they hide under the leaky umbrella of OB at smart business schools – dishing up ideas, nearly all of which are derivatives of the real academic disciplines. There is practically no idea, theory or method that has not been borrowed from psychology or economics. Does this mean there are necessarily no clever thinkers in the area? Perhaps, like the Japanese manufacturers, they are brilliant imitators of others. OB researchers and writers take good ideas, improve them and market them brilliantly.

But OB as a whole is incoherent and unsubstantive. The chapters in an OB book seem unconnected, having little or nothing to do with one another. Topics can be arranged in any order. So OB researchers work on an enormous number of topics, each with many variables, which are unrelated to one another.

But when OB people come up with good ideas they don't confirm, expand or refute them. No school develops; no movement ensues even if the idea is good, the theory useful and the method-ology innovative. When the topic gets difficult, the researchers move on, bored, to some new 'cutting-edge' ideas. So OB becomes a sort of specialist, highbrow news. It is desperately faddish.

There are more specific accusations that can be made against OB.

1. Political Correctness:

This may involve anything from a doctrinaire denial of biological influ-ences on human behaviour to laments about the fashionably oppressed. We need an intellectually honest history of OB and some realistic appraisal of why topics go in and out of fashion. OB seems particularly eager to jump on any politically correct bandwagon, like diversity, espousing the accepted view. Fashion and acceptance, not veridicality, seem the important criteria for researching and writing about a topic.

2. Anecdotes, not data:

There is too much on stories, case studies, parables and anecdotes and not enough emphasis on the data to substantiate theories and concepts. Medicine, like business, is eager to use case studies but it is (hopefully) an evidence-based discipline. Case studies make interesting reading and they are extremely useful for teaching. But in science we develop from hunch to hypothesis to theory to law. We move from observation and induction to verification and falsification. OB researchers need to develop and test theories more. Yes, it is a young science, but that is no excuse for slinking away from systematic data-gathering to test theories.

3. No powerful theories:

A theory is a network of falsifiable causal generalizations. But OB has a messy stew of ideology, buzz words and doctrinaire statements. What theory regularly leads to is the prediction of empirical relationships and generalizes across topics/phenomena. Theories in psychology and economics – dissonance theory, equity theory, social-exchange theory – are warmly embraced but never bettered by OB theories. OB has lots of models that are boxes loosely connected with arrows but these are no substitute for real theories. We need theories of motivation and of organizational structure. We need, but do not have, OB-generated, real theories of job stress and organizational structure.

4. Derivative methodology:

Most psychologists collect their own data to test hypotheses. And they choose the most appropriate methods to do so. Many economists analyse others' large data sets with sophisticated econometric models. OB does neither. However, some are simply methodological critics not collectors of their own data. The focus should be on what we know rather than how we found out about it. Methodology is a tool, but an important one for doing research. OB research is difficult – there are lots of related and confounding factors, but OB really needs to explore them sensitively and thoroughly.

5. Identity:

OB does not know what it is and what it isn't. Its incoherence means it never rejects ideas, many of which are pretentious bunk (critical theory, grounded theory). Marxists, feminists, psycho-biologists, ethno-methodologists, all can find a cosy nest in OB. Everybody is welcome, all ideas are equally important and all approaches are equally good. There are no rules, no limits and no quality control. All this exacerbates the identity problem.

6. Marketing:

OB people certainly know about marketing their ideas. Take the gurus of OB – Peters, Goleman, Handy. They know the power of the press, the virtue of spin and they use it to the full to further their cause. OB courses are well attended and OB departments are often highly rated within business schools because of the business that they attract. Marketing is important because often the ideas are ephemeral and vaporous – there is a constant need for marketing because there are constantly new products on the market.

7. Attempting tractable rather than important problems:

OB people know the difference between tractable and those intractable, but perennial, problems of business that are pretty unsolvable. So they go for those pretty important ones where they can make a difference. And this is a fairly good strategy. To make a small but significant difference is surely the right thing to do.

Journal and book authors need to state major findings clearly, free of organo-babble, statistical jargon or ritualistic propitiations for long-dead heroes of the revolution. What OB needs is some pretty simple things really: a set of criteria to determine success and failure, attempts to solve important problems of moderate difficulty, and serious comparability to determine if one 'solution' is better than another.

Faced with a group of high-flying managers, one often notices a curious generational effect. The Young Turks love technical solutions to all business problems and are deeply critical of all OB. Struggling early-middle-aged managers are often obsessed by organizational structural issues, which drives them to look for solutions there. It is often the older and more powerful executives who know that most problems at work are human relationship problems – and they are naturally, at least initially, attracted to OB, often to be disappointed.

Why England?

There are many misconceptions about migration to Britain. It isn't widely known that, in nearly every single year since the Second World War, more people have left Britain than migrated to these shores. Also, most people are unaware of which is the biggest migrant group – the Irish.

The issue that provokes the most interest, however, is why people migrate to, and emigrate from this sceptred isle in the silver sea. Probably the most common motives are economic and political – people come for a better standard of living and the benefits of stable democratic government. How then does one explain the motives of people from rich stable democracies like America, Australia, Canada and New Zealand choosing to leave their place of birth to live in Britain? What possible reason could people have for choosing this green but damp island that has lost an empire but has not found a role in the world?

It is not the BBC, *The Times*, the theatre, the pub life, the sense of history or the visible remains of Europe's *ancien régime*. It certainly isn't the pound stabilized by the EMS, housing prices or the incorruptibility of our civil servants!

The particular joys of living in Britain lie in four particular characteristics of the people: The first is irony. The fact that few, even English-speaking peoples (especially Americans), understand irony demonstrates its unique prevalence in England. So many characteristics attributed to the British are a direct consequence of irony. The British love of understatement as well as being treacherous (perfidious Albion) can both be partly attributed to a love of irony. Humour and diplomatic talk with heavy use of irony mean that Englishmen can converse with one another in simple plain English before a group of foreigners who, despite prefect command of the tongue, would not understand what they are really saying.

Irony can be what Freudians call a 'defence mechanism', in that we can talk about important issues using words to express something different or opposite to it – important things can be discussed in frivolous terms, and vice versa. Love of irony is classless – even cockney rhyming slang could be seen to be a form of irony. But it is dramatic irony – that attitude of delicious detached awareness of incongruity – from farce to tragedy that exploits the potential of irony most.

The second is scepticism. Some countries, their peoples and their cultures seem imbued with naïve enthusiasm, embracing all that is new as if it were necessarily better, while others seem cynical in the face of change. I like the observation contrasting the British and Americans, which suggested the best feature of the Americans was their enthusiasm and the worst their naïvety, while the best feature of the British was their scepticism and the worst their cynicism, and that too many transatlantic mixes led to naïve cynicism rather than enthusiastic scepticism.

The disinterested sceptic agnosticism of the English is admirable and seems to apply to the 'state' religion as much as it does scientific enterprise. This is why entrepreneurial preachers, modern gadgets and miracle cures do not do as well here as elsewhere. Disinterested doubt seems to me a highly mature cynicism. It is perhaps this scepticism that in part explains why the great 'isms' like communism and Catholicism have not easily taken root here.

The third is stoicism. There is a famous prayer that asks that we are given the courage to change the things we can change, the serenity to accept the things we cannot change and the wisdom to know the difference. Stoicism steers the road nicely between instrumentalism, which attempts to change everything (even the unchangeable), and fatalism that does not attempt any change (even the changeable). Some cultures believe that everything is curable, everything is achievable and nothing is impossible, while others seem to accept their fate and have learned to be helpless.

The English, more than many other people, are able to distinguish between the two and are stoical in the face of the intractable problems. That is what makes the British so steadfast under attack, so resilient when things are going wrong. The British are well known for their self-control, their apparent indifference to pleasure and pain, which is the essence of the virtue of stoicism. The very sangfroidness of the English makes them particularly irritating to most hot-blooded Latin peoples.

And the fourth is tolerance. This is not to imply that the British are free of racism, sexism and various other forms of prejudice and discrimination. But there is in Britain a sense of 'live and let live', an acceptance of the eccentricities of others and a respect for their privacy. The British respect a person's right to behave – in terms of dress, religion, etc. – just as one wishes, providing, of course, the rights of others are not infringed.

Not everyone will agree that the British are tolerant compared, say, to the Swedes or, say, the Dutch. And perhaps legal evidence may be brought to bear in the case that the British are the very opposite of tolerant, especially with foreigners. But it is the day-to-day, one-to-one contact with the English that shows them to be most tolerant. They appear to accept the oddities of other people's behaviour much more readily, despite its contrived unusualness.

Irony, scepticism, stoicism and tolerance are all manifestations of phlegmatism. The Greek physicians Hippocrates and Galen categorized people into four types: melancholic (pessimistic, sober, rigid), choleric (restless, excitable, impulsive), sanguine (sociable, responsive, carefree) and phlegmatic (thoughtful, controlled, reliable). But the medieval writers believed phlegmatism, one of the four humours, to cause sluggishness, dullness and apathetic coldness, indifference and imperturbability. Clearly, not all aspects of phlegmatism are virtuous and one must learn to stoically tolerate the good with the bad.

It is, then, not the rain, the beer or the tea in England that makes it such a desirable home but phlegm, that thick mucus supposedly secreted in the respiratory passage of the British, which makes them and their island home so attractive. Ironic isn't it?

Work ethic

Your grandfather called it the *work ethic* and approved of it strongly; your father talked about *conscientiousness*, which he too thought was a good thing; you talk of the benefits or necessity of *hard graft*, but what about your children? – what will they think about the work ethic?

Every generation laments the decline of the work ethic, which it believes to be the cause of current economic and moral decline. But what is the work ethic? And what does it mean to endorse or reject it? More specifically, how does it affect behaviour at work?

The idea of the Protestant work ethic (PWE) was conceived by the German sociologist Max Weber (1905), who saw it as part of the explanation for the origin of capitalism. He pointed out that the Catholic countries of Europe were (and are) poorer than the Protestant countries because of what they believed in – notably aestheticism, procrastination of gratification, rationality, etc. People who believe in the PWE tend to be achievement-and-success-orientated, stress the need for efficacy and practicality, tend to be anti-leisure, and are conservative and conscious about wasting time, energy and money.

It has been argued that PWE-believing parents socialize their children by rewarding them for success, independent rational behaviour and postponement of gratification. They therefore become economically successful, which thus explains the relationship between the PWE and economic growth.

It is said that Weber provided the moral and religious justification for the accumulation of wealth. Weber was a polymath, whose training in economics, the law, sociology and other related disciplines enabled him to understand the complexity of organizations.

The so-called Protestant work ethic can be summarized as follows: a universal taboo is placed on *idleness*, and *industriousness* is considered a religious ideal; *waste* is a vice and *frugality* a virtue; complacency and *failure* are outlawed, and *ambition* and *success* are taken as sure signs of God's favour; the universal sign of sin is *poverty*, and the crowning sign of God's favour is *wealth*.

The broader meaning of the work ethic typically refers to one or more of the following beliefs:

* People have a normal and religious obligation to fill their lives with physical or intellectual toil. For some, this means that hard work, effort and drudgery are to be valued for their own sake; physical pleasures and enjoyments are to be shunned and an ascetic existence of methodological rigour is the only acceptable way to live.

- Men and women are expected to spend long hours at work, with little or no time for personal recreation and leisure, which is in effect wasted time.
- A worker should have a dependable attendance record, with low absenteeism and tardiness.
- Workers should be highly productive and produce a large quantity of goods and service for their employer or themselves.
- Workers should take pride in their work and do their jobs well, whatever they do.
- Employees should have feelings of commitment and loyalty to their profession, their company and their work group.
- Workers should be achievement-orientated and should constantly strive for promotion and advancement. High-status jobs with prestige and the respect of others are important indicators of a 'good' person.
- People should acquire wealth through honest labour and retain it through thrift and wise investments. Frugality is desirable; extravagance and waste should be avoided.

For all sorts of reasons people these days strongly accept or reject the work ethic. It certainly has little to do with Protestantism but clearly a lot to do with religion and morality. There also certainly appears to be a strong Islamic and Judaic work ethic, very similar to the Protestant one.

But for the manager and potential selector of employees, should one seek out or reject those who endorse the PWE? What do we know about the work ethic at work? We know those who believe in the PWE are more likely to be workaholics. Indeed, they are often proud of the fact, believing that to be a workaholic is to be religiously virtuous, a form of patriotism and an acknowledged way to be influential, healthy and wise. But having workaholics is a double-edged sword. They may be intense, energetic and driven but also more concerned with presenteeism than efficiency. Indeed, psychoanalysts have seen the chronic workaholic as an obsessive-compulsive, neurotic characterized by a sharp, narrowed focus of attention, endless often pointless activity, ritualistic behaviour and a strong desire to be in control. They can be intolerant, impatient, inefficient and prone to break down.

But the PWE endorsers will tolerate tedious work longer than those who don't believe in the ethic. Hard graft, after all, is a worthwhile activity. There are, however, three most interesting factors associated with the work ethic at work that may also be a mixed blessing. Believers tend to favour competitiveness over co-operativeness. This may make them poor team players. Trust many, love a few, but always paddle your own canoe. Teamwork on an equal basis doesn't come easily to them.

More importantly perhaps is the work-ethic believer's sense of social justice. People who endorse the work ethic have been shown to make a very clear and dramatic distinction between equality- and equity-based pay schemes. The former suggest that work rewards (i.e. pay) should be distributed equally regardless of input or output. The latter believe that all rewards should be distributed in direct proportion to effort.

Those who endorse the work ethic believe in performance-related pay and in performance management in general. They can be greatly offended by systems that seem to reward people – i.e. service-related pay – but take no account of effort. It is quite simple in the eyes of the believer – the harder you work, the more you get. Not the longer your service or the more you deserve it (and certainly not 'from each according to his ability and to each according to his need'). Rather, to each according to his input and from each according to his effort.

If the work-ethic believer is in an organization that does not have an equity-based system, it is possible that he/she will reduce his/her effort to the lowest common denominator, even go absent to ensure that equality of input matches the equality of output. Believers are very sensitive to reward – distributive and procedural – because at the heart of the belief system is that each individual is personally answerable to his or her maker.

A final feature of the work ethic at work concerns retirement. Because work has always been their central focus, they tend not to have a rich out-of-work life. And so retirement is a threat. Without work they have no identity, no structure, no purpose. And, knowing this, they cling on to work for dear life – not accepting severance packages, not taking early retirement – not going under any circumstances.

To seek out and employ those who believe in the work ethic may not be as good a thing as it first seems. They may be moral, hard-working types who struggle in when ill and when transportation is bad and are happy to stay after work. But they are often poor team players, pretty intolerant of those who do not share their views and can confuse the means with the end. And they may not be too much fun to be around!

Work rage

Listen to people speak about their work. They talk about:

- tackling new problems
- grappling with new materials
- wrestling with new technology
- sinking their teeth into a presentation
- looking for sales staff with more punch
- wanting an aggressive marketing policy
- making a killing in the stock market
- knocking the audience dead with a speech
- capturing a market segment
- taking advantage of a gap in the market.

The language of work is the language of aggression, of domination and of control. Freudians see a basic aggressive urge that underlies all our work. They note that we struggle to control our environment, to organize, tame and master it so that we can overcome our funda-mental insecurity about survival. This is the fundamental reason why we work. Our drive to work is a way of compensating for early infan-tile helplessness. Further, this aggressive drive is a catalyst for our language at and around the workplace.

Our language at work stresses an adversarial relationship – with the physical, social and emotional environment. We transform ma-terial and people. When we build things we call it work; when the desired change is destructive we call it rage. Aggression always involves some change in an external object: life to death, tall to small, unblemished to blemished, pristine to damaged. All aggressive drives aim to transform the present state of something.

But, say the Freudians, who love paradox, both construction and destruction represents attempts to manipulate both things and people, to some changed goal. Hostile aggression, the more primitive, focuses on negative change. Creative aggression, whose object is to change the present to enhance or create future life – is called work. The more aggressive, determined and single-minded we are about achieving our goals (of security) the more effective we will be at work.

Our language therefore reflects the way we symbolize our work. And it enables us to master not only our immediate environment, but also (through communication) people that are separated from us in time (the past and future) and space (far-off places).

For those whose testeronic aggressive instinct is high, the purpose of the present is not to enjoy but to be acted upon. You act on the current state of affairs – you manage it – by controlling it, changing it, commanding it, directing it. One must think ahead, put perceptions (fears) into words (strategic plans) and constructively change and control. After all we 'work someone over', 'give him the business'. We 'master our brief', attend master classes, talk of an orchestra 'maestro' and revere the old Dutch masters. We master skills and some worship the Lord who is Master-of-us-all.

Our fundamental aim, agree the socio-biologists, is to ensure survival and even enrichment of ourselves, immediately family and kin. We work for them. So when thwarted, frustrated and rendered ineffective we express aggression, hostility and destructive rage.

So all forms of working are rooted in the state of being against. We are, all of us at work, in the exploitation business. The work 'exploit' means to selfishly utilize for personal profit.

It is therefore no surprise that we talk such a lot about stress at work. If work is a constant battle it can easily lead to frustration and exhaustion. In a curious way, those outward-bound-type courses get it right because the philosophy underlying many of them is that management is about courage. It is also about emotions. Most of us like to think that business is ruled by the head, not the heart – that people make rational and logically decisions and act upon them.

You do not need either a lot of experience or tremendous insight to know that most business decisions are either psycho-logical or pretty illogical. Cowardice, vanity, sloth, covetousness and the other sins are as likely to inform business life decisions as hypothetical deductive or inductive reasoning. And the emotions that inform these decisions are as likely to be negative as positive.

Anger, born out of frustrations or fear, is ever present at work. Road rage, air rage, supermarket rage are often linked to work rage. Whistle-blowing and litigation can be born of rage that comes from feeling unfairly dealt with.

The point Freudians make is that the issue of rage is largely unconscious, surfacing in our work idioms, adages and aphorisms. Past generations were probably more aware of work rage and they understood more than we do that work was often about survival. We may have sublimated all the rage into 'stress-talk' and the stress-industry that lives off it.

Working for monsters

What was it like working for Robert Maxwell? How does one cope with the capricious, irascible, vain bastard one may find as a boss? Is there any upside in working for charismatic but deeply egocentric and selfish entrepreneurs? Sure, they make the workplace exciting but that is often because they are unpredictable.

The monster boss certainly makes life more interesting. Life is a roller coaster, not humdrum tedium. Further, they often provide excellent learning opportunities – some call this stress; others learn to call them 'developmental opportunities'. But most of all they test your people skills and patience. Dealing with shoddy workmen, hypochondriacal staff and poor customer service appears a real 'doddle' once one has mastered the monster from hell.

There is a whole range of books about dealing with difficult people. Nearly all provide a supposedly valid taxonomy of types: the *sniping saboteur* (who identifies your weaknesses and exploits them), the *cocky-knows-it-all* (who talks and never listens and can't be proved wrong), the *abominable no-man* (who is doubtful, discouraging, despondent and deadly to be around) and the *whingeing whiner* (who carries around with them neurotic negativism).

Some books list these types alphabetically and their titles tell it all: the *abdicator* boss, (who zealously overdelegates) or the *meddler* boss (who is the opposite, namely a chorus interventionalist). The opposite of the *apathetic* boss (who is passive and indifferent) is the *quarrelsome* boss (who resists everything).

But those books never help one with bosses, particularly the larger-than-life characters that become well known. What is often the case is that there is a yawning gulf between the reputation of these 'super-bosses' so carefully crafted by the in-house spin doctors and the reality one hears only from bitter, sacked employees who are happy to whistle-blow on their boss after the event.

How can you manage the boss and make your life at least tolerable, if you work for an 18-carat monster? The answer is in understanding 'where they are coming from'. The secret lies in reading and responding to their moods, foibles and weaknesses, in understanding their needs and ultimately in anticipating their obnoxious behaviour before it occurs.

Consider some well-known characteristics, and consider how your particular monster fits in. For instance, take *sociability*, the extent to which your boss really likes socializing with others. The boss who scores low on this attribute is probably hard to get to know, perhaps a little shy, careful and ponderous. They may have to pretend to be outgoing, but they are not. In fact, they hate it. Those bosses who are very high on sociability are easy to be with and easy to get to know, but it is unlikely that they are interested in what you are saying. They prefer talking to listening. They like being the centre of attention. They are social gadflies. Do not expect long, serious conversations with the charming extroverted sociopath.

Similarly, on a simple *likeability* or agreeableness dimension, bosses who score low like to argue with and challenge you. Combative, distrustful and moody, they are often the embodiment of the monster boss. Privately they are more honest than publicly. Deeply disagreeable, they like a scrap. They push, demand, cajole – and, as a result, really get things moving along. On the other hand, the manager who scores on likeability is full of charm, agrees with everything you say but tends to progress things slowly, if at all. Conflict-averse, those high on likeability prefer people to be supported rather than challenged.

The boss who *is intellectually dim* tends to resist new ideas and innovation. These types are not really interested in data and evidence and prefer simplistic, well-rehearsed answers. Being low on IQ as well as EQ is surely being seriously short changed. Sufficient IQ is the minimum requirement in certain jobs. Some monsters are just thick – and know it, but most have masses of low cunning. Bright bosses accept the necessity of change and development. They are often interested in evidence and data and encourage their collection.

Similarly, the extent to which your boss is *ambitious* must dictate how he or she acts. The steady-as-you-go boss, lacking in ambition, avoids initiatives and is careful of being shown up. Security is traded off against ambition and they are ambitious neither for themselves nor for their staff. But the highly ambitious boss likes to 'run with the bull'. They may be opportunistic but it is pretty certain their eyes are on their superior and not on you, their subordinate. Your best hope is to be seen to be helpful and influential in your boss's career. Monsters are amoral and opportunistic. They lay down their friends' lives for their own.

Personal adjustment, or, as politically correct American psychologists have now learned to call it, 'negative affectivity', is a very important facet of human behaviour and requires careful monitoring. This is neuroticism. It can take many forms: phobia, anxiety and depression. Many monsters are neurotic and this is obvious in their hypochondria and moodiness.

Those a wee bit low on adjustment need reassurance and support. In fact, it may well be that a bit of role-reversal occurs, in the sense that you become the parent and the boss becomes the child. But adjustment is another word for stability, and the very instability of the low-adjustment boss presents problems. Neurotic bosses take very careful handling. But psychotic bosses, particularly psychopaths, are worse. They are characterized by a total lack of conscience and empathy – by brutal, uncaring, thuggish behaviour.

Stable, adjusted bosses can take feedback calmly and can deal with crises. They are often characterized by those wonderful British characteristics of phlegmatism and stoicism. Indifferent to pain and pleasure, bulls or bears, successes or failures, the adjusted, stable boss is a much-appreciated rock in the sea of business troubles.

Finally, there is *prudence* or conscientiousness: beware the imprudent manager. They don't follow through, they don't pay their bills and they can be wildly incautious about financial arrangements. Their incompetence may easily lead to financial, if not moral, bankruptcy. The overprudent manager may, on the other hand, be too tightfisted and short-sighted to take any kind of business risk. Most monsters are both: mean with your pay, overgenerous with their own.

Working for monsters means careful monitoring. You have to learn to read the signals – to move away from them when moody, to charm when in a good mood. But following in their wake as they crash through organizations and the stock market can bring real benefits. May you live in interesting monster managerial times.

Writers die young

To a large extent, the stereotype of the tortured young novelist is correct. Hunched over a ramshackle desk in a forlorn garret, the writer is the epitome of the obsessive, self-denying artist. Prepared to forsake food, warmth and (alas) personal hygiene in favour of expressing themselves, writers too often seem heroic failures. The problem is that few even get into print let alone produce bestsellers. And many take to drink and drugs on the way.

In fact, students of the writing process often note how businesslike successful writers are. They do not wait for inspiration; they check into the spare bedroom much as people go to the office. Many set themselves manageable but challenging targets of, say, 800 words or three pages each day. And they keep at it until the target has been achieved.

Many writers invent reinforcement schedules or treats to keep them going. The dry sherry before lunch after the target was achieved was one writer's little peccadillo. Another always stopped at a point that was easy to pick up the following day. This ensured the start went well, which is pretty important.

Studies on the longevity of people in different professions have a lot to offer in an understanding of stress at work. Firefighters, journalists and cabbies do not live as long as monks, potters and gardeners, for obvious reasons. Various studies of professional stress have confirmed studies on longevity, which show that artists die young. Composers, dancers, musicians and painters tend to have shorter lives but writers die first. In one econometric study, it was shown the average longevity of established writers was a mere 61 years (10 to 15 years less than average).

But why? What factors may lead to writers being unhappy, stressed and adopt a lifestyle that leads to an early death? And what implications does this have for other jobs? One important distinction is to understand the product and the process – what you do and how you do it. Compared to many other artists, both the product (the book, paper) and the process of writing are less satisfying than for visual or performing artists.

Compared to other artists and, indeed, most other professions, the creative process is most lonely and least interactive. Many writers have admitted that writing breeds loneliness, the feeling of not being appreciated, and despair. It is isolating, remorseless and relentless. One retreats from life in order to write about it – a very curious irony.

Paradoxically, most writers are deeply interested in other people, from whom they cut themselves off. Further, they need self-confidence to continue, which can easily be undermined by no feedback. And they often also need an ability to fantasize about imaginary lives. There is a simple solution to this situation that many writers soon find – alcohol. Unlike other jobs, drinking at work is neither illegal nor dangerous. Writers rather like Faulkner and Hemmingway noted how alcohol sharpened the 'dull flatness' of the everyday.

Musicians', actors', dancers' even painters' performances are rapidly noticeably diminished by drink. But this is not the case with writers. Indeed, there is a host of psychiatric tomes on drink and the writer, one of which rejoices in the amusing title of *The Thirsty Muse*. The lonely writer who sets his or her own schedule may see drink and drugs as an aid to the creative process. And up to a point they may be right. But judging and maintaining the optimal amount eludes most.

A major problem, for the writer in particular, is how long the product takes to complete. Compare the musician, actor and dancer with the writer. Even including rehearsals, the performance is completed in a fairly short time and there may be a high number over a lifetime. And they receive feedback, approbation being the most desirable. As a result, they can feel loved, admired and appreciated, which fuels self-esteem and the ability to withstand the odd failure and rejection.

Even compared to composers and sculptors, writers seem very slow. Haydn composed over 100 symphonies (and 70 string quartets) in a lifetime; Moore did 13 serious sculptures in the last two years of his life. Apart from Barbara Cartland, the number of books by celebrated writers seems pitifully few compared to other artists.

So why do writers die young? The answer lies in part because their work provides little short-term satisfaction but rather a fair degree of pain based on loneliness, lack of appreciation and support, and monotony. Equally, the job or process is almost uniquely suited to a lifestyle that allows, even encourages, an overabundance of immediate gratification incompatible with good health.

Great writers are observant, vigilant craftspeople. But like everyone else they need friendship, support and appreciation for their skills. And they need to be discouraged from taking to the demon drink to help them through the difficult process of writing.

Journalists have certain advantages and one major disadvantage over writers. Many have good colleagues, a convivial work climate and extensive feedback on their output. But they do have a far worse tyranny – the deadline. Any job involving deadlines is associated with stress and attempts to alleviate stress, often with alcohol, after the event. Freelancers, however, rarely have the advantages and only suffer the disadvantages. Curiously, many journalists say they need the deadline to get productive and do their thing. Perhaps the best novelists have self-imposed deadlines.

So, it is not a case of 'don't put your daughter on the stage, Mrs Worthington' but 'don't encourage her to scribble for a living or marry a scribbler'.

Xmas parties

The Christmas party season is a time for lechery, sloth and indolence. It is also a time of gift exchange, office parties and excessive shopping. So many presents are bought that some shops make more money during this period than during the rest of the year put together. And the party season now even begins in late November.

Family Christmases can be beastly – a celebration of gluttony and drunkenness, greed and envy, maudlin sentimentality, self-deception and boredom. It is bad enough to endure one's tedious relatives (God gave us our friends but the devil our relations), but it is the presence of those ever-jolly goodwill-towards-all-men types that is particularly insufferable. Punctuated only by the Queen's Speech and some 'blockbuster' high-adventure film (with a very desirable and sublimating amount of death and violence) on TV, there is the dreadful monotony of small talk with dull provincials, being forced to play some incomprehensible board game, or attempting either to assemble or repair a very expensive electronic toy without the necessary tools or the instructions.

Little wonder, then, that the rates of both suicide and homicide increase at the Yuletide, no doubt because of the disappointment caused by the yawning gap between the bleak reality of Christmas and either the media image or the rosy (and hence biased) memory of warm, exciting and jovial festivities of a secure and ever retreating childhood. Murder increases perhaps as a result of the heightened tensions from the proximity of one's relatives, the disinhibiting effect of booze and the cramped conditions in many front rooms.

The office Xmas party, at least in Britain, has a rather poor reputation – at least for morality. What causes ordinary, staid, respectable adults to go in for Mardi Gras type behaviour (erotic dancing, clumsy fondling, verbal declarations of passion) is not at all clear.

It may be the stress of the pre-Christmas period in general. It might just be the only time of the year when the organization sponsors a party with free, even drinkable, booze. It may be the conspicuously hung mistletoe branches, which somehow license otherwise unacceptable behaviour.

What is always the most interesting, even surprising, thing about the office party is who pounces on whom. No one is surprised if the 28-year-old consultant makes a pass at the busty secretary. The real surprise is the balding, middle-aged, middle manager from stores who clumsily gropes his colleague's wife in the staff kitchen.

For female staff, the three types who are most dangerous and most likely to make a surprise move are the following: *Mr Veneer* – nobody is more delighted that large numbers of women are reaching senior business positions, for Mr Veneer is playing a numbers game. He invites a constant stream of women out on his expense account, knowing that he will strike it lucky sooner or later. A suave, practised, married womanizer, he is the archetypal salesman. Finding a quiet corner at the party, he will get down to business straight away with such opening tactics as, 'My wife lives in the country and I have a flat in town', 'I fancied you from the first moment I saw you'. Naturally, his second wife doesn't understand him.

Mr Invisible – he is frequently part of the female's peer group, or perhaps a colleague whom she has known vaguely for years. More probably a gauche, balding, quiet married man, Mr Invisible needs four pints of lager before he is able to say, 'I have decided to have an affair with you'. 'I'd like to have you on my team, but I'm not sure you could handle it', or even, 'I know you are available'. He likes to give the impression he has never done anything like this before – and in fact might not have. A middle-class trainspotter, he is able to remain invisible behind an anodyne or innocuous personality.

Mr Flamboyant – the professional bachelor/divorcé of a certain age who drives a red Porsche and is the 'Boss'. He would like everyone to think that he can pull endless women because he is sexy, not because he is loaded. He will be fashionably dressed at the party and probably drink Martinis. His opening gambit is, 'What's so great about young men? or 'My last girlfriend was 22'. He has, of course, done this many times before and likes his target to know it.

But all this may be too sexist. As therapists are finding out, many a bewildered man is unable to cope after being picked up at a party, taken home for the night and then unceremoniously dumped by the new assertive female. It is no longer particularly rare, or even unacceptable, for the woman to make the first move. However, no femme fatale would be crude, vulgar and presumptuous enough to make her first move at any place as obvious as the office party.

Printed and bound by CPI Group (UK) Ltd, Croydon, CR0 4YY

13/04/2025

14656562-0005